PLANNING AND DEVELOPMENT IN MODERN LIBYA

PLANNING AND DEVELOPMENT IN MODERN LIBYA

Edited by

M. M. BURU, S. M. GHANEM
AND K. S. McLACHLAN

The Society for Libyan Studies

AND

MIDDLE EAST & NORTH AFRICAN STUDIES press limited

Published by Middle East and North African Studies Press Ltd.
Gallipoli House, The Cottons, Outwell, Wisbech,
Cambridgeshire PE14 8TN, England

The Society for Libyan Studies
c/o The Institute of Archaeology
31-34, Gordon Square
London WC1H 0PY
England

ISBN 0 906559 19 7

Also distributed outside the UK by
Lynne Rienner Publishers Inc.
948, North Street
Boulder, Colorado 80302, USA

Printed by Whitstable Litho Ltd., Whitstable, Kent

CONTENTS

CONTENTS (Continued)

Acknowledgements

The editors are deeply indebted to many individuals and organisations for their assistance in both aiding the original symposium and supporting the publication of this volume. Principally, of course, we wish to thank the contributors of the consituent chapters of the book, who have undertaken revision of their materials and been patient with the editors during their preparation of the manuscript. The editors hope that their ideas have been adequately and fairly represented.

Publication of this book would not have been possible were it not for the generousity of the Society for Libyan Studies. That body kindly agreed to act as co-publishers and to subsidise some of the costs of the project. The editors are happy to acknowledge the debt they owe to the Society and its continuing role as supporter of, among other things, research activities in history and the social sciences concerned with Libya.

Additional editorial work has been undertaken by George Joffe, Anne McLachlan and Ruth McLachlan, for which the editors are grateful. Typing of the manuscript was done by Katherine Leclercq and maps prepared by Elizabeth Johnson.

The views expressed in the individual papers are the opinions of the authors and do not necessarily coincide with those of the editors or of the Society for Libyan Studies. Boundaries and/or frontiers depicted on maps are not authenticated. They represent only the lines generally described by individual authors and should be taken as in any way authoritative definitions of national or international frontiers.

All transliterations in the volume have been made consistent with normal practice, place names following the system adopted in the *National Atlas of the Socialist People's Arab Jamahiriya* and personal names presented in their conventionalised way. Deviations from these norms was accepted where authors were insistent on their spelling of particular words in Arabic.

List of Tables

List of Tables (continued)

List of Figures

CONTRIBUTORS

Ali Abdussalam	Professor of Economics, Gar Younis University, Binghazi, Libya
Tony Allan	Reader in Geography, School of Oriental & African Studies, London
Mohamed M. Alawar	Lecturer in Geography, Al-Fateh University, Tripoli, Libya
Hosney A. Benzabih	Doctoral research student, School of Oriental & African Studies, London
Mukhtar M. Buru	Professor of Geography, Al-Fateh University, Tripoli, Libya
Shukri M. Ghanem	Senior economist, Libyan Academy of Sciences, Tripoli, Libya
Charles C. Gurdon	Writer and doctoral research student, School of Oriental & African Studies, London
George Joffe	Writer, broadcaster and Middle East editor, Economist Intelligence Unit, London
John S. Latham	Director, Environmental Remote Sensing Applications Centre (ERSAC), Livingstone, Scotland
Amin Marghani	Writer on aviation affairs in the Middle East and North Africa
Keith McLachlan	Senior Lecturer in Geography, School of Oriental & African Studies, London
Misbah Oreibi	Deputy Observer of the Arab League Mission in Geneva
Bob Price	Regional planing consultant for the Middle East, Finnmap Oy, Helsinki
Stuart Watkins	Project manager for the Sabha Regional Plan, Finnmap Oy, Helsinki, Finland
John Wright	Writer and broadcaster on Arab and energy affairs based in London

INTRODUCTION

Libya is one of the very few Arab oil-exporting states to have retained a strong faith in the value of social and economic planning. Uniquely in the region, too, the country has been committed to regional planning. The present volume has been designed to trace the modern economic history of Libya with special reference to change, development and planning since independence in 1951.

This work represents the efforts of a group of seven Libyan and eight European research workers, all of whom have deep interests in academic and/or field programmes in Libya. They, together with other scholars, took part in a two-day symposium entitled 'Libya: Research Papers into Economic Development' held at the School of Oriental & African Studies, University of London in February 1984. Selected papers presented at this meeting have been revised and integrated into this volume. A number of papers were specially commissioned for the present book so that a balanced coverage of the topic could be offered.

In addition to chapters by established academics, the editors have encouraged younger researchers to participate so that the most recently available field work could be incorporated into the text. It is a pleasure to welcome several authors who do not normally take part in debates of the kind elaborated in this book. They are representatives of companies which have been involved in setting up regional plans for the 1980-2000 long-term plan period in Libya, working as consultants to the Secretariat of Municipalities. Very little of the findings and recommendations of the consultants are yet available to the public at large and it is hoped that the material in this book will be a useful indication of the style of regional planning that has been current in Libya over the period 1980-1985.

A contribution is made here to topics normally disregarded in the literature. In addition to some new light thrown on the workings of the Libyan economy, ground is broken by review of the country's non-hydrocarbon resources and the evolution of Libyan air transport.

All the participants in this volume are engaged in continuing research into planning and development, offering the prospect that some of the ideas and attitudes examined here may be further expanded at a later date.

PART ONE: RECENT HISTORY OF RESOURCE DEVELOPMENT

Chapter 1

TRADE & MIGRATION BETWEEN MALTA & THE BARBARY STATES DURING THE SECOND OTTOMAN OCCUPATION OF LIBYA (1835-1911)

E.G.H. Joffé

The Maltese archipelago is located in the middle of the channel linking the western and eastern portions of the Mediterranean - 44 miles south of Sicily, 185 miles north of Tripoli and 158 miles east of the coastline of Tunisia. All commercial routes, whether running north-south or east-west, pass close to its shores and it could be considered, therefore, from geographical considerations alone, to have considerable potential as a commercial nexus, both for local and for long-distance trade. Conversely, the archipelago provides an ideal position from which to control commercial maritime activity from a naval point of view as well. Indeed, the turbulent history of the area has shown that it is ideally placed to participate in the complex social, economic and military relations that have linked the regions and populations surrounding the central Mediterranean basin.

During the prehistoric and classical periods, the Maltese archipelago clearly did play a major role in commercial activities between the North African coast and the Italian peninsula and, 'There is no doubt that Malta was highly prosperous for a long period under Roman rule'[1]. The same was also true of the Roman provinces in Libya and Tunisia until, with the arrival of the Vandals in the mid-fifth century, economic decline set in for the next one hundred years[2]. The effects of the decline were to persist thereafter, since military considerations were to predominate over commercial ones for the next twelve centuries. Once Islam had spread over North Africa, Malta - except for a short period between 870 and 1090 when the archipelago itself was part of the Muslim world - became part of the 'forgotten frontier' that ran through the Mediterranean, separating Islam and Christendom[3]. By the sixteenth century, the division became formalised in the institutionalised warfare of the Corso, particularly once the Order of St.John of Jerusalem had installed itself in Malta after 1528. It was only with the explusion of the Order in 1798 by Napoleon, en route for Egypt, that the geographic imperatives of Malta's position were able to reassert themselves and that commerce between the archipelago and North Africa became, once again, of primary importance.

In fact, these imperatives had never completely given way to political pressure. In the thirteenth century, the Aragonese commercial empire had integrated Malta and North Africa into its web and the patterns established then lasted up to the arrival of the Knights of St. John of Jerusalem, despite the Reconquista and the bitterness it engendered in the Muslim world during the fifteenth century[4]. Even the knights continued commercial contacts throughout the period of their occupancy of Malta. The situation was, in part, forced on them by the deficit nature of the Maltese economy. The simple fact was that Malta could not provide for itself. Once the population rose significantly above 10,000, the island was no longer able to satisfy its alimentary requirements and, from the late fifteenth century, grain had to be imported. As early as 1530 the Pope gave the Order permission to trade with Barbary[5]. Commercial contacts with North Africa were also regularised in the sixteenth century, with safe-conducts being issued to Muslim merchants to permit trade with Malta. By the eighteenth century, despite the continued importance of corsairs, close contacts had been established between the Grand Master of the Order and the Beys of Tunis and the Qaramanli pashas of Tripoli. The Barbary coast had become an obvious alternative to Sicily as a source of food - despite the ideological problems that such a solution posed[6].

This was particularly important in the case of Tunisia, where trade from the 1740's up to the 1790's was particularly active[7]. It was mainly concerned with wheat and livestock and, until the recrudescence of the Corso in the closing years of the century, it grew rapidly in importance. It had to be carried on in ships registered with third nations, but, nonetheless, began to play a vital role in the Maltese economy. The case of the Regency of Tripoli was more complex. Here, the importance of the trans-Saharan trade meant that Tripoli was more interested in contacts with Europe than with Malta, but Maltese co-operation was essential in ensuring that such a trade could be continued without constant interference from corsairs licensed by the Order[8]. However, here too, food supplies for Malta provided an essential element of contact between the authorities in Malta and Tripoli.

By 1800, however, the picture had changed completely. After a brief French occupation, Britain took over Malta and now the North African littoral took on a commercial role as part of British concerns during the Napoleonic wars. In fact, this was in line with long-held British views of Malta's importance:-

> 'By the late seventeenth century, contacts between England and Malta, originally initiated in the 1580's by the British pirate-merchants, had reached a more mature

stage of development, to the point of attracting official recognition from London. The English Government had started to appreciate the value and significance of Malta's strategic position and its potential as a base for English naval operations in the central Mediterranean'[9].

The corollary of this was that the new naval squadrons based on Malta required secure food supplies - particularly in meat and grain - and that, given the control of Italy by Napoleon, Sicily could not be considered a secure source. Tripoli was therefore chosen instead and, from 1803 onwards, a significant trade began between Tripoli and Malta in livestock and grain [10]. At the same time, Malta began its career as a major entrepot for British goods destined for the vast European markets bordering on the northern Mediterranean shore, but which, from 1806 onwards, was officially closed to Britain by the Berlin decrees, issued by Napoleon as part of his attempt to crush Britain by isolating her from her major markets. In this context, the certainty of food supplies from the Barbary states was an essential component of the military-commercial policy that Britain pursued as part of her strategy to defeat Napoleonic France [11].

CONTACTS BETWEEN MALTA AND BARBARY UNTIL 1835

Throughout this early period, relations between Malta and Tunisia remained on the commercial level, sustaining the active level of trade achieved during the latter years of the Order in Malta. By 1800, for instance, some 500 head of cattle and over 20,000 hectolitres of cereals were being exported annually to Valletta and, although this trade experienced fluctuations, it represented a trend that was to continue[12]. In so far as the Berlin decrees and British control of the Mediterranean severely interfered with traditional patterns of trade between Tunisia and Europe - where the most important centres of commerce were Leghorn and Marseilles - Britain was able to develop a considerable commerce in manufactured goods through Malta. Nonetheless, the departure of the Order from Malta did little to alter commercial relations at the start of the nineteenth century.

However, the presence of Britain in Malta did presage major changes to come. Trade was regulated now by a treaty signed between Britain and Tunis in 1762, which itself repeated the terms of an earlier 1751 treaty - rather than by the comfortable personal correspondence that had characterised relations between the Order and the Beys of Tunis. This automatically meant that a European power would be able to use this formal relationship to interfere in the domestic concerns of the Regency, once it felt powerful enough to do so. The occasion came in 1816, when Admiral Exmouth enforced the decisions of the European powers by preventing further enslaving of Christians and insisted on an end to corsairing[13].

The Exmouth treaty marked a dramatic turn in Tunisia's commercial relations with Europe and, over the next fifteen years, 'On passait d'une économie stable et équilibrée en 1815 à une économie de traite de type colonial en 1830'[14]. Commercial relations which had involved a trade surplus for Tunisia were transformed into a deficit and France came to dominate, both in trade and in political relations. By the 1840's it was clear that France was determined on creating a colonial relationship of some kind with Tunisia and the British role was confined to protecting its commercial interests there - specifically those with Malta - and with looking after the interests of British subjects there, mainly Maltese who, from the 1830's onwards, began to appear in Tunisia. The first major group settled in Porto Farina in the 1840's, but there were soon important groups to be found in all the major coastal cities, particularly in Tunis itself[15]. Trade with Malta had increased, but was still substantially based on livestock supplies, with irregular deliveries of cereals and olive oil.

The situation in Tripoli had developed in a completely different direction. Although Tripoli, like Tunis, had begun to supply livestock and grain on a regular basis after 1803, the trade, which initially was a monopoly of the Qaramanli pashas, had soon been taken over by Maltese migrants to the Regency. This had been achieved by consular pressure on the Pasha, on the grounds that the 1751 treaty which governed commercial relationships between the Regency and Great Britain (and thus, by extension, Malta as well) required free trade and the Pasha's monopoly prevented this. Further attempts to reverse the situation by increasing taxes and duties on exports to Malta met with threats of the British fleet being called in 1811 and, by the end of 1814, these commercial considerations had become subsumed into a wider political conflict. The arrival of a new figure on the Tripolitanian scene, Consul Warrington, marked a new attempt to force Tripoli into a British political orbit. It coincided with the destruction of traditional sources of revenue for the Regency, as had been the case with Tunis, and with the failure of Pasha Yusuf Qaramanli's attempts to find an alternative[16].

With the end of corsairing, financial settlements of outstanding claims against the Regency were met by mortgaging its future agricultural produce. The first example of this occurred in 1817 when the future barley harvest of Binghazi was mortgaged against a debt incurred by the Pasha when he could not settle a Hanoverian claim. The barley was to be sold in Malta. This process, soon to be codified in the *tizkera* system - a *tizkera* being the promise to settle debts against future income, usually from agriculture - was to provide an ideal means of exploiting the growing weakness and dependence of the Regency[17]. The *tizkeras* became objects of speculation, particularly in the hands of the growing Maltese community in Tripoli, now some 1,500-strong[18] and thus an additional weapon in Warrington's hand when they were not honoured at face value. Further speculation occurred as a result of the Pasha's decision to debase the Tripolitanian coinage, in a desperate effort to pay his growing debts to Maltese merchants and thus satisfy British claims against him, and, by the end of the 1820's, the currency had been ruined. Only Spanish coinage was trusted and thus another element of economic independence had been lost.

The signature of a treaty with France in 1830, which gave Britain a commercial rival in Tripoli, led to a final set of demands on the Regency that finally broke the Qaramanli dynasty. Warrington insisted on the settlement of 200,000 pounds' worth of debts and backed up his demands with threats of a naval bombardment. The response was the abdication of Yusuf Qaramanli and the Manshiyya rebellion in 1832. By 1835, the Ottoman empire had become extremely concerned over events in the Regency of Tripoli, particularly by the apparent rivalry between Britain and France for control of the Regency - although the British Government refused to countenance Warrington's schemes for British occupation. In mid-May, 1835, the Ottomans reoccupied Tripoli and brought the Qaramanli dynasty to an end, an action which also ended a series of British manoeuvres which stemmed directly from the alteration in trade patterns inaugurated by the British authorities in Malta in 1803[19].

MALTESE-NORTH AFRICAN TRADE 1835-1881

While these developments were taking place, fundamental changes were occurring in Malta's trading patterns. The end of the period of the Napoleonic wars saw Malta now firmly located as a major entrepot for the Mediterranean, taking its essential food supplies from Tripoli, Tunis and - for wheat - Egypt. After 1812, The Adriatic and then the Black Sea began to take over the grain trade, as Malta began to supply not just her own needs but also those of Britain. Malta had now become integrated into an east-west trade pattern and the north-south pattern that had characterised the previous period began to diminish in importance. In addition, peace meant that the Maltese monopoly on Mediterranean trade - through the issue of permits which were essential if a merchantman were to avoid seizure by the British navy - had now ended. However, after 1813, the Napoleonic trade boom ended and, together with an outbreak of plague in Malta, this led to a decline in commercial activity:-

> 'It must be made clear from the outset, that the great stagnation that followed after 1814 was caused by the

peace and the subsequent abolition of the Licence System. Malta was merely a place where merchandise could be deposited, in transit from other places. When other ports were opened, Malta remained isolated in the middle of a 'closed' Mediterranean Sea...The island depended on transit trade and upon this depended its economic prosperity'[20]

The stagnation lasted up to the mid-1830's and, during it, the North African trade became correspondingly more significant. Nonetheless, trade patterns in the Mediterranean had irrevocably altered, with the Mediterranean becoming more and more a funnel for the transfer of primary products from the Levant to Europe, particularly Britain and France. Grain was a major element in this trade and the grain ships leaving Alexandria would, on occasion, call in at the North African ports, although Malta was a more likely centre. Nonetheless, 'Malta was included, more than often, merely for shelter and for furnishing provisions. She had little to offer as a market'[21]. The same was true for North Africa.

As a result, the relative importance of North Africa remained high. The plague, which broke out once again at the end of the 1830's, led to Sicily becoming unattractive as a source of supply and thus Tripoli grew in importance. Although Tripoli also closed its ports to Maltese trade on occasion, as did Sicily more frequently, port dues there were non-existent, whereas Sicilian ports put up their dues because of the plague. In 1837, for example, Tripoli allowed access to Maltese vessels despite plague in Malta, whereas Sicily refused[22].

At the same time, Maltese merchants in Tripoli became involved in the trans-Saharan trade, for which Tripoli was the main outlet, with three major routes finding their terminal points there - the other main route passing through Morocco[23]. By the 1840's, just as trade generally in the Mediterranean was improving, 'The trade with the Barbary states was one of the most progressive and prosperous in the years of revival'[24]. The Maltese in Tripoli acted as middle-men for British merchants in Malta or for Maltese there who had contacts with British merchant houses in the metropolis. The middle-men had contacts with Libyans, either in Tripoli or in major markets on the desert edge, such as Ghadamis or even with centres to the south of the desert. Thus, the importance of Malta to the success of the trans-Saharan trade was considerable. Although the Maltese had no direct involvement in the slave trade - worth between 10,000 and 20,000 dollars annually in the 1820's, with 2,000 being exported from Tripoli as late as 1842[25] - they did handle much of the ivory, ostrich feathers and gold dust that passed to Europe, items which, by 1850, had become more significant than slaves (Table 1.1). In fact, it was probably this that persuaded the British consul in the 1850's to ensure that the Maltese did not become involved in the slave trade - as several migrants

Table 1.1 Libya's exports - 1850

	Quantity	Value (francs)
(1) <u>Local produce</u>		
cereals (hectolitres)	212,700	1,496,000
cattle (head)	11,787	408,000
olive oil (kilograms)	1375,800	742,000
butter (kilograms)	460,000	406,000
(2) <u>Produce from Africa</u>		
slaves (numbers)	2,708	759,000
ivory (kilograms)	77,000	754,000
gold dust (grams)	109,000	360,000

(3) TOTAL VALUE OF EXPORTS - 6 mn francs/£250,000*

Source: Cachia A., 1945, Libya Under the Second Ottoman Occupation, Government Press, Tripoli, pp.167-8.

* £1.00 = 24 francs

apparently intended to do - rather than any moral considerations urged by the Anti-Slavery Society in London. Slaving was only eradicated from Tripoli in the 1890's.

The critical development occurred in the 1840's, as steam-shipping came to dominate Mediterranean trade. Not only did this ensure that the vast grain-producing areas of the Black Sea would be open to North European markets, but it also gave Malta a new significance as a bunkering station, a position that the archipelago retained up to 1880, when improved ship design made bunkering a more infrequent consideration. Now Tripoli and Tunis became minor elements in the Maltese trade patterns, acting essentially as supply-points, with Tripoli playing a far more important role than Tunis, as, under Ahmad Bey, Tunis looked towards modernisation and French aid - a policy which was to lead directly to European supervision of Tunisian finances after 1869, the year in which the Suez Canal was to open and ensure that Malta's true role for the next fifty years would relate to its strategic significance in imperial communications between Britain and India (Table 1.13).

The role of North Africa in Maltese trade is shown in Tables 1.2, 1.3, 1.4, 1.5 and 1.6. Thus, although regularly outclassed by Russia, Turkey and Egypt as a source of imports - and by Sicily in 1840, but never thereafter - Tripoli and Tunis continued to lie between fourth and seventh in importance throughout the latter part of the nineteenth century. In 1864, the French consul in Malta reported that:

> 'L'importation se compose principalement de céréales pour la consommation provenant de Russie, Turquie, Barbarie et Egypte, de boeufs et de quelques cheveaux provenant

Table 1.2 Malta-North Africa: imports and exports

	Imports (Landed (£)				Exports (mainly re-exports) (£)			
Year	Total	Algeria	Tunisia	Libya	Total	Algeria	Tunisia	Libya
1860[a]	2981947	1730	...	273713	2380820	-	...	632112
1870[a]	4097269	2568	32422	149859	3627694	18119	41226	61575
1880	840425	48410	102690	40305	10703921	85162	7874	29113
1890	778573	...	21217*	80435	22144067	...	12865	6068
1891	1019088	...	18278	179216	34955977	...	22349	6947
1892	1040832	...	16276*	144483	11742579	...	29844	27025
1893	1468065	...	46977*	57445*	12275141	...	64129	21180
1894	735822	...	67328	65297*	13086085	...	17911	3844
1895	802891	1755*	33980*	56859*	13231813	85	28728	14855
1896	885315	4071*	29318*	91289	11886149	-	40697	8450
1897	905006	...	23186*	39293	11008876	...	133346	12734
1898	880164	...	29309*	31046	9379140	...	71384	8790
1899	976330	...	45516*	59263	5449501	...	6112	10761
1900	992704	215	28261*	81259	6471567	97	4034	20073
1901	1299309	29	67935*	138002	8683126	22	25107	44747
1902[b]	293495	16	12411	16358	1879338	-	12411	16358
	1261650	7286	73548*	92784	5349576	256	8417	47130
1903[b]	1318430	1076	35277*	99364	6145883	47016	7511	65778
1904[b]	1468858	...	15423*	70373	8444024	10710	34983	63427
1905[b]	1142047	188	35042*	84126	7156848	2	36920	77982
1909[ba]	1006518	1054	27633	94336	81469	20	4909	42141[c]
1911[ba]	2413687	5122	57393	55975	750422	180	12987	64195[c]
1912[ba]	2614566	6106	107563	7559	977656	268	13760	71962[c]
1913[ba]	2510934	3410	87574	4656	1053854	609	15348	47061[c]

Table 1.3 Selected imports: North Africa to Malta

Units: Cattle - number of head, except in 1896 when this was measured in 'cantari' (1 cantar = $1\frac{1}{3}$ cwt)
Other - number of head.
Wheat & Barley - measured in 'salme' (1 salm = 8 bushels).
Oil - measured in 'caffisi' (1 caffiso = $4\frac{1}{2}$ gallons).

	Libya					Tunisia				
Year	Cattle	Other[a]	Barley	Wheat	Oil	Cattle	Other[a]	Barley	Wheat	Oil
1870	9,692			4,898					5,457	
1880	5,137		65,635	4,100		4,115		16,520	21,960	
1890	9,293		30,000			1,603				
1891	13,802		10,000			565		10,000		
1892	14,609				15,811					11,077
1893	5,153					5,000				
1894	6,242	220			19,539	7,132	223	906		13,859
1895	5,138				17,582	1,685		1,522		17,072
1896	(21,053)	203	1,139			(5,888)	198			5,976
1897	5,750				8,768	2,481				
1898	5,653					3,542				
1899	5,943					4,125				
1900	8,762	2,764	923	107	7,873	na	na	na	na	na
1901	11,767	3,354	1,200	76	13,397	6,761	448	105	4	448
1902[b]	347	472	1,415	27	978					
	8,216	4,364	4,431	586	3,419	7,904	467	344	1	12,580
1903[b]	7,931	2,981	5,105	142	631	3,260	276	222	6	10,205
1904[b]	5,721	2,651	546	2	9,965	1,039	249	66	13	793
1905[b]	6,870	1,503	8,996	303	16,254	3,912	344	6		1,392
1909[b]	15,494	648	469			na	na	na	na	na

Source of the Table 1.2 Colonial Office, Blue Books, Government Printing Office, Valletta.

a: The import figures for 1860 include both landed imports and re-exports and are thus not directly comparable with later figures.

b: The figures given for these years are for fiscal years, from April 1 of one year to March 31 of the successive year. The initial figure for 1902 is for the first three months of that year. All figures for preceding years are for calendar years.

* Here total imports into Malta are equivalent to imports actually landed for local consumption. In all other cases, some imports were re-exported.

c: Only dutifiable imports and exports from bond listed for 1909 to 1913.

Source of the Table 1.3 Colonial, Blue Books, Government Printing Office, Valletta.

a: Includes sheep, mules and horses.

b: These are fiscal years, all previous years are calender years; the first figure for 1902 is for the first three months of the year.

Table 1.4 Malta's trade in 1840

(1) Major imports

Nationality	Value (fr)	Vessels	Nature of Cargo
Britain	7.0 mn	147	supplies, alcoholic drink,
Two Sicilies	3.3 mn	601	food, firewood, wine
Russia	2.4 mn	45	corn, iron
Turkey	1.1 mn	21	corn, wood
Egypt	1.1 mn	68	barley, maize, cotton
Libya	0.7 mn	90	animals, oil, skins

(2) Major exports

Britain	2.7 mn	119	corn, cotton, skins,
Libya	2.3 mn	50	oil corn, tobacco
Turkey	2.3 mn	61	coal, supplies
Tuscany	1.2 mn	26	corn, cotton, skins
Egypt	1.0 mn	25	coal, wood, iron
Two Sicilies	1.0 mn	146	supplies

Source: MAE (Corr. Cons. & Comm.) Malte 20 (1839–42) Rapport à M. le Cos, Francais à Malte, Malte - 17 Aug. 1841.

Table 1.5 Libya's imports and exports in 1898

Imports (francs)*			
Britain (Malta)	2,168,000	Britain (Malta)	3,500,000
France	1,800,000	France	3,067,000
Turkey	1,600,000	USA	800,000
Italy	1,200,000	Turkey	517,000
Austria	550,000	Algeria	257,000
Germany	300,000	Tunisia	247,000
Tunisia/Morocco	300,000	Italy	200,000
Belgium	250,000	Others	1,350,000
Others	872,000		
Total	9,040,000		9,938,000

Source: Cachia A., op.cit., p.169.

* £1.00 = 24 francs

Table 1.6 Malta's trade patterns

1860: Major ranked importers (£)

1.	Russia	1,265,074	4.	Barbary	273,713
2.	Turkey	687,519	5.	Sicilies	238,045
3.	Egypt	419,622	6.	UK	37,630
			7.	Sardinia	20,254

Major ranked export destinations (£)

1.	UK	1,847,970	4.	Barbary	32,112
2.	Sicilies	158,322	5.	Belgium	12,926
3.	Sardinia	89,776	6.	Gilbraltar	11,943
			7.	Portugal	10,000

1870: Major ranked importers (£)

1.	Russia	1,877,997	5.	Italy	171,722
2.	Turkey	1,371,037	6.	Tripoli	149,859
3.	Austria	209,279	7.	UK	65,724
4.	Egypt	186,083	8.	Tunis	32,422

Major ranked export destinations (£)

1.	UK	2,099,366	5.	Italy	169,917
2.	France	719,414	6.	Spain	77,569
3.	Gibraltar	19,702	7.	Tripoli	61,575
4.	Belgium	195,642	8.	Tunis	41,226

1880: Major ranked importers (£)

1.	Russia	6,179,886	5.	UK	105,497
2.	Egypt	1,471,691	6.	Tunis	104,057
3.	Tripoli	688,100	7.	Algiers	48,988
4.	Italy	236,428	8.	Turkey	31,034

Major ranked export destinations (£)

1.	UK	3,759,333	5.	Italy	114,467
2.	Belgium	2,553,706	6.	Spain	104,605
3.	France	2,156,193	7.	Algiers	85,162
4.	Gilbraltar	1,267,751	8.	Tripoli	29,113

1897: Major ranked importers (£)

1.	Russia	6,780,262	5.	Tripoli	112,295
2.	Turkey	3,198,883	6.	Austria	51,826

3.	Italy	211,697	7.	Greece	49,247
4.	UK	150,473	8.	France	44,599

Major ranked export destinations (£)

1.	UK	1,784,834	5.	Tripoli	12,734
2.	France	457,901	6.	Turkey	3,992
3.	Tunis	133,361	7.	Greece	771
4.	Italy	41,999	8.	Russia	292

1900: Major ranked importers (£)

1.	Russia	4,413,829	5.	Tripoli	113,472
2.	Turkey	2,097,186	6.	USA	47,144
3.	UK	305,010	7.	Egypt	25,431
4.	Italy	179,444	8.	Tunis	28,261

1900: Major ranked export destinations (£)

1.	UK	1,100,924	5.	Tunis	4,034
2.	Italy	92,569	6.	Turkey	673
3.	Tripoli	20,073	7.	Russia	305
4.	Egypt	12,869	8.	USA	60

1930: Major importers (rank order)

1. UK
2. Italy
3. British colonies
4. Germany
5. Tunis
6. USA

Domestic export destinations (rank order)

1. Netherlands
2. Italy
3. Germany
4. British colonies
5. Tunis

Re-export destinations (rank order)

1. Egypt
2. Tunis
3. Italy
4. UK
5. Libya

1938: Major importers (rank order)

1. UK
2. British Empire (Australia)
3. Romania
4. Italy
5. Germany

Domestic export destinations (rank order)

1. UK
2. Netherlands
3. Turkey

Re-export destinations (rank order)

1. UK
2. Egypt
3. Libya
4. Italy
5. Tunis

Source: Annual Reports and Blue Books, Government Printing Office, Valletta.

> de Barbarie; de grains et semences d'Egypte, de Barbarie, de Russie, d'Italie, de Syrie'... [26]

A similar position was maintained by exports to North Africa, where European destinations predominated before Tripoli and Tunis came into the lists. However, these gross figures conceal the underlying nature of the trade pattern, since neither they, nor the French consul quoted above, indicate the significant difference between transit trade and landed goods. In fact, the absolute figures for trade with Black Sea ports - six times as great as those for North African destinations on average - arise from the vast amounts of wheat involved, quantities of up to 2 million salmes on average throughout the latter part of the nineteenth century. Nor was this wheat for local consumption, since it formed the bulk of the export trade to Britain and other North European ports. In 1870, for example, grain imports from Russia totalled 682,534 salmes, from Turkey 412,747 salmes, from Austria 68,442 salmes, from Egypt 39,758 salmes, with Tripoli and Tunisia contributing 4,898 salmes and 5,457 salmes respectively. Of these totals, which together came to 1,216,521 salmes, only 101,250 salmes were actually landed - less than 10 per cent of the total [27]. In 1880, Russia provided 1,635,973 salmes, as against 4,100 salmes from Tripoli and 21,960 salmes from Tunis.

However, North Africa reigned supreme in the livestock and oil trades (Table 1.3). In 1880, for example, of the 10,202 cattle landed at Malta, Tripoli supplied 5,137 head, while Tunis supplied 4,115 head. The importance of olive oil imports, for trans-shipment, from Tunisia and Tripoli continued to be important - apart from climatic factors - until the French occupation of Tunisia in 1881, when Italy came to dominate in the trade. In fact, for North Africa the problem was always climatic. In the Regency of Tripoli, particularly, the uncertainty of the harvests - only four out of ten were considered to be adequate[28] - meant that it could not be relied on for wheat and barley supplies. As far as animals were concerned, the supplies were usually adequate, except when drought struck, as in 1871 and 1892. The animal trade was thereafter suppressed for several years and supplies had to be found from elsewhere, usually from Turkey. In 1881, drought struck Binghazi and the livestock trade there with Egypt was similarly affected. Indeed, the trade from Cyrenaica to Egypt was much more significant than that from Tripolitania to Malta, with up 30,000 head of cattle a year going to Egypt[29]. However, given the territorial differentiation between administrations in the two Vilayats and the complex taxing systems used in Ottoman Libya, the livestock trade in Cyrenaica operated quite independently from Tripolitania and the benefits were equally localised, particularly as they were often farmed out[30].

One critical element that led to the dominance of Tripoli in the commercial affairs of Malta was the institution of the esparto trade in 1868. Esparto grass, which grows widely throughout the Tripolitanian littoral and in southern Tunisia as well, became important as a raw-material for the British paper industry. Soon a major trade grew up, with an esparto market being held in Tripoli on Mondays and prices being dictated by the prices offered by British paper manufacturers. A price of 55 to 72 shillings per ton in Britain meant prices of 9 to 17 piastres per quintal in Tripoli, with freight charges to Britain standing at 9 to 11 shillings per ton by the end of the century. Between 1902 and 1911, average annual production stood at 30,000 tons, although, by this time, the harvesting of the esparto, which involved pulling it up by the roots, had drastically damaged its potential as an export crop. Much of the esparto exports went out via Malta[31].

The Tunisian esparto exploitation never achieved the same significance, partly because local political conditions before the French occupation made collection far more difficult. Esparto was traditionally used for local, rural needs[32] and the British consul in Tunis decided to attempt to organise its collection in 1871 - or so he told the Foreign Office[33]. However, the trade was never as considerable as that in Tripolitania and, following the French occupation, it was essentially taken over by French interests and no longer satisfied the British market. Certainly there was not the close interrelation between producer and consumer as occurred in Tripoli, where British firms, mainly based in Liverpool, London, Grimsby and Sutherland sometimes had their own warehouses actually in Tripoli itself.

It is clear that the forty-six years between the fall of the Qaramanli dynasty in Tripoli and the French occupation of Tunisia was a period in which Malta's role in the export trade of North Africa was of primary importance. Partly because of its own domestic needs for food supplies and partly because of its major role as a transit centre, Malta dominated the region to the south of it and, 'C'est ainsi que pendant le second et le troisième quart de ce siècle Malte avait réussi à accaparer le monopole presque complet du commerce d'une grande partie des pays barbaresques'.[34] Despite the change from trade within the central Mediterranean to a more strategic role, both in the British-Black Sea grain trade and in the links with India, Malta's role with North Africa remained preponderant. However, the French occupation of Tunisia in 1881 was to close this potential market to British and Maltese commercial interests, although the Maltese themselves became a major component in the new European community that the French were to create there.

MALTESE-LIBYAN TRADE AFTER 1881

Ironically, the impending decline in Malta's trade as a result of factors related to technological improvements in shipping at the end of the nineteenth century, coincided with the closing of the Tunisian markets. By the 1890's, the decline in Malta's maritime trade was evident. The temporary boom created by the Suez Canal had been compensated for by the reduced need for Malta's bunkering facilities and, apart from a short-lived boom during the First World War, the decline became permanent[35]. In fact, the growing French colonial empire in North Africa was also to contribute to Malta's decline, as a 1912 Royal Commission reported:-

> 'Before the creation and development of the commercial harbours of Algiers and Tunis and, in the East, of Alexandria and Port Said, in the beginning of the twentieth century, Malta used to be the principal commercial centre of the Mediterranean where goods were brought and whence they were distributed to the Barbary coast and Sicily. In the opening years of the twentieth century, however, competition became more severe every year and most of the commercial activity was lost to the developing ports on the North African coast'[36].

Even coaling was substantially lost to Algiers by 1900. Tunis ceased to be a significant import source and consistently fell below Tripoli, both in terms of imports and exports (Tables 1.2 and 1.5; note also the decline in Maltese trade from 1891 as shown in Tables 1.2 and 1.7). Only the trade with Tripoli continued as before and, indeed, under-went expansion.

Table 1.7 Malta's imports and exports

Year	(£) Imports	(£) Exports	(£) Locally consumed imports
1850	602,215	281,823	
1851	506,146	192,066	
1860	2,981,947	2,380,820	
1870	4,097,269	3,627,694	
1880	11,459,019	10,703,921	840,425
1890	23,679,321	22,144,067	778,573
1891	35,591,999	34,955,997	1,019,088
1892	12,633,038	11,742,579	1,040,832
1893	13,732,030	12,275,141	1,468,065
1894	13,773,783	13,086,085	735,822
1895	13,099,978	13,231,813	802,891
1896	10,472,139	11,886,149	885,315
1897	10,895,639	11,008,766	905,006
1899	6,668,961	5,449,501	880,164
1900	7,434,289	6,471,567	1,026,829
1901	9,915,254	8,683,126	1,299,309
1904	9,735,859	8,444,024	1,335,831
1905	8,388,492	7,156,848	
1906	7,470,606	6,250,787	1,219,819

Source : Colonial Office, Blue Books, Government Printing Office, Valletta.

THE 1891-1892 ANOMALY

The one contradictory feature in Malta's trade pattern after 1881 is the sudden peak that occurred in 1891. In many respects it seemed to act as a final peak in a trade pattern that was never to recur, for after the massive rise in that year - one-third greater than the previous year, three time greater than the average for the succeeding decade and almost four times greater than the preceding decades - trade steadily declined until 1899, briefly to recover in the initial years of the present century and then to fall again until the First World War.

One obvious explanation for this is to be found in the pattern of Turkish and, more importantly, South Russian, trade with Malta. As Table 1.8 shows, trade with Russia and Turkey closely followed over-all trade patterns for imports into Malta, while exports, particularly of wheat and other grain, to Gibraltar and thereafter Britain, closely followed over-all export patterns. Exports from Russia and Turkey, which varied between one-half and one-third of the total up to 1890 and three-quarters thereafter, consisted almost exclusively of trade in grain. In 1891, for reasons that are not immediately apparent, trade with Russia doubled over the previous year and quadrupled over the previous decade to 22.3 million, out of a total of

35.6 million - itself one-third up on 1890. Turkish trade, at 8.8 million pounds, was double its usual level, but about the same as it had been the previous year. Thereafter, trade with both countries fell, as did over-all trade, as Britain entered the late nineteenth century slump (Figure 1.1).

However, the reason why such a maximum should occur in 1891 is less easy to determine. Indeed, only a tentative explanation can be proposed here, for it relates to factors far from the Mediterranean basin. Firstly, the predominance of Russia in the British grain trade had really come to an end. Not only was there the massive potential of the United States to satisfy burgeoning demand in Britain, where three-quarters of all grain consumed was imported after 1880, - a factor that had steadily grown in importance since the end of the Civil War two decades earlier - but wheat from Canada and Australia was also becoming available to the British market. By the end of the decade, Australia, Canada and the USA were to dominate in the British market and Russia and Turkey had become relatively insignificant.

However, in 1890, an event had occurred which, temporarily at least, had made US grain unattractive to British importers. In that year, the USA adopted the MacKinley tariff, a rigorous system of protection, and Britain began to look for alternative trading partners where the principles of free-trade would still apply. The growing dependence on the US grain trade was an obvious candidate for replacement by alternatives and it seems that, temporarily at least, a return was made to Russian sources of supply. It did not last for long, although imports of grain from Russia continued at a relatively elevated level for the rest of the century. In the end, the growing Atlantic dominance in trade patterns was to reassert itself and Russia had, by 1900, sunk into insignificance.

Interestingly enough, the pattern of North African trade with Malta mirrored that of over-all trade, particularly with respect to Maltese imports from Tripoli and Tunis. However, the reasons for this cannot be linked to issues concerned with British-US commercial relations, since the items involved were different. Whereas the Russian/Turkish trade was based on grain, Tripoli/Tunis exports to Malta were primarily based on cattle for local consumption, although grain and oil played an important role as well, as can be seen from Table 1.9. However although Tripoli enjoyed a major rise in cattle exports to Malta in 1891 and 1892, the total number of cattle imported into Malta during the 1890's, and early 1900's remained relatively constant, only showing a slight rise after 1901. From 1890 until 1900, Russian supplies of cattle averaged 3,766, with a fall of towards 2,000 head annually as Turkish supplies took over. Supplies from Tripoli during the same period, however, averaged 8,035 annually, or 6,492, if the two exceptional years of 1891 and 1892 are excluded. The balance of supplies of live cattle came initially from Austria and Hungary and later from Turkey. After 1900,

Fig. 1.1 Maltese imports from Russia and Turkey

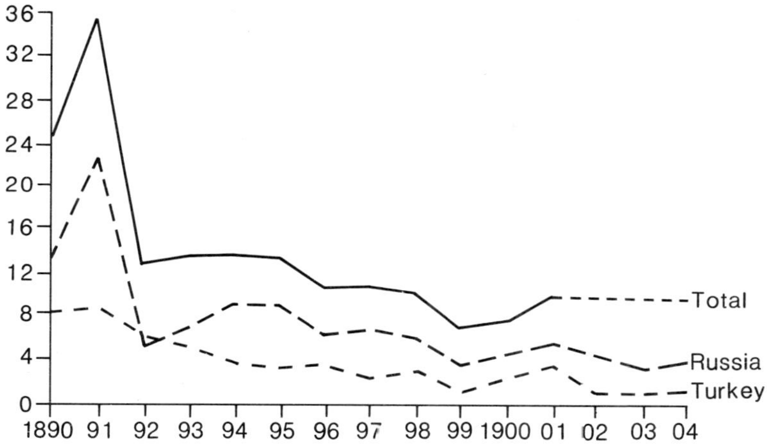

Fig. 1.2 Maltese imports of cattle

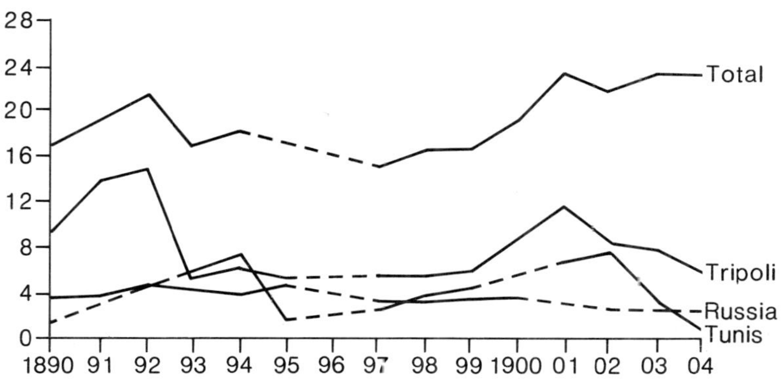

Table 1.8 Maltese imports from Russia & Turkey

(£)

Year	Total	Russia	Turkey
1890	23,679,321	13,610,348	8,016,972
1891	35,591,999	22,314,148	8,752,618
1892	12,633,038	4,961,352	5,566,285
1893	13,732,030	6,916,697	5,247,606
1894	13,773,783	9,084,644	3,700,824
1895	13,099,978	8,853,897	3,290,863
1896	10,472,139	6,012,473	3,672,000
1897	10,895,639	6,780,262	2,319,883
1898	10,025,131	5,813,894	2,910,842
1899	6,668,961	3,556,297	799,689
1900	7,434,289	4,413,829	2,097,186
1901	9,915,254	5,062,299	3,614,733
1902	...	4,341,571	804,634
1903	...	3,265,190	882,613
1904	9,735,859	3,902,952	986,658

Table 1.9 Maltese imports of cattle

(head)

Year	Total	Russia	Tripoli	Tunis	Turkey
1880	10,202	...	5,137	4,115	...
1890	16,605	3,481	9,293	1,603	...
1891	19,316	3,619	13,082	...	...
1892	21,279	4,235	14,609	...	...
1893	16,826	4,178	5,153	5,000	...
1894	18,464	3,951	6,242	7,132	...
1895	...	4,617	5,138	1,685	...
1896	15,118	3,029	5,750	2,481	...
1897	15,118	3,029	5,750	2,481	...
1898	16,653	3,190	5,653	3,542	
1899	16,787	3,532	5,943	4,125	1,925
1900	19,227	3,827	8,762	2,930	2,240
1901	23,231	...	11,767	6,761	...
1902	22,037	2,684	8,216	2,930	2,098
1903	23,489	...	7,931	3,260	9,312
1904	23,390	2,413	5,721	1,039	10,422

Source (For Tables 1.8 & 1.9) Blue Books, Government Printing Office, Valletta.

Fig. 1.3 Libyan Trade with Malta

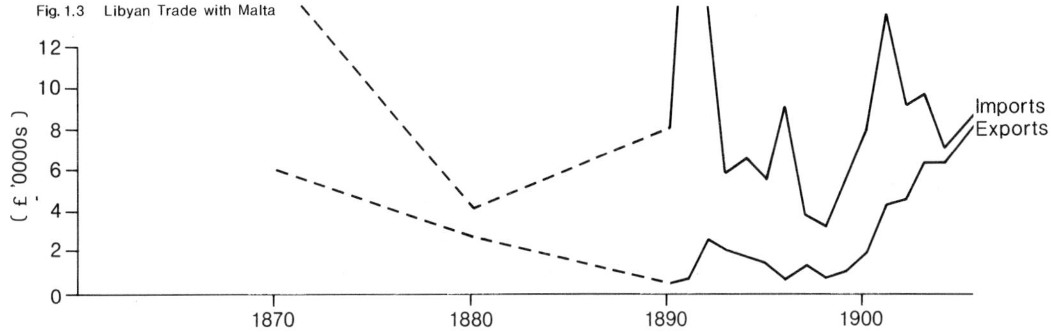

Fig. 1.4 Malta's import and export trade

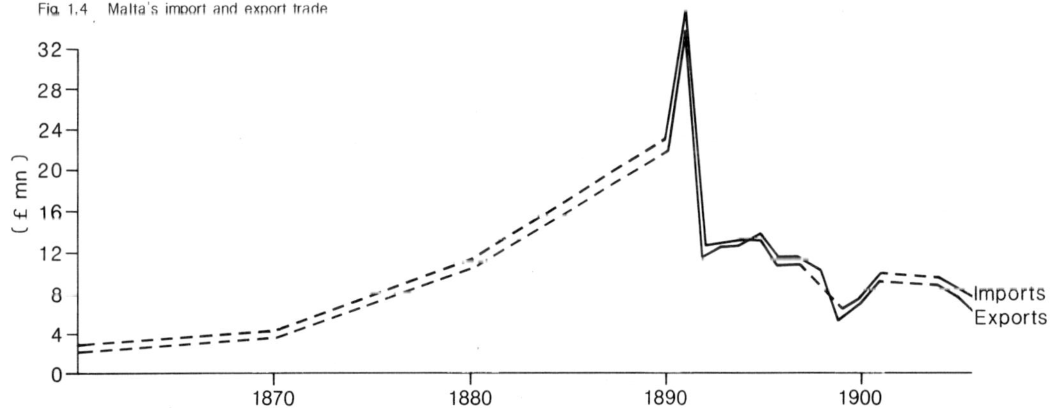

live cattle were slowly replaced by frozen meat from Australia.

The importance of the abnormally-high imports of cattle from Tripoli in 1891 and 1892 (see Figure 1.2) in the over-all value of exports from North Africa is evident once the relative values of different kinds of imports are considered. In 1895, for example, cattle from Russia were worth 10 pounds per head, from Tripoli 8 pounds per head and from Tunis 7 pounds per head. Wheat from Russia was worth 1.4 pounds per salme, barley from Tunis cost 0.8 pounds per salme and saggina from Tunis was available at 0.9 pounds per salme. Thus, unless grain formed a major element in the over-all trade picture by volume, the role it would play in over-all value was minor. This was exactly the situation with North Africa, where, in 1895, imports of wheat from Russia, of 125,415 salmes were worth 175,581 pounds as against 4,617 cattle worth 46,170 pounds - almost four times as much. In the case of Tripoli, 5,138 cattle imported into Malta were worth 41,104 pounds while the balance of the trade was made up from 17,582 caffisi of olive oil worth only 10,110 pounds - just the reverse of the Russian example. With Tunis, these relative values were even more striking with 1,685 cattle worth 11,795 pounds, 1,522 salmes of barley worth 1,218 pounds, 3,792 salmes of saggina worth 3,413 pounds and 17,072 caffisi of oil worth 10,243 pounds.

From these figures, it is quite clear that the sudden surge in Libyan exports to Malta (Table 1.3 and Figure 1.3) was due solely to Malta's internal requirements and to a failure to find suitable supplies elsewhere - probably because of the relatively-low prices available in North Africa. In addition, it was due to the domination of livestock in the trade pattern, unlike the situation with other suppliers, such as Russia or Turkey. Furthermore, the increased level of supply of livestock from North Africa failed to maintain itself after 1892 because of a severe drought in Tripoli and Tunis. Quite simply, supplies from North Africa were not available to satisfy the evident demand and the Maltese turned elsewhere. Equally certainly, the global issues of North American British trade played no role in the local trade patterns between Malta and North Africa at this time.

THE TWENTIETH CENTURY OPENS

From 1898 onwards, the British-Maltese trade continued to dominate with barley, for the distilleries of Scotland, esparto top for Britain and livestock playing the major role for Malta. (Tables 1.5 and 1.10). Nonetheless, Libya's trade had become much more diversified, as Table 1.8 demonstrates, and many other nations now played a significant role. In addition, since the British-Maltese trade was so involved in primary materials, it was very easily affected by climate and the 1892 drought depressed trade for several years afterwards. Nonetheless, after 1900, there was a steady growth in trade.

Table 1.10 Libya's major trade partners 1900-10, (Turkish lira)

Country			Average annual value
Britain	Exports	barley and esparto	135,000
	Imports	manufactures, ironware, tea, drugs.	91,000
Malta	Exports	coal, paraffin	
	Imports	cattle, eggs, fruit, poultry	
Germany)	Imports	tea, glass, ironware, textiles	110,200
Belgium)		matches, textiles	
Austria)		sugar, timber, textiles, meths.	
	Exports	barley, esparto, citrus	6,436
Turkey	Exports	mats, henna, citrus, samne, textiles	57,760
	Imports	flour, cereals, butter	65,000
France	Exports	poultry, eggs, henna, quails, citrus, ostrich feathers	64,400
	Imports	flour, tea, silk, bran, sugar textiles	48,000
Egypt	Exports	cattle, henna, mats	13,960
	Imports	rice, sugar, wool	11,680
Tunisia	Exports	henna, silver, eggs, mats, textiles, citrus	12,800
	Imports	hay, oil, soap, dates, caps, textiles	18,000

Continuation of Table 1.10

Italy	Exports - poultry, silk cocoons, samza (olive residue), hides, skins, bones, scrap metal	
	Imports - flour, bran, coffee, drugs, wine, silk, textiles, hardware, paper, pasta, potatoes, food, furniture, marble, lavastone	
Total Average Annual Trade -		
	Exports	379,400
	Imports	475,680

Table 1.11 Italy's trade with Libya, 1905-10 (Turkish lira).*

Exports	123,520	158,040	121,040	128,840	117,360	176,000
Imports	26,120	22,800	42,160	27,040	64,240	128,000

Sources: For Table 1.10 and 1.11. Cachia A. op.cit., pp. 170-174.

* £1.00 = 0.96 TL

In part, the climatic problems were compensated for by the continued buoyancy of the trans-Saharan trade which continued until the start of the twentieth century. From 1872 until 1881, it had been operating at about 40,000 Turkish lira per year, but dropped after the French occupation of Tunisia, until in the 1890's the annual level was in the order of 24,750 Turkish lira[37]. By 1911, it had fallen below 10,000 pounds per year, mainly because of the French occupation of the central African sultanates of Kanem and Waddai in 1904, the opening of the Kano-Lagos railway and the French occupation of Timbuctoo. The Italian occupation of Libya finished it for ever[38].

The major ports for Libya now were, in order of importance, Tripoli and Binghazi which handled a vast range of goods, including ivory, gold dust, ostrich feathers, hides, sponges (30 per cent of all sponges produced in the Mediterranean and of a much higher quality than those in Tunisia), wool, carpets, matting, salt, barley, citrus fruits, dates, soda (natron from the Fezzan) and livestock; Al Khums and Zlitan specialised in the esparto trade and then Zuwarah, Misratah, Marsa Susah and Darnah which handled grain, salt and cereals. They were served by a series of local shipping lines which depended on the destination of the goods involved. The British trade was handled by chartered ships, the Maltese trade by an Italian company, the Societa Generale di Navigazione, and a Maltese company, Pace. German, Belgian and Austrian trade went via Malta, Turkey and Egypt made use of the Maltese and Italian lines, while the French trade went via Tunisia and the Italian via Genoa[39].

Now, however, political considerations once again entered into commercial considerations. Italy had been casting envious eyes on Libya after the French occupation of Tunisia in 1881 made it impossible for Italian colonial ambitions to be satisfied there. The Italian collapse in East Africa at Sadowa in 1896 made Libya seem even more attractive and, once the major powers - Britain and France - had decided their policies over the occupation of North Africa after 1904, Italy clearly decided that Libya was to become its own colonial destiny. From 1907 onwards, Italian commercial activity became predominant, with Italian shipping representing 45 per cent of the total tonnage using the port at Tripoli and with Libyan-Italian trade doubling between 1906 and 1910. This did not mean that over-all trade grew, in fact it had begun a gentle decline. and the growth in Italian trade was achieved at British expense[40] (Table 1.11).

At the same time, a policy of 'peaceful penetration' began by means of the operations of the Banco di Roma. The eighteen branches of the bank, set up after 1907, purchased land and set up local industries, while new shipping lines appeared, financed by the bank[41]. The bank even extended its activities into Binghazi and began to take over the remnants of the trans-Saharan trade[42]. All in all, the essential economic underpinning for a colonial presence had already been created by the time the Italian occupation came in 1911, in response to French moves to institute its Protectorate in Morocco. Indeed, had it been delayed, other powers might have disputed the Italian claim to pre-eminence in Libya. Tripoli already had six banks - French, Maltese, Italian and German - there were twenty-four commercial agencies there, together with hospitals and schools to service a European population of 4,403, including 918 Italians, 2,623 Maltese, 664 French, 105 Greeks, 150 Spaniards and 43 Austrians [43].

Thus, by 1911, British commercial predominance in Libya had been replaced by Italy. Once again, as had been the case in the first thirty-five years of the nineteenth century, commerce was used very effectively to provide the basis for European interference in Libyan affairs and, in this case, to prepare the ground for colonial occupation. The Maltese, who had played such an important part in the previous period, as merchants and speculators, had grown in numbers from the 1,000-odd there in 1850, to over 2,000 by 1911. Their activities had also changed, for now they were involved in petty trade and in construction, or crafts [44]. They had, in fact, ceased to be the representatives of imperial power and had, instead, become part of the complex ethnic mosaic which played an essential role in the institution of colonies of settlement in Libya and Tunisia during the twentieth century.

THE MALTESE PRESENCE IN TUNISIA AFTER 1881

Population pressure in Malta has always meant that there has been a significant component of migration in the activities of the Maltese themselves. Even under the Order of Malta, attempts were made to settle the excess population elsewhere, including the West Indies in the seventeenth century [45]. Once the British occupied Malta, attempts were made to encourage migration to the Ionian islands as well as a renewed attempt to persuade Maltese to move to the West Indies, but private migration chose the southern Mediterranean instead. In fact, until the First World War, most Maltese chose to migrate to North Africa, particularly to Egypt, Tripoli, Tunis and Algeria. Although the Egyptian migration tended to be seasonal initially, this was not so much the case with the other North African states, where the first migrants appeared in the first decade of the nineteenth century in Tripoli, during the 1820's in Tunisia and in the 1830's in Algeria.

The initial choice of Tripoli was directly related to the British presence in Malta and to the fact that return to Malta was easy. In the case of Tunis, the first major settlements really began in the 1840's and 1850's and coincided with the modernisation of aspects of the Tunisian state undertaken by Ahmad Bey and his successors. In Algeria, the cause was quite simply the institution of French rule after 1830 which encouraged the Maltese, always staunch Catholics and determined to preserve their cultural identity, to migrate there in the security of European control. Migration patterns and flows also followed recessions in Malta, themselves dependent on trade and there was thus a dramatic rise in migration in the 1870's.

In Tunisia, the initial settlement at Port Farina in the 1840's was rapidly followed by the establishment of a community in Tunis itself, on the edge of the medina, where it formed, 'un lumpen-prolétariat qui croupissait dans la misère'[46]. Once the Protectorate had been installed, the Maltese population grew rapidly, from 6,500 in 1881 to 11,300 by 1911. (see Table 1.12). Its members began to acquire property, having control of 15,295 hectares of land in 1900 and owning 424 buildings in Tunis by 1903. Nonetheless, it remained substantially an artisan and petit-bourgeois group. In Sfax, for instance, there were 56 workers, 28 craftsmen and 10 farmers out of a total population of 246[47]. In the south, a similar pattern appeared with 91 tradesmen and 81 craftsmen out of a total population of 198 in Gabes, and similar figures in the military territories to the south of Gabes itself. In Djerba there were 86 tradesmen and 250 fishermen, gardeners, craftsmen and restaurant owners, out of a total population of 348[48].

Clearly then, the Maltese in Tunisia played an essential but lowly, role in the creation of a French-dominated European community in the country. Their importance lay in the fact that they provided a weight against the Italian presence in Tunisia during the early years of the Protectorate. The French authorities certainly saw matters in this way and continued to consider the Maltese presence important until, in 1921, all foreigners in Tunisia were obliged to accept French citizenship or accept the permanent status of being foreigners. Of the 13,520 Maltese in Tunisia, 5,000 took French nationality, while 7,500 remained British. From that date the Maltese community in Tunisia declined. Nonetheless, it had played a counterpart role to Maltese trade with Tunisia, in ensuring that the eighteenth and nineteenth century links between Tunisia and Malta should continue at a degree of closeness that was belied by their cultural diversity. To that extent, Maltese migration and trade played an antiphonal duet in Tunisia, as in Libya, during the nineteenth century.

CONCLUSION

This paper has attempted to show that, under British colonial occupation, Malta rediscovered its identity as an island in the central Mediterranean. Despite the profound cultural differences engendered by being a Christian outpost, the Maltese, once given the opportunity, soon exploited the possibilities for trade and migration offered by the Regencies of Tripoli and Tunis.

Table 1.12 Maltese migrants in North Africa

	1820	1842	1850	1865	1881	1884	1885	1891
Algeria								15,000
Constantine		3,000		6,000			12,000	11,649
Algiers		2,000		4,000			3,000	2,772
Oran								256
Tunisia					6,500			11,527*/11,706
Tunis		2,000		5,000			8,000	
Souss		250		500			1,000	
Sfax		250		500			1,000	
Other		500		1,000			1,000	
Gabes								
Djerba								
Terr.milit.								
Tripoli								
Binghazi		200		500		300	500	
Tripoli	1,500	800	1,095	1,500			2,000	
Total**		20,000		40,000			55,000	

		1900	1901	1906	1911	1921
Tunisia***	10,330		11,700	7,311	11,300	13,520
Gabes	196			137	198	
Djerba	345			245	348	
Terr.milit.	59			36	83	
Tripoli		1,900			2,600****	

Continuation of Table 1.12

* This figure is taken from Sammut C. (see below).
** These figures are for all Maltese migrants throughout the Mediterranean.
*** Alternative figures are given in Sammut C. (see below). (1906-10), p.330).
**** This figure includes some Britons.

<u>Sources:</u> Price C.A., 1945, <u>Malta and the Maltese,</u> Melbourne, p.230 for 1842, 1865 and 1885 figures.
Martel A., 1965, <u>Les Confins Saharo-Tripolitains de la Tunisie,</u> PUF, Paris, Vol.II, p.94 for Tunisian figures 1896-1911.
Fallot E., 1896, <u>Malte et ses Rapports Economiques avec la Tunisie,</u> (Revue Tunisienne) for 1891 figures.
Sammut C., 1973, 'La Minorité Maltaise de Tunisie: ethnie Arabe ou Européenne?', Galley (ed.), <u>Actes du Premier Congrès d'Etudes des Cultures Méditerranéennes d'influence Arabo-Berbère,</u> SNED, Algiers, p.424 for 1906 Tunisia figure of 15,326 (UK) and 11,700 (France).
Segré C.G., 1974, <u>Fourth Shore,</u> Chicago UP, USA, p.41 1900.
Bonello J., 1976, <u>Maltese Emigration 1981-1921,</u> RUM, p.14.

1881 Tunisia figures.
Others: SHM BB 1938 for 1884. PRO FO 101/37 for 1820 and 1850.

Table 1.13 Malta's import and export trade in 1856

Country	Imports (£)	Exports (£)
Britain	64,873	1,017,642
Russia	666,642	4,305
Two Sicilies	243,201	8,471
Turkey	695,893	23,610
Egypt	671,768	10,707
Libya (Barbary)	100,533	184,085
	2,724,999	1,838,448

<u>Source:</u> Mifsud J., 1973, <u>The Maritime Trade of Malta 1800-1900,</u> Royal University of Malta, (Msida), (B.A. Hons. dissertation), p.174.

In the case of Tripoli, the initial British interest in victuals for the island of Malta and the British navy stationed there soon gave way to an attempt to interfere in the internal affairs of the Regency by way of Maltese commercial and speculative interests. Eventually this was to lead to such instability and rivalry between Britain and France that the Ottoman empire stepped in and replaced the Qaramanli dynasty in Tripoli. Thereafter, British interest was strictly limited to commercial ends and was eventually replaced by Italy. The Maltese who had migrated there formed a petit-bourgeoisie and artisanal class, numbering about 2,000 by the time Italy occupied Tripoli in 1911.

Tunisia underwent a different experience, partly because of the much greater pressure that France could exert after 1830 and the French occupation in Algiers. After the French occupation in 1881, British influence - never very strong - declined. In addition, the trade between Tunis and Malta, never as regular as that with Tripoli, further declined. Migration, on the other hand, increased, as the Maltese community, under economic pressure in the Maltese archipelago and with the reassurance of European occupation in Tunisia itself, spread through the Regency. It functioned mainly as a surrogate settler class, providing petty services and crafts for the French army and the growing French and Italian interests settling there.

In short, as the central Mediterranean region came under European influence or colonial control, Maltese trade and migration acted as two interlinked aspects of European penetration which, although overshadowed by the much more important east-west trade in which Malta acted as a staging post in British imperial and commercial concerns, were, nevertheless, critical in aiding the absorption of North Africa into the European trading sphere. In part they played a major role in preparing North Africa for colonial occupation, while, at the same time, North Africa became the social and economic hinterland for Malta itself.

REFERENCES

1. Blouet B., 1981, *The Story of Malta*, Progress Press, Valletta, pp.28-35

2. Abun Nasr J., 1975, *A History of the Maghrib*, CUP, Cambridge, p.45.

3. Hess A.C., 1978, *The Forgotten Frontier, a History of the Sixteenth century Ibero-African Frontier*, Chicago UP, Chicago USA.

4. Braudel F., 1972, *The Mediterranean and the Mediterranean World in the Age of Philip II*, Fontana, London, 2 Vols., p.116

5. Mallia-Milanes V., 1975, 'British Merchants'

Initial Contacts with Malta: a Reconsideration', in *Melita Historica*, VI (4), p.360.

6. Joffé E.G.H., 1984, 'British Malta and the Qaramanli Dynasty (1800-1835)', paper submitted to the *First ACOS Conference*, Tunisia, p.3

7. Valensi L., 1963, 'Les Relations Commerciales entre la Régence de Tunis et Malte au XVIIIème Siècle', *Cahiers de Tunisie*, *43*, 3, pp.74, 77.

8. Valensi L., 1963, *Le Maghreb Avant la Prise D'Alger*, Flammarion, Paris, p.63

9. Scerri D., 1978, 'Aspects of Anglo-Maltese Relations Under the Later Stuarts', in *Storja 78*, Valletta, pp.6-7

10. PRO, Kew, FO 76/750-753

11. Blouet B., *op.cit.*, p.164.

12. Valensi L., 1963, *op.cit.*, pp.78,79.

13. Mantran R., 1961, *Inventaire des Documents d'Archives Turcs du Dar el-Bey*, Tunis, PUF, Paris, p.111

14. Kraiem M., 1973, *La Tunisie Précoloniale*, STD, Tunis, Vol.II, p.73.

15. Joffé E.G.H., *op.cit.*, for details

16. Folayan K., 1979, *Tripoli During the Reign of Yusuf Pasha Qaramanli* University of Ife Press, Ife-Ife Nigeria, p.61.

17. PRO, Kew, Fo 101/37.

18. Joffé E.G.H., *op.cit.*
Abun Nasr J., *op.cit.*, p.201

19. Mifsud J., 1973, *The Maritime Trade of Malta 1800-1900*, RUM, Msida, (B.A. Hons, dissertation), p.46.

20. *Ibid.*, p.102.

21. *Ibid.*, p.106

22. Wright J., 1969, Libya, Benn, London, p.114

23. Mifsud J., *op.cit.*, p.135.
See also Lafera V., 1976, *British Malta*, Acquilina, Valletta, Vol.I, p.184 for similar comments on the North African trade.

24. Folayan K., *op.cit.*, p.88

25. Ministère des Affaires Etrangères, 22 December 1864, *Corr. Comm. 23 Malte 1858-1863*, pp.121-146

26. Colonial Office, 1870, *Blue Book*. Apparently, Egyptian grain was not attractive because of the impurities it contained. Archives of Malta, LIB 1185.

27. Wright J., *op.cit.*, p.115

28. Cachia A., 1945, *Libya Under the Second Ottoman Occupation*, Government Press, Tripoli, p.168

29. *Ibid.*, p.85.

30. Wright J., *op.cit.*, p.115.
Cachia A., *op.cit.*, p.140

31. Valensi L., 1977, *Fellahs Tunisiens*, Mouton, The Hague, p.214

32. PRO, Wood, 20 April 1871, Kew, FO339/108/133.

33. Fallot E., 'Malte et ses Rapports Economiques avec la Tunisie', *La Revue Tunisienne*, Tunis, No.1896, p.10.

34. Blouet B., *op.cit.*, p.114

35. Fenech D., 1973, *A Social and Economic Review of Malta During the First World War 1914-1918*, RUM, Msida, (B.A. Hons. dissertation), p.5

36. Cachia A., *op.cit.*, p.150

37. Wright J., *op.cit.*, p.114

38. Cachia A., *op.cit.*, pp.164-165 and pp.170-174

39. Gam   M., 1980, *Ramadan Sweiheli, Vie et Oeuvre d'un Personnage de la Résistance Libyenne*, Maitrise, Paris III, p.19.

40. Al-Horeir A.S., 1981, *Social and Economic Transformations in the Libyan Hinterland During the Second Half of the Nineteenth Century: the Role of Sayyid Ahmad Al-Sharif Al-Sanusi*, California, (Ph.D.thesis), p.209.

41. Gamoudi M., *op.cit.*, p.12

42. *Ibid.*

43. PRO *Police Registers for Tripoli, 1847-1855*, Kew, FO 101/18.

Cachia A., *op.cit.*, p.110

44. Zammit J.C., 1968, *Maltese Migration in the Nineteenth Century*, RUM, Msida, (B.A. Hons, dissertation), p.13

45. Sammut C., 1973, 'La Minorité Maltaise en Tunisie; Ethnie Arabe ou Européene?', *Actes du Premier Congrès d'études des Cultures Méditerranéennes d'influence Arabo-Berbère*, SNED, Algiers, p.426.

46. Skik H., 'Les Maltais en Tunisie', *ibid.*, p.88.

47. Martel A., 1965, *Les Confins Saharo-Tripolitains de la Tunisie*, PUF, Paris, Vol.II, p.95

48. *Ibid*

Chapter 2

THE ROLE OF INDIGENOUS FARMING IN THE AGRARIAN STRUCTURES OF TRIPOLITANIA IN THE NINETEENTH AND TWENTIETH CENTURIES

Keith McLachlan

INTRODUCTION

This article has as its objective on examination of agrarian structure and the type of agriculture in western Libya during the period after 1850. It is suggested that the end of the Qaramanli rule in 1835 opened the way for a more progressive approach to agriculture and the rural community. Operation of the Ottoman land codes from the middle of the century had a delayed but perceptible effect in Tripolitania. By the end of the nineteenth century, enclosure of land within private gardens and increased involvement with settled farming characterised rural areas of the best-watered coastal strip. Turkish administrators were taking a positive attitude towards improvement of Libyan farming that further assisted a gradual transformation of productivity in agriculture.

It is possible to argue that the processes of agricultural change followed a pattern that was distinctively Libyan. But in the years after 1911, development took two quite separate paths; one indigenous and the other colonial, whether that authority was Italian or British. The nub of the arguement is whether Libyan farmers created their own internal dynamic of growth in agriculture entirely divorced from adjacent colonial activities, or whether they simply mimicked foreign innovations.

The limitations of the physical environment placed strong constraints on the speed and direction of Libyan development in agriculture. Water was the key factor. The volumes of water available for irrigation were limited to those drawn from shallow aquifers. In its early phases of change, the new agriculture was concerned with a limited range of mainly traditional crops. And both water-lifting for irrigation and levels of yield from crops were inhibited by relatively primitive technology used by farmers.

An issue explored in this article is, to what extent is there a logical and universal progression of Libyan agricultural change from the early years of the present century? It is an observed fact that rural groups who were described as pastorallyorientated semi-nomads at the turn of the century were practising advanced commercial farming under settled conditions as early as the period immediately following the Second World War. It might be adduced that the type of shifting cultivation and semi-nomadic herding that comprises the base level from which later change took place was a complex reaction to cultural predilections, political insecurity, the inhibitions of communal land - or water - ownership, and an agricultural land-use system of an extensive kind. Under the more or less benevolent impact of the Ottoman land codes and Turkish encouragement of farming, land-holding became increasingly private in the coastal areas. Settled cultivation grew in extent. Herding became progressively less important as a contributor to farm incomes.

By 1945, the great majority of Tripolitanians were settled. Cultivation was generally irrigated from much-improved means of water-lifting which, after 1955, was mechanised using diesel pumps. Indicative of the established nature of the settled rural community, land fragmentation was increasingly a problem[1]. The coming of independence opened up yet another phase of change. Libyan farmers began to purchase former Italian farmland, where they intensified production through a substitution of full irrigation for the semi-irrigation practised by the Italians[2]. The cropping pattern in Tripolitania changed in response to this as larger areas were brought under groundnuts, citrus and fodder crops. In effect, the Libyan farming sector spread southwards onto the steppelands though at the cost of land abandonment in the fertile coastal oases.

Since 1970, the Libyan farming sector has survived with difficulty in Tripolitania as water-levels have dropped alarmingly, security of land tenure has diminished and freedom in marketing has been taken away from farmers.

The cycle of development in Tripolitanian agriculture has, therefore, been largely independent of the European colonial influence. The ultimate sign of this has been the absorption of Italian colonial farms into the indigenous system in a process that changed the intensity of land-use, the nature of irrigation and the types of crop grown. It is a paradox that the harshest blows stuck against the prosperity of Tripolitanian agriculture have come with growing oil wealth and heavy state involvement in rural development. By the early 1980's, Libya's richest agricultural land was under threat of failing water supplies. The continuum of progressive change in local farming had also been rudely shattered and the future put in considerable doubt.

THE EARLY CHANGES IN FARMING

Turkish and Italian writings concerned with the middle and late nineteenth century suggest that the traditional economic and social frameworks of the Tripolitanian regions survived intact throughout the political vicissitudes that struck the area during the closing decades of Qaramanli rule, the restoration of Turkish government after 1835 and the encroachments of European penetration as the Italian invasion introduced the experience of colonialism after 1911[3]. Local practices of land-holding, for example, were little influenced by the effects of the Ottoman Land Codes of 1858 and their associated decrees affecting taxation while the majority of the rural population, then engaged economically in various forms of herding activities, were entirely untouched by such interventions by the ruling power. It was only at the turn of the nineteenth century that it was possible to discern the beginnings of basic changes in Tripolitanian Arab economic life. Individuals and groups within tribal units were, by that time, becoming persistent in their claims to retain permanently shares of tribal (communal) land in their own possession and increasingly turned away from former tradition in which communal lands were sub-divided annually between tribal members, who had merely a right to usufruct. From this movement came the emergence of private ownership of land[4], a process fostered by the Turkish administration, which had brought a period of prolonged peace to Tripolitania.

The advent of the Italian colonial regime was the most important foreign influence causing economic change. Systematic attempts at detribalisation in the coastal and Jebeline districts in the twenty years following the Italio-Sanusi wars were pursued actively under the governorship of Marshal Balbo in the 1930's. He effectively reduced the power of local ruling families and eliminated the military strength of the tribes[5].

The mass employment of Arabs in the public services, army, industry, and Italian-controlled agriculture was more insidious and far-reaching than the planned detribalisation by the Italian authorities, for the Arab was offered employment outside the tribal system which pressure in other quarters compelled him to take. The general effect of Italian contact was that most tribal groups lost the full economic allegiance of their members.

The so-called 'boom' period after 1955 stimulated further indigenous economic change, mainly in the urban sphere in Tripolitania, but also to an increasing extent in rural areas. The presence of relatively cosmopolitan markets in Tripoli, and successes in the export of groundnuts and olive oil stimulated further investment in agriculture, particularly in the Arab sector during the 1960's.

Land development for agriculture in Tripolitania began in the late decades of the nineteenth century. The clear dating made possible by the move from nomadic to sedentary occupance helps the assessment of the amount of investment in the oases very considerably. From the writings of Europeans who visited the Qaramanli court at Tripoli and from subsequent works by European travellers concerning conditions in the second Ottoman period, it appears that in nomadic times Tripolitania contained a series of small palm oases strung along the length of the littoral [6 7 8]. Garden culture was limited to the immediate vicinity of the villages and carried on by small groups of peasants. After that time, the palmeries were extended to form a more or less continuous strip along the littoral [9]. This change in the nature of the oases was brought about by steady investment in agriculture.

The transition from traditional semi-nomadic occupance to modern Arab commercial farming was not an unbroken process. There were several critical breaks affecting it which resulted from modifications in the scale and direction of investment over time. Evidence taken from a land-use survey of the oases and a companion questionnaire survey [10] indicated a broad but discernible pattern of human and capital investment during the years preceding the arrival of oil revenues after 1951.

The first phase in the process of development was the traditional semi-nomadism which was located mainly in the peripheral and inner steppe lands of Tripolitania. In the social and economic framework of Libya in the years before the Italian conquest, the rural areas of Tripolitania were essentially self-sufficient. The nomadic tribes were adjusted to the necessities of the pastoral life from which they gained a living, at times good, more frequently indifferent and often poor, depending upon the vagaries of the climate and the availability of pasture and water for the flocks [11].

The surplus available from this economic activity was correspondingly small. Where the environment permitted an easy living, as for instance in the Jabal Al Akhdar areas of Cyrenaica, or where trade routes brought an influx of wealth, this was used to support tribal friction and periodic warfare. The net result of these factors was to militate against the accumulation of capital and to tie the majority of the population engaged in pastoral occupance to the basic necessity of providing food and shelter.

The forces of nomadism which dominated the interior steppes, and the necessities of the semi-nomadic life precluded profitable agricultural utilisation of the coastal oases. Production of agricultural goods was limited by the short-term nature of tribal settlement in any given area, and the yields from the crops which were cultivated under the system (mainly grain and fodder) were poor, corresponding closely to the ill-developed technical standards known to the semi-nomads [12]. During the later years of the nineteenth century semi-nomadism became a less dominating social routine and growing preoccupation with arable farming brought in its train a greater geographical centralisation in the coastal oases.

A second phase of economic change is characterised by the maturing of several diverse but inter-related factors, individually minor, but in total sufficient to change both location and alignment of economic activity. Pressure of family claims to retain particular plots of land on a permanent basis was increasingly accepted by the tribal group. Annual division of tribal lands amongst the constituent members ceased, though significantly, for oasis land alone. Over a period of time, investment by individuals and small family groups in private land in the oasis belt of the littoral provided an alternative economic interest for people of the semi-nomadic tribes. The gradual nature of the transition from tribal to private land-holding deserves emphasis, for tribal control of the steppe lands continued until recent times and preoccupation with livestock herding in not insignificant areas of the western area left a measure of the economic and social power of the tribal unit unimpaired.

The processes of economic evolution were reflected in an altering approach to land-use and consequently in changes in the value of agriculture on different categories of land. The indigenous revolution which later saw the sedentarisation of most of the peoples of rural Tripolitania, also witnessed a great re-alignment of land-use zones. The erstwhile cropland of the steppe relapsed, under shifting cultivation, to unimproved grassland or to scrubland in the non-agricultural category. The unimproved grasslands of the peripheral steppe were reclaimed for use as intensively-cultivated land. That is, initial movements resulting from social and economic change engendered major changes in land-use [13]. In effect, during the gradual process of sedentarisation, the peripheral steppe lands tended to lose value as a zone of shifting cultivation since dryland cultivation in the climatically favoured areas of the littoral grew in importance.

The crucial change in occupance from nomadism in the steppe to sedentary life in the oasis areas had effects upon agricultural production and yields. Opportunities for irrigation increased as the tribes settled in the oases. Less time spent by the nomads in pursuit of pasture for their flocks meant more time in the oasis gardens and greater scope for the development of agricultural techniques.

Production of crops under shifting cultivation was hedged in by several rigid considerations. In the first place, the physical geography of the region miltated against a reliable return from seed broadcast in the steppe areas. A basic feature of shifting agriculture in Libya has always been the wide spatial dispersion of sowing areas made necessary by the localised nature of rainfall in the interior. Thus it was the practice in nomadic tribes to allocate scattered plots of territory amongst its members so that any one family unit could have maximum security against the failure of all its crops. The main sources of steppe-grown cereals were the beds of wadis or large wadi-depressions of the inner steppe. While wadi-sown cereals are less subject to the dangers of rainfall failure, they tend to be exposed to dangers of heavy run-off. In addition to these hazards, the instability of crop production was enhanced by the variability of rainfall itself. In the Bani Walid and Bir Dufan areas and all the steppe areas inland from the coastal plain, variability of rainfall averages 40 to 50 per cent. Hence even with scattered sowing of grain there is a high incidence of crop failure.

In the oases, these limitations brought about directly and indirectly by the climatic regime are less severe. Most obviously, rainfall at coastal stations is greater than at those in the steppe zone. In the oases, the incidence of rainfall throughout the agricultural year is, on average, better distributed than in the steppe for cereal cultivation. Variability, too, decreases rapidly from the steppe to the coast. These three factors - improved rainfall incidence, variability and quantity - mean that production may be concentrated in smaller areas of the oases with the added advantage that the flood risk, high in the steppe, is here reduced[14].

Concentrated agricultural production in the oases brought about a decline in the importance of the herds. Sedentarisation meant that the agricultural year ceased to be governed by the annual cycle of pasture seeking; forms of full or semi-nomadism became modified to seasonal nomadism or transhumance. Corresponding to these modifications of nomadism as society developed, sedentary agriculture increased in economic importance in the oases and production rose. As more time became available for prolonged residence in the oases, so it was more in the farmer's interest to give priority to his interests in arable farming. In simple terms, this resulted in most farmers sowing and harvesting their seed when the climate was most propitious rather than when the herding cycle permitted it. Residence in the oases also made possible the storing of grain surpluses from one year to the next.

The rate and direction of indigenous investment in agrarian land development was limited by continuing livestock operations in the steppe lands. While semi-nomadism tended to be replaced by seasonal transhumance, full sedentarisation had not taken place. The Tripolitanians still resisted the idea of sedentary life[15] and even the settled farmers regarded themselves as men of the steppe. This is an important attitude since it encouraged large-scale investment in livestock on the one hand and on the other hand a disinclination to invest in the oases, which were still thought of as temporary resting grounds.

As the Arabs moved to the oases, so the necessity arose for basic reclamation of garden areas, particularly, the enclosure of family and individual holdings. Reclamation of this nature usually involved an extension of palmeries, which were associated with, or which result from, the construction of wells. Similarly, time and labour in the oasis land was spent on other features of reclamation such as levelling the terrain and providing access to paths and roads within the oasis.

But investment in irrigation facilities remained at a low level[16]. Water was obtained either by part rights or by purchase. The well systems used were simple and shallow bores which had been constructed during the era of communal ownership, and which had devolved to use by various tribal fragments. The virtual communal ownership of wells found in early developing areas reduced the value of the individual farms, since low availability of water during the critical dry-periods restricted agricultural activity to a limited varietal specialisation of crops. The access to a well may have been limited to one day in seven or eight, a factor which closely confined irrigated cropping to the 'kitchen garden' and the date rows.

In 1959-60, just before the dawn of the oil era, the average investment per farm unit in irrigation and reticulation systems in Al Khums and the Sahel Al Ahmed areas amounted to 15 pounds per year equivalent, indicating the low average involvement in irrigation technology where many small farmers still had limited access to an irrigation water supply[17].

The changing attitude of farm operators towards landholding as the processes of economic change accelerated, was governed by the necessities of a self-sufficient economy. In Tripolitania, fragmentation of farm-holdings arose naturally from traditional habit and environmental pressure. Annual division of tribal lands had been undertaken as security against crop failure and at the time of permanent allocation of tribal lands amongst members, similar precepts prevailed. Availability or non-availability of water supplies occasioned differentiation in land values within the oasis, especially in view of the small proportion of oasis land in relation to the vast steppes of the interior. Self-sufficient minifundia farm organisation, which emerged from dryland cultivation units observed in the immediate post-sedentarisation period, also tended to exaggerate real differences in land. In general, land-holdings in the steppe become adjuncts to an oasis-based economy.

There was a further increase in intensity of utilisation of agricultural land, with the passage of time. Dryland culture was replaced gradually by inter-cultivation and double cropping techniques. Cropland activity tended increasingly to be concentrated exclusively in the oases, where dryland orchards and gardens were converted to intensive orchard and field cropping.

Underlying the development of minifundia farming and lateral expansion of crop production was the irrigation potential of the oasis lands. Scientific reports produced by Italian missions in the early years of the century indicated that development of irrigation was extremely limited. Contemporary Italian photographs show that much of the littoral was open land planted with occasional palms[18].

Development of irrigation facilities changed this picture quite radically and construction of wells together with reclamation of dryland into irrigated gardens was undertaken to bring about lateral expansion of cultivation. Minifundia farming was so strongly developed that the Italio-Libyan struggles of the 1920's caused only slight disruption to economic life. Two decades earlier in the latter years of Ottoman rule, similar strife, brought on by Turkish attempts to enforce taxation laws, had caused temporary evacuation of the littoral. This is a pertinent index of the changes brought about by the use of irrigation in agriculture.

The major sector of Arab investment was in water supply. Once the provision of reticulation facilities had been effected earlier, a desire arose for the greater use of irrigation which could be met only by construction of wells owned and worked by individual farmers. As farmers increased their knowledge of irrigated farming, so the water demand became more pressing. To cater for the more intensive use of irrigation, the water-distribution system was extended, especially in advanced areas where two wells per farm unit were general. Expenditure on wells and other fixtures showed an appreciable decline at this stage and in most cases changes represented an improved use of facilities already in place.

The rate of agricultural investment tended to be slow corresponding to the self-sufficient character of operations in this phase of agricultural evolution. Capital normally became available only through sale of fortuitous surpluses of produce. The situation was one of apparent conservatism, since irrigated garden culture provided an undemanding living in an early emergent, self-sufficient economy. The deep entrenchment in non-commercial agricultural activity was terminated when land-use was changed from provision for family needs to exploitation of farm-holdings for profit.

Farm units orientated primarily towards the production of cash-crops for the commercial market were indistinguishable in physical form from farms at a less advanced stage, but nonetheless represented some of the most intensively utilised agricultural land in Tripolitania. Inter-cultivation of palm and olive plantations implied an equal emphasis between the two activities. Tree crops were used for commercial production, and varietal specialisation in field crops compared favourably with those cultivated on larger, often foreign-owned, commercial units.

Domestic demands upon the produce of the gardens were still met by the farmer, but the increased availability of water for irrigation gave scope for production of consistent surpluses mainly for the market. The number of crop varieties cultivated remained more or less stable with the change from traditional to a form of transitional farming, but varietal specialisation came about through concentration upon one or two commercial crops on a scale which diminished the role of other subsistence crops.

In the self-sufficient economy in Tripolitania, funds for capital investment accrued from earnings made in years of favourable weather and from off-farm earnings. In a commercial economy, there was a clear change in the character of investment. Commercial operations in the oases offered a relatively sure return on capital each year some of which was available for re-investment in the farm unit. Hence there was a consistent rate of capital investment in agriculture as opposed to the earlier, erratic expenditure on the farm.

At the same time, capital used for investment in the farm business was drawn from sources other than agriculture. Thus, among the effects of installation of motor pumps for irrigation and specialisation of cropping for market, were a corresponding decline in the steppe and livestock holding and a diminishing reliance upon family labour.

Another type of capital investment at this commercial stage of agrarian change was the rationalisation of irrigation facilities to cater for the greater use of water. It was usual for the well-head to be strengthened, and the adjoining storage basin to be enlarged and sealed with cement. A similar process was applied to the irrigation channels where the lines of movement were re-orientated and the channels lined for greater efficiency.

The culmination of Arab agricultural development in Libya before the oil era was expressed in the 'hawaza' farms. These large-scale, irrigated units were concerned entirely with production for the commercial market. The land-use pattern associated with this particular phase of farming activity diverged from earlier forms as a result of the decline in the importance of traditional tree crops, such as dates. On the other hand, intensiveness of land-use through enhanced specialisation of crop varieties did increase, as in the case of quality vegetables and cash-crops such as groundnuts.

The position of intensive commercial farming in Tripolitania immediately preceding the dominance of the Libyan economy by oil may be illustrated by the relatively small areas given over to advanced systems of production. The intensively-cultivated areas, (non-inter-cropped) were represented by two different cultural elements; the Arab gardens and the mezzadria plots of Italian-run concession farms. Clearly, Arab gardens showed appreciable variations in intensiveness of land utilisation corresponding to the stage of development attained by, and the aptitude of, the individual farmer. Nonetheless, the varying style of land-use was more apparent in the choice of varieties of seed and degree of agronomic sophistication than in the types of crop cultivated. From the point of view of intensity of land-use alone, the divergences were less appreciable.

Thus whereas the 'kitchen-garden' element of the minifundia unit later changed from the total cultivated area of a holding to a parcel of 'garden' within a larger farm, subsequent moves to hawaza units were marked by the elimination of the domestic garden and the practice of palm inter-cultivation. To this extent, intensity of land utilisation decreased. The application of new techniques, particularly in irrigation and use of fertiliser, brought about a greater intensity of field crop cultivation.

The distribution of hawaza units was sparse. Pre-1961 in the Misratah-Al Khums area, for example, there were only three or four farms of this nature located within the traditional oasis. But the advances in technique introduced into indigenous farming through the operation of these farms was as important for its educative effects upon the mass of small farmers as it was for absolute production. The results of these technical improvements were illustrated by yields of barley in quintals per hectare on comparable land which rose from 3.5 in rain-fed gardens to 11.5 in advanced transitional oasis farms and to 17 in hawaza areas.

The situation regarding investment was complex, but there were several discernible trends present. The amount of capital required to permit the smooth accession of farm units to hawaza status was large, but at that time in Tripolitania, there could be three main ways - (a) government investment in ex-Italian demographic settlements or the availability of ex-Italian farms where the investment in land development had already taken place (b) accrued capital resulting from tenure of tribal or public office (c) funds accumulated from consistent trading gains usually supplemented by monies gained in urban employment.

Capital investment was directed, in broad terms, to the modernisation of traditional Arab farms into improved production units or creation of farms of a kind that Libyans had gained familiarity with during colonial rule. Rationalisation of the farm business was brought about by means of consolidation of land-holdings, the provision of reliable and plentiful supplies of water for irrigation and matching standards of distributing water about the farm area.

Tripolitania offers an interesting case-study in the economic geography of North Africa by virtue of its position before 1961 as an emergent economy moving under pressure from internal and externally-stimulated change from traditional to transitional farm and land resource management. The course of economic change, in so far as it was expressed in agricultural land-use, can be charted in a realistic way through physical characteristics of the individual farm or farming region. In effect, the mosaic-like nature of rural evolution can be determined with some accuracy to give both the location of, and the spectrum covered by, farm types within any region. Unlike the generalised models available, of which Rostow[19] is the prime instance, an analysis at the farm level indicates, as in Libya, that different farmers in the same area may be involved contemporaneously in primary herding, primitive cultivation and sophisticated horticulture.

Perhaps the most important variable in this North African environment was the application of improved techniques to water extraction and irrigation practice. These two factors, above all else, strongly influenced the patterns of change in rural Libya before 1961. Ownership of water in private hands was a major change from previously existing situations and opened the way up for more rapid and effective exploitation of irrigation on farms. Thereafter increasing ability to lift, store and distribute water on private land-holdings separated advanced from less advanced farmers within the Libyan rural sector.

During the six or seven decades from the first emergence of sedentary farming on a wide scale throughout Tripolitania to the beginning of the period of oil wealth, dated for convenience to 1961, there was a gradual but perceptible alteration in the way that the land and water resources of the area were owned and used. Towards the end of that period there was evidence that a dynamic of change had been set in motion that was purely a Libyan (as opposed to colonial) phenomenon. Still deeply dependent on agriculture for food and export products, Libya appeared to be modernising itself from within and making increasingly good use of very limited physical resources [20]. Unconstrained exploitation of the soil and water endowment was precluded by the limited availability of capital and credit in the hands of both people and government. In consequence, damage to the environment through expanded use of underground water resources was extremely small.

Introduction of augmenting levels of oil revenues into the economy, with increasing local effects during the 1960's, was to upset all optimistic forecasts concerning development of agriculture. The uneven but nonetheless visible continuum of indigenous economic advance in the rural sector was destroyed by the allocation of large sums from the national economic plan to agricultural projects. The dismal prognostications of the World Bank that oil income would bring more problems to the country than it would solve and that there would be growing discrepancy between rates of growth in urban and rural sectors proved in the end to be close to the realities achieved [21]. By the 1980's, agriculture provided few jobs for Libyans, contributed insignificantly to national income and at the same time large areas of the former oasis land had been abandoned as water resources were grievously over-exploited.

There must be seen to be something of a double irony in contemporary developments in Tripolitanian agriculture. Any flowering of indigneous farming that appeared to be so full of optimism to observers in the late 1960's [22], has been constrained by the parallel agricultural economy - that represented by state development of settlement or production units. Private farming has had to contend not only with the economic vicissitudes brought on by the oil economy [23], but with competition for scarce resources with the state sector.

Colonial agriculture, begun by the Italians and maintained by the British Military Administration, appeared to have begun to disappear after 1951. The process was slow at first. Gradually, however, Italian farmlands were absorbed into the new Tripolitanian agriculture. At times this was undertaken both too expensively and too precipitately, financed by soft loans from the Agricultural Bank. The important factor was that, for the first time since 1911, there was a single unitary agriculture throughout the province. Small-scale developments at Wadi Ka'am [24] and later land reclamation under NASA, the National Agricultural Settlement Authority [25], were designed to buttress the private sector even though initiated by the government.

In more recent years, the state has taken over land from Italian owners [26] and remained the operator of sequestrated farms. It has established large-scale production estates and settlement units, of which it has retained control and ownership. The state has, in effect, recreated the bimodal agricultural system, with its holdings on the one hand, lavishly constructed and heavily subsidised in operations, existing separately from the private farms, where enterprise is difficult and constraints abound. It might be suggested that the public domain in modern Libyan agriculture has become the natural successor to the former colonial system. In some ways, state agriculture has acted on the Italian model. It has gone deeper for water and moved south to find vacant land. It ignores almost entirely the needs of the local private farmers and, certainly in respect of its profligate use of underground water supplies, has been developed at the cost of diminished current and future water availability to private farms.

For the purposes of this analysis, it is sufficient to note that the re-emergence of a protected arena of agricultural activities by the Libyan state has led to a deceleration in the dynamic of development and change in Tripolitanian agriculture. The private sector has by no means been strangulated as yet, but the outlook is poor. Structural and institutional problems for farmers are considerable. The water problem, explored elsewhere in this volume, is generating an imperative for major alterations in the form of farming on the Jifarah Plain. Whether private farming will be used as a vehicle for putting a more water-conscious agricultural system into place or will be used as a scapegoat for the need for radical upheavals in the agrarian structure, remains to be seen.

REFERENCES

1. Theodorou N., 1954, *Indigenous and Italian Farm Enterprises in the Azvia Area*, FAO, Rome.

2. Allan J.A. McLachlan K.S. and Penrose E.T., 1973, *Libya: Agriculture and Economic Development*, Cass, London p.97

3. Cachia A.J. 1945, *Libya under the Second Ottoman Occupation*, Tripoli. Cachia notes the work of Hafez Pasha (1899-1903) in registering land p.55 and the agricultural developments under Ahmed Rassem Pasha (1882-98). See also Cachia, A.J. Chapter XIII, pp.109-116.

4. Qureshi A.I., undated, *System of Land Rights and Taxation in Tripolitania*, UN, Lib/TA8.
5. Evans-Pritchard E.E., 1949, *The Sanusi of Cyrenaica*, OUP, Oxford, pp.225-226.
6. Tully R., 1816, *Narrative of a Ten-Years Residence at Tripoli in Africa from the Original Correspondence in the Possession of the late Richard Tully* (The British Consul), London.
7. Cowper H.S., 1897, 'Further Notes on the Tripoli Hill Range', *Geographical Journal*, London, Vol.7, pp.620-633
8. Chemali I., 1916, *Gli abitanti della Tripolitania*, Ufficio politicomilitare, Tripoli.
9. Maugini A., 1931, *Le Colonie Italiane*, Rome, p.35. He suggests an area of suani of 17,000 ha.
10. McLachlan K.S., 1961, *A Geographical Study of the Coastal Zone between Al Khums and Misratah Tripolitania*, (Ph.D. thesis), Durham
11. Cachia A.J., *op.cit.*
12. Clarke J.I., 1960, 'The Siaan: Pastoralists of the Jifarah in Willimot S.G. and Clarke J.I. (eds.) *Field Studies in Libya*, Durham, pp.52-59.
13. Fox J.W., 1956, *Land-Use Survey: General Principles and a New Zealand Example*, Bull. No.49, Geog.Series No.1
14. Vivoli G., 1939, *I cereali nell' Africa settentrionale Italiania*, Tripoli.
15. Brehony J.A.N., 1960, 'Semi-nomadism in the Jabal Tarhunah', in Willimot & Clarke, *op.cit.*
16. British Admiralty, 1920, *A Handbook of Libya*, HMSO, London, p.97.
17. McLachlan K.S., 1961, *op.cit.*
18. Franchetti, 1914, *La Missione Franchetti nella Tripolitania: Il Gebel*, Societa Italiana per lo studi della Libia, Firenze-Milano
19. Rostox W.W., *The Stages of Economic Growth - A Non-Communist Manifesto*, CUP, London
20. Rowland F. and Robb E., 1945, *Survey of Land Resources of Tripolitania*, British Military Administration, Tripoli
21. International Bank for Reconstruction and Development, *The Economic Development of Libya*, Washington D.C.
22. Allan J.A., et al., 1973, *op.cit.*
23. Birks S. and Sinclair C., 1984, 'Libya: Problems of A Rentier State', in Lawless R. and Findlay A. (eds), *North Africa*, London, pp.241-275
24. McLachlan K.S. 1960, 'Wadi Caam Project' in Willimot, and Clarke, *op.cit.*
25. El-Ghonemy M.R., 1967, *Land Policy in the Near East*, FAO, Rome
26. Wright J., 1983, *Libya: A Modern History*, London, p.149

Chapter 3

ITALIAN FASCISM AND LIBYAN HUMAN RESOURCES

John Wright

The Italian conquest of Libya and the Libyan people started with the 1911 assault on Turkish Tripolitania and Cyrenaica by the liberal state. In the early euphoria and facile optimism aroused by the invasion, when the Italians still had high hopes of enlisting local support, the Libyans had been assured with benign simple-mindedness that 'Italy is your father because it has married Tripolitania, which is your mother'.[1]

But by 1930 Italian disillusionment after nearly twenty years of intermittent warfare, rebellion and oppression, particularly in Cyrenaica, was reflected in the comment of Libya's Governor, Marshal Pietro Badoglio, to his second-in-command, General Rodolfo Graziani, '...penetrating the soul of this people is very difficult'.[2] And later: 'But now the way forward has been made clear, and we have to follow it to the end, even if the entire population of Cyrenaica has to perish.' [3]

Although a leading industrial power, Italy between the world wars sought solutions for her economic and social difficulties in agricultural regeneration, including colonial agriculture on the marginal and money-absorbing soils of Libya. There were strategic and demographic arguments for doing so, at least so far as Libya was concerned; other arguments may be found in the nature and loyalties of Fascism. For Libya, the results of Fascist colonial policy were far-reaching: conquest at all costs, followed by the sudden arrival of large numbers of Italian settlers, and the rapid and intensive development of the colonial infrastructure.[4]

Italian colonial policy in Africa in the late 1930's reflected these and other considerations. The long, bloody and unpleasant conquest of Libya had only recently ended, while the swift if superficial conquest of Ethiopia was an even newer achievement. If in Libya the Italians had always to be wary of new outbreaks of unrest, in Ethiopia they faced constant rebellion from warlike peoples in a difficult and distant country. Practical considerations of security thus seemed to demand just, but uncompromisingly firm, dealings with African subjects. The need to settle at first thousands, and ultimately hundreds of thousands of landless Italian peasants on the best lands in Libya and Italian East Africa as a supposed solution to metropolitan demographic problems, reinforced the need for domineering strong-handedness and overt demonstrations of racial superiority by rulers never wholly sure of themselves. Then Fascism itself provided the appropriate ideology for a new Roman imperialism, while naturally denying African subjects the political freedoms and aspirations that metropolitan Italians themselves could no longer claim.

Yet what might have been excessively harsh everyday practice was usually tempered by more benign and realistic considerations, not least of them Fascism's concern with its own international standing and reputation. The conquest of Libya and the extension of Italian rule over large Muslim minorities in Ethiopia meant that Italy had by 1936 become a leading 'Muslim' power, conscious that its imperial record provided a means of enhancing or damaging its image in Islamic opinion everywhere, but most particularly in the increasingly nationalistic Arab World. Mussolini's self-proclaimed role of 'Protector of Islam' (1937) found an echo in the realisation by many Italian colonial officials of the need for a more humane and at least socially and economically more constructive policy towards Rome's Muslim subjects in Libya and elsewhere. This was an attempt to make some amends for the harm done to Italy's reputation by the long conquest of the colony and the death or exile of many thousands of Libyan patriots. Morever, by the mid-1930's the colonial administration had come to realise the value of the Libyans themselves as an essential source of manual and menial labour and as recruits for the conquest of Ethiopia that the Italians themselves were unwilling, or unable, to provide. Combined with these practical considerations was the genuine desire for Africans' social and economic advancement. Not least of the objectives in promoting such advancement was the need to make Italy's African Empire, with Libya foremost, a showplace of efficient Fascist management and an example to other colonial powers of the constructive collaboration possible between racially, technically and culturally 'superior' white settler colonists on the one hand and Italy's emerging African subjects on the other, with the two races developing along parallel, wholly separate, but mutually beneficial lines. Such demonstrable achievement would in turn reinforce Italian claims to undertake the similar sympathetic and effective administration of other African colonial territories.

Yet the role the native Libyans were expected to play in this new Fascist scheme of things was never clearly defined. If Badoglio in 1930 could write about (if not necessarily act upon) a policy of genocide, by the time Air Marshal Italo Balbo became Governor of Libya four years later, the Libyans had at least been recognised as an essential souce of manual labour for the ambitious colonial development schemes, as recruits into the lowest ranks of the burgeoning civil service, and as soldiers for service in Ethiopia. Much as they might have liked to do so, the Italians could not ignore the Libyans.

Soon after the nominal conquest of Ethiopia in 1935-6, it became clear that Rome's subjects in North and East Africa were destined to live under a form of Fascist *apartheid* (although in actual practice Italian rule was so short-lived that the intended system never went fully into effect). In 1939 Martino Mario Moreno defined two principles of Italian policy in Africa[5]:

1. Quantitative and qualitative affirmation of the Italian race;
2. Collaboration with the natives without mixing[6].

The Fascist Colonial Institute itself counted four principles considered to inspire Fascist native policy in Africa:

1. Clear and absolute separation between the Italian and African races;
2. Collaboration without promiscuity;
3. Humanity in respect of past errors;
4. Absolute severity towards future errors[7].

As late as 1941, an Italian commentator wrote:

> Fascist native racial policy is separatist, but also associative-collaborative; it is a just middle way between the excesses of domination and the excesses of assimilation; it fulfils social, ethical and juridical criteria; it is based on racial differentiations that the natives themselves would not want narrowed, while human justice necessitates that they are not widened[8].

Mussolini himself expressed it with headline brevity: *'Umanità sì, promiscuità no'*.

In the view of an American commentator, 'assimilation' was used by the Italians to mean a change in the mental outlook of the natives:

> ...it implied a desire to impress the native with the greatness of Italian civilisation; it sought to gain his respect for Italy's colonising ability; and it attempted to convince him of the singular privilege of being under the domination of modern Rome[9].

In the specific case of Libya, it was felt that things had to be ordered there:-

> ...so that the native population and the new conquering race remain in respect of each other as two parallels, each one making for its own objective, with no reciprocal crossing of paths. The purpose of the lawmaker and the government of Libya must be to demonstrate that the two civilisations, the Christian and the Muslim, can live together side by side, by means of mutual and reasonable tolerance. In its relations with native society, the Italian Government must not devise new methods, but must make use of those

> already existing in the country. A policy inspired by such ideals cannot but give good results and, moreover, is the easiest to follow[10].

Balbo, who was certainly the most attractive and sympathetic of the various leading Fascists sent to conquer and/or administer Libya between 1922 and 1943, and the one most responsible for the colony's notable material development, foresaw by 1938 the need to make provision for the Libyans' moral advancement and civil evolution 'such as to create a spiritual rapport between the conquering power and its Muslim subjects'. He believed that the northern Libyans (he had a generally poor opinion of the Fezzanese) could not continue to be treated as mere colonial subjects; rather he foresaw - on the Roman imperial model - the promotion of such subject peoples first to the rank of 'allies' and then to the status of fully-fledged citizens [11]. Balbo in 1938 envisaged something of an ideal future when he asserted:-

> We will not have rulers and ruled in Libya. Instead we shall have Catholic Italians and Muslim Italians, united in the common fold as constructive elements in a great and mighty organisation, the Fascist Empire [12].

But if this was Balbo's vision, the actual administration of the colony, even under his governorship, showed no signs of evolving along such lines.

The Italians often appeared particularly sensitive about their role as colonial masters. Unlike most other European colonial rulers, they had little experience of governing subject peoples. Moreover, Italian claims to be heirs to a 'higher culture' with which they intended to enlighten Africans did not greatly impress Rome's own colonial subjects. The pastoral peoples of Libya, Somalia and Eritrea, with their traditions of oral rather than visual culture, were unlikely to appreciate the splendours of an Italian civilisation that usually make the greatest superficial impact on outsiders for visual rather than linguistic or literary values, and which are not easily transferred to an African environment anyway. It may indeed be argued that the opposite is true of British and French cultures, and that their literary-linguistic impact on African colonial peoples has accordingly been that much greater.

Then the social gap, the differences in physical appearance, manners and outlook, at least between southern Italians and north Africans, was in many instances too narrow for Italians as a race to be readily accepted as in any way 'superior' to their colonial subjects, especially in Libya. The willingness of Sicilians and other southern Italians to work alongside the locals on the dock-sides of Tunis and Alexandria, or indeed at many other menial tasks, may have helped to establish a certain social rapport, but never the degree of respect that colonial rulers expected [13]; in 1930, even the Italian beggars of Tripoli found it hard to maintain their 'superiority' over their Libyan counterparts[14]. Yet with so many of their own peasants being sent to Africa to continue to till the soil there - a white peasant settler 'without native labour, down on his hands and knees, squeezing the grain out of the soil'[15]- how could Italy expect to assert the 'racial superiority' it claimed for its own people in the East African Empire or in Libya in the late 1930's?

Although a Fascist writer asserted that Italian colonial policy had been 'instinctively racialist' ever since Italy had become active in the Red Sea in the 1860's[16], the fact remains that Fascism itself, although always avowedly imperialist, was not originally racialist[17]. But in 1936, with the conquest of large, diverse and perhaps rather frightening populations in Ethiopia, closer association with an overtly racist regime in Nazi Germany, and resentful of sanctions imposed by the 'Jewish-dominated' League of Nations, the official attitude to race changed sharply. In January 1937, the Cabinet approved a law for 'maintaining the prestige of the race' and for regulating relations between Italians and African natives[18]. The main concern of the lawmakers seems to have been to prevent 'relations of a conjugal nature' between Italians and Africans, with the objective of 'preserving, on national territory as well, the purity of the arian race...preserving it from pollution by semitic blood or that of other inferior races'[19]. Such regulations seemed to reflect in particular a new-found horror of producing socially and physically degenerate half-castes on the Portuguese or French pattern[20]. But the problem seems in practice to have been less one of keeping the natives in check than of preventing the naturally gregarious Italians from becoming over-familiar with them.

This new-found obsession with race was obviously mainly concentrated on the East African Empire. The colony of Libya, lying on Italy's so-called 'Fourth Shore' on the opposite side of the Mediterranean, was recognised as 'a land inhabited by Arab peoples of the white race, of higher culture, and held in control by the rigorous moral precepts of the Muslim religion'[21]. Balbo himself conceded that '...the Arabs and Berbers of the coastlands constitute a population...capable of assimilating the spirit of our laws and evolving onto the stage of a more advanced social order'[22].

Nevertheless, this recognition of their 'superior' status earned Libyans no special 'racial' privileges, compared with other Italian African subjects, but the right, from mid-1939 onwards, to apply for so-called 'Special Italian Citizenship' *(Cittadinanza Italiana Speciale)*. In January 1939, the four coastal provinces of Tripoli, Misratah, Binghazi and Darnah became an integral part of the Italian kingdom. This nineteenth Italian region contained all the Italian agricultural settlements, existing or planned, and nearly all the native population, apart from some 40,000 in the centre and south. The object of the new arrangement was to impress on Italian settlers (then arriving in the colony in their thousands under state sponsorship) that they were not going into exile, or becoming mere 'colonists', but would be making their new lives in another part of Italy[23]. Further reasons were stated to be 'the continual manifestation of loyalty on the part of the Muslim population' and the need to provide for its assimilation. This need was to be met through offering the formal equality of citizenship - although, according to a British observer at the time, '...there is small prospect, immediate or remote, of the Arabs attaining personal equality with the Italians'[24].

There were relatively strict qualifications for application (for instance, literacy in Italian and/or a period of military or public service). For it was obvious, if never openly stated, that citizenship was to be confined to those who had in some way actively demonstrated their acceptance of, and identification with, Italian rule. Hardly surprisingly, the petty privileges conferred by Special Citizenship were not valid outside Libya.

> Citizenship...in its spirit affirms that the Libyan in his own country is what the Italian Citizen is in the fatherland, without however having to divest himself of any of the rights and duties deriving from his religion, any more than those racial values that we defend on his behalf, just as we defend ours[25].

If a Fascist commentator[26] could claim that Italy had 'spontaneously granted' in Libya what the Muslims of Algeria had long been ineffectively demanding of their French rulers, such half-truths ignored the peculiar social conditions that had been created in Libya as a result of the harsh and still recent twenty-year war of conquest.

> The structure of Libyan society had been undermined by the years of fighting, by the flight of refugees...by internal migration in response to new economic pressures, and as a result of the deliberate Fascist policy of destroying the power of the Sanusi Order, abolishing the traditional tribal assemblies, and weakening the authority of the sheikhs and other traditional leaders. As a result, Libyans could only look for leadership and guidance to the domineering and authoritative Fascist regime that imposed its will throughout Italy and the Empire...[27]

Because the traditional native leadership was 'ruined, dead, or in exile', as a British observer noted in 1938, 'only a humbler class is left - a class which has always served, and which is at the moment serving a new master'[28]. Thus the Libyans, like the Italians themselves, were to be considered as a 'proletarian race' and were to make their contribution to the building of the new Roman Empire through their manpower and their acquired manual or martial skills. Ideally, Libyans were to be settled as a docile population of small-holders and skilled or semi-skilled workers. But it was also recognised that the nomads and semi-nomads, driven from their best range lands to make way for Italian colonists, had to be left at least some closely-supervised freedom to lead their traditionally mobile lives on less-favoured lands set aside for their exclusive use [29].

The Italians deserve some credit for their religious policy in Libya. The government of the colony eventually took over all the religious authority of the *Caliph al-Islam* and/or the Head of the Sanusi Order. As Balbo put it, 'Italy has thus taken upon itself the religious protection of its Muslim subjects, by virtue of its dignity as an Islamic power' [30]. The official attitude to the Sanusi Order was particularly harsh and hostile because it was the main source - in Cyrenaica, effectively the sole source - of resistance to the Italian conquest and occupation. But in other respects, the Italians had always been willing to tolerate Muslim practice and observance. Although the Roman Catholic Church largely endorsed Fascist colonial policy, and tended to site its churches conspicuously, it was specifically forbidden to proselytise in Libya - a lesson perhaps learned from its singular lack of success in French North Africa. The colonial government, besides restoring many mosques and shrines, built several new mosques. Such gestures were not necessarily appreciated by the Libyans, who questioned the worth of such acts by Christians, and who anyway saw them as motivated more by the necessity of appeasement than by genuine piety. The Italian authorities took upon themselves many other duties and functions intended to express their goodwill towards Rome's Muslim subjects; it is impossible to judge to what extent such activities achieved their desired object [31].

But in taking on the self-appointed role of 'Protector of Islam' at a ceremony in Tripoli in March 1937, Mussolini - reinforced by the increasingly strident Arabic language broadcasts beamed to the Middle East by *Radio Bari* - seems seriously to have expected to impress Muslims everywhere with Italy's sympathetic attitude towards Islam in general and its religious policy in Libya in particular. It was an image presumably intended to contrast with the striking failures of contemporary British policy in Palestine and Egypt and with growing French difficulties in Algeria and Tunisia. If some observers at the time were led to the desired conclusion that Mussolini's new policy was 'no empty theatrical gesture, but a serious bid for the patronage of the Muslim World' [32], there was little hard evidence by the late 1930's that the necessary groundwork had really been laid in Libya [33].

In common with many Africans, the Libyans were brought by their experience of European colonialism into fuller contact with the outside world, with some of the new ideas, practices and institutions of the early twentieth century. If the ways and means of such contact were often abrupt, crude and abrasive, this was an almost inevitable process in the Libyans' own cultural, social and economic evolution. It was, moreover, a process not necessarily made any more difficult or unpleasant simply because it occurred under a particular form of Fascist colonial rule rather than under any other system of politics or administration.

The demand for labour created by the Italians' ambitious

colonial development and settlement schemes of the late 1930's brought many Libyans into the modern cash economy for the first time, and in many instances enabled them to acquire more than basic manual skills. The Italians always hoped to incorporate the Libyans into a new and more productive agricultural system. In the event, Libyan settlement plans were not successful, mainly because the Italians failed to provide resources and finance and because potential Libyan settlers were more interested in job prospects in public works, the army, the civil service, or on private Italian concessions. And, because Italian metropolitan workers were neither cheap nor abundant, the authorities had to take on more native labour - a practice that may not have accorded with Fascist colonial ideology, but which was a basic logistical and economic necessity, even if the quality and reliability of the labour were not high[34]. The scale of Libyan involvement in large public works can be judged from the building of the Tunisia-Egypt coast road (the *Litoranea* or *Via Balbia*) in 1935-37, which involved 4,510,000 man days of paid work, of which Libyan workers accounted for 4,080,000[35]. And a British observer found in 1939 that:-

> The Arab population in Libya today is less poor than it has ever been in the past. There is no unemployment... everywhere that one travels, from the Tunisian frontier to the Egyptian, they are at work. At seven lire a day, on the roads, the houses, the aerodromes, the aqueducts, clearing the bush and erecting the civic centres and new military barracks and military stores that are springing up from one end of Libya to the other[36].

But employment fluctuated sharply with the seasons and with the demand created by particular development projects. One result of Italian policy was the emergence of a rootless population of rural migrants, trying to make a living on the fringes of the modern cash economy. And Italian colonialism also 'accentuated the existence of a two-level economy. In the interior, tribal life; in the large cities...a Western economy'[37]. Balbo's declared long-term policy was nevertheless to bring the native workers and producers into the same corporative and syndicalist system that controlled the trade and labour of the mother country.

Apart from the organisation of their work and wages, the greatest direct impact of Fascist colonial rule on some ordinary Libyans was felt in the fields of military service and education. The Ottoman Turkish administration had never been able to raise regular recruits in Tripolitania or Cyrenaica, although the Libyans gave the Turks remarkable service as irregulars in the Italio-Turkish war of 1911-12 and again during the First World War. Military units were raised locally almost from the beginning of the Italian occupation. But, understandably, they did not always undertake the subjection of their fellow countrymen with particular zest: Eritrean *askaris* were found more effective and reliable. But, conversely, Libyan troops fought hard and bravely in the conquest of Ethiopia. In February 1936 Libyan and other colonial troops were recognised as 'reserves of the first order for our every expansion to come'[38]. A Libyan Division was formed in 1935; of the 9,500 men in its ranks, 9,100 were Libyan volunteers. In the course of fighting in the Ogaden in early 1936, the division took part in 22 engagements in which one third of its men were killed or wounded[39]. This surprising demonstration of loyalty prompted the regime to take a more generous view of the role Libyans might yet be expected to play in the expanding Fascist scheme of things[40].

The Fascist administration has been much criticised for its alleged failure to educate the Libyans, and until the end of the conquest in the early 1930's 'there were virtually no schools worthy of the name outside Tripoli'[41], although there were certainly more than there had been under the Turkish administration. The main purpose of the Fascist education policy seems to have been to produce relatively large numbers of Italian-speaking pupils, instilled with 'respect and devotion' for Italy, but knowing little more than the three R's. By the 1939-40 academic year there were over 20,000 Libyan pupils in 121 state elementary schools, for the school was to be 'the principle agency which carried Italian civilisation to the natives'[42]. There were only three secondary schools in the whole colony: the Turkish-founded Arts and Crafts Schools in Tripoli and Binghazi and the Higher Islamic School in Tripoli. This school had a religious and Islamic legal curriculum, and the Italians' objective in founding it in 1935 was to provide the necessary future Muslim functionaries and teachers, with no further call for students to go to Egypt and Tunisia to acquire the education they needed, as well as the ideas that in the official Italian view they could well do without. Moreoever, if one of the purposes of Fascist education was to provide more soldiers, then suitable grounding was undoubtedly provided by the *Gioventù Araba del Littorio*, founded by Balbo in 1935 as a Libyan youth organisation modelled on the *Balilla*.

An American commentator on Italian colonial education policy judged in 1943 that:-

> ...Italy went to considerable expense and effort to provide elementary education for natives. In this respect she compared favourably with such colonial powers as France, England and Belgium. However, she did not provide facilities for post-elementary education to the same degree as did the latter powers[43].

Such opinions contrast sharply with those of other writers. While the Italians themselves claimed that the Libyans' spoken and written Arabic greatly improved during their rule, a British commentator in 1948 thought that 'though the Italians might point with pride to the number of schools in existence (in Libya), Arab children finished their studies with a good grounding neither in their own language nor in Italian[44].

These two quotations epitomise the difficulties of evaluating the worth of Fascist rule in any of Italy's African colonies, but most particularly in Libya. While other of Rome's former colonial subjects now seem able to take a fairly detached view of their experience of Italian colonialism in general and Fascist colonialism in particular, the Libyans have a special memory for the years 1911-43 and above all for 1922-43. Moreover, the record has been much distorted by the adverse, even hostile, international attitude to Fascism and all its works, and specifically in the case of Libya by the official control of the collective memory and written record. These are distortions that, despite the efforts of a newer generation less inhibited about probing into the recent past, make it hard for the historian to disentangle fact from opinion, hearsay from evidence, conclusion from propaganda.

REFERENCES

1. Naitza G.B. 1975 , *Il Colonialismo nella Storia d'Italia*, Florence, p.88. Proclamation by General Caneva to the Arabs of Tripolitania, Tripoli, 15 January 1912.
2. Goglia L. and Grassi F., 1981, *Il Colonialismo Italiano da Adua all'Impero*, Rome-Bari, p.349. Despatch from Badoglio to Graziani.
3. *Ibid.*, p.353.
4. Wright J., 1982, *Libya: A Modern History*, London, pp. 36-37.
5. Goglia L. and Grassi F., *op.cit.*, p.334. Mario Martino Moreno, 'high colonial functionary, orientalist and scholar of great versatility and intelligence, was one of the most capable and brilliant directors of the Ministry of Italian Africa'.
6. Moreno M.M., June 1939, 'Politica di Razza e Politica Coloniale Italiana', *Gli Annali dell'Africa Italiana*, No.2.
7. Istituto Fascista dell'Africa Italiana, *Nozioni Coloniali per gli Iscritti alle Organizzazioni del PNF*, Trento, pp.112-116.
8. Di Camerota P., 1941, *La Colonizzazione Africana nel Sistema Fascista*, Milan, p.83.
9. De Marco R., 1943, *The Italianization of African Natives. Government Native Education in the Italian Colonies, 1890-1937*. (Ph.D. Thesis), Colombia University, New York, pp.7-8.
10. Balbo I., 4-11 October 1938, *La Politica Sociale Fascista verso gli Arabi della Libia*, Report to the Convegno Volta sull'Africa, Rome.
11. *Ibid.*
12. *Ibid.*
13. Norman J., 1965, *Labour and Politics in Libya and Arab Africa*, New York, pp.17-18.
14. Holmboe K., 1936, *Desert Encounter*, London, p.83.
15. Steer G., 1939, *A Date in the Desert*, London, p.162.

16. Moreno M.M., *op.cit.*
17. Preti L., 1965, *I Miti dell'Impero e della Razza nell' Italia degli Anni '30*, Rome, p.19
18. Istituto Fascista dell'Africa Italiana, *Nozioni* etc., pp.112-116.
19. *Ibid.*
20. Moreno M.M., *op.cit.*, Piccioli A., August 1938, 'La Razza e L'Impero' in *Gli Annali dell'Africa Italiana*, Anno I, Vol.II.
21. Istituto Fascista dell'Africa Italiana, *Nozioni*, etc., pp.112-116
22. Balbo I., *op.cit.*
23. Moore M., 1940, *Fourth Shore*, London, pp.167-168.
24. *Ibid.*, p.168.
25. 1943, 'La Politica Indigena dell'Italia', in *Gli Annali dell'Africa Italiana*, Anno VI, Vol.II.
26. Moreno M.M., 'Politica di Razza'.
27. Wright J. *op.cit.*, pp. 39-40.
28. Monroe E., 1938, *The Mediterranean in Politics*, London, p.168.
29. Ongaro G., June 1939, 'Pastorizia e Colonizzazione Musulmana della Libia', in *Gli Annali dell'Africa Italiana*, Anno II, No.6.
30. Balbo I., *op.cit.*
31. Evans-Pritchard E., 1963, *The Sanusi of Cyrenaica*, Oxford, pp.203-204.
32. Macartney H., and Cremona P., 1938, *Italy's Foreign and Colonial Policy, 1914-1937*, London, p.187.
33. Monroe *op.cit.*, pp.168-169.
34. Segré C., 1974, *Fourth Shore. The Italian Colonization of Libya*, Chicago, pp.154-155.
35. Pottier R., 1937, *La Tripolitaine vue par un Français*, Paris, p.225.
36. Steer G., *op.cit.*, p.164.
37. Lombardi P., 1982, 'Italian Agrarian Colonization during the Fascist Period', in Joffé E.G.H. and McLachlan K.S. (eds.), *Social and Economic Development of Libya*, Wisbech, 1982, p.107.
38. De Marco, *op.cit.*, pp.22-23.
39. Bovini M., April 1939, 'Valore Militare delle Truppe Libiche nelle Operazioni dell'Ogaden' in *Rassegena Sociale dell'Africa Italiana*, Anno II, No.4. see also Del Boca A., 1978, *La Guerra d'Abissinia 1935-41*, Milan, pp.176-178.
40. See Mussolini's reply to his presentation with the 'Sword of Islam' at a ceremony in Tripoli, 18 March 1937. (Ambrosini G., 1937, *I Problemi del Mediterraneo*, Rome, p.182.)
41. Moore M., *op.cit.* p.179
42. De Marco, *op.cit.* p.86.
43. *Ibid.*, p.89.
44. Rodd Lord R. of, 1948, *British Military Administration of Occupied Territories in Africa during the Years 1941-47*, London, p.287.

PART TWO: COMMERCE TRADE AND ECONOMY

Chapter 4

FOREIGN TRADE AND DEVELOPMENT POLICY IN LIBYA

M.I. Oreibi

In this paper I aim to do two things. The first is to look at the development of foreign trade in Libya over the last decade or so, and the second is to provide a general picture of its development policy and the trends that can be discerned in relating the two. As a general rule, there were no firm trends in the development policy of the early 1970's. It is only in the last part of that decade that the development policy trend began to take shape. Foreign trade, being a crucial factor in development, is used here not only to assess discernable trends in policy, but also to see how effective efforts to develop the Libyan economy have been and what the problems hindering these effforts are.

No attempt is made here to analyse trade figures, nor to discuss Libya's commercial, monetary and fiscal policies in any depth and how they, in turn, affect development policies. The Libyan economy is passing through a delicate stage of development. Although in the last few years the economic system has taken a definite shape, neither the development policy in general nor the foreign trade policy in particular seem to have been adjusting sufficiently to the new pace. This, in fact, is a reflection of the sudden nature of the changes that occurred after 1976. It takes time for bureaucracy to adapt itself to dramatic changes in institutions and policies, such as those which affected the Libyan economic system during the 1970's, especially the 'popularisation' of the economy. I am using the word 'popularisation' to mean that Popular Committees took over control of the economy. Socialisation may serve the purpose, but it is certainly a special type of social order.

TRADE AND DEVELOPMENT

It was Professor Robertson who coined the catch-phrase 'foreign trade is an engine of growth'. Economic expansion of the industrialised countries was very closely related to the growth of foreign trade. The whole structure of trade theory was developed in order to justify and promote the participation of all countries in international trade, and to demonstrate its potential.

The different degrees to which countries are endowed with natural resources give each nation comparative advantages in the production of certain goods, while not of others. On the basis of these differences in natural resource, international division of labour contributes to increases in world production. Economic gains from trade, as a result of specialisation, would be divided among participating countries. Trading countries would be producing beyond their normal capacity, thus increasing economic welfare. There would be no government interference with technology freely-available to all countries and no factor mobility between nations.

Foreign trade is not universally advantageous. There are those who gain and those who lose in any economy that opens its doors for foreign trade. The economists' consensus is that the net gains more than compensate for these losses. This is the case in a closed economy opening up for trade. But economists who happen to be from the industrialised countries talk about the gains for the international economy as a whole.

Table 4.1 Value of exports and imports in current prices 1950-81, (millions of US Dollars)

	Exports (F.O.B)	Imports (C.I.F)
1950	11	20
1955	13	40
1960	11	169
1965	796	320
1970	2,366	554
1975	6,840	3,542
1976	9,561	3,212
1977	11,423	3,773
1978	9,907	4,603
1979	16,085	5,311
1980	22,128	6,836
1981	15,659	15,466

Source: 1983; Handbook of International Trade and Statistics, and September 1983, International Financial Statistics.

Since industrialised countries were more advanced and therefore the dominant partners, they absorbed all the gains from international trade. Whenever welfare was mentioned, it meant the welfare of dominant, powerful societies. Indeed, a whole gamut of analytical tools has been developed in order to justify the unequal exchange of international trade. Comparative advantage is the centre of trade theory. Thus the result of trade theory analysis is that the comparative advantages of developing countries are governed by the raw-materials with which they can supply their industrialised counterparts.

World division of labour, for efficiency and better allocation of world resources assigns specialisation in labour-intensive, primitive modes of agricultural production to the peripheries. Only recently have the traditional views on comparative advantages come under more serious scrutiny: 'trade explains factor endowments, rather than factor endowments trade'[1]. The basic attack on the traditional trade theory came from economists who represented the losers in an unequal exchange equation. Amongst the important contributors were: H. Myint, R. Prebish and S. Amin. Comparative advantage is a dynamic concept and is largely man-made. This does not mean that natural resources should be ignored, since they bring great advantages in manufacture and production to the country in which they occur, thus giving it a natural advantage.

Questioning the basic tenets of the traditional trade theory does not, in any way, reduce the importance of international exchange. Historically, trade-led growth has been a bulwark of development policy in both industrialised and developing countries.

Trade promotion or outward-looking development strategies proved very effective in transforming the stagnant economies of many backward countries into dynamic, fast-growing ones. The success stories in the last two decades of Hong Kong, South Korea, Taiwan, Singapore and Brazil demonstrate the effectiveness of their outward-looking policies [2]. Import substitution as a developmental policy is also a trade-based alternative. As domestic production is directed towards reducing imports, so trade expertise and industrial infrastructure gains will soon spill into exports. The unfair, unequal conditions and distribution of gains from international trade do not in any way detract from the fact that some trade is better than no trade at all. And, with the above-mentioned reservations, trade has always been an engine of growth.

Developing countries tend to have many serious difficulties in financing their trade. Huge balance of payment deficits simply cannot be made up for by foreign exchange earnings from their dwindling exports. Borrowing from international capital markets is the only escape route for those who have the access to it. This source of finance has been over-used and problems have accumulated not only for those who borrowed liberally, but also for those who lent and, consequently, for the world economy as a whole. The huge debts accumulated by some developing countries, particularly in Latin America, have become a source of great instability in the world economy.

Fortunately, Libya has no financial constraint on its foreign trade. Since the early 1960's the trade balance and the balance of payments have registered surpluses, in spite of the remarkable increases in imports and unilateral transfers by expatriates. (See Table 4.1).

The discovery and development of oil changed the position of the country from that of a deficit economy looking for foreign financial aid to that of a surplus economy exporting capital and generously aiding other needy, developing countries[3].

Import and export planning is closely connected with general planning in the economy. In a planned economy this relationship becomes very important as export performance and imports required are both organically interwoven into the economy as a whole.

As imports complement internal production, both production and consumption rely on the planned level of imports. A shortage in imports of capital goods and intermediate goods would seriously interfere with achieving the targets of economic growth. The reasons why the planned level of imports may not be achieved are basically financial and technical.

Financing imports is not a problem for Libya. There might be liquidity crises from time to time, but cash-flow difficulties can be dismissed as a factor affecting imports. The balance of payments is benefiting from the higher price-levels of hydrocarbons and the reasonable level of production, creating a surplus which supports a high level of reserves and a higher level of imports (Table 4.2). There are other technical and administrative bottle-necks, mainly infrastructural, that slow down the arrival of necessary goods at their final destinations, such as poor transport facilities and the huge geographical distances separating population centres. There are other administrative obstacles that ought not to be forgotten, the lack of trained personnel in the administration of ports, services, supplies to ships, unloading and conducting the formalities of releasing goods from customs to mention only a few.

However, great efforts are being made to reduce these impediments. The size and number of ports have been greatly increased. Ships are no longer queuing for their turn for long and the time needed for ships to enter the harbour has been greatly reduced. Labour shortages have been compensated for by more intensive use of machines and the utilisation of containers. Administrative complications are less acute as the government importing agents have replaced private contractors, so the implementation of the imports formalities does not raise as many problems as it used to do. Important as they are, all these efforts did not eliminate the significance of technical factors in delaying the delivery of goods, and reducing the waste in Libyan ports.

Whether for production or consumption purposes, imports are necessary for the development of the economy. The rates of growth of both exports and imports have been exceptional in Libya (See Table 4.2).

The discovery and development of the oil industry accounts for these high rates of growth in imports as well as exports.

Table 4.2 Annual average growth-rates of exports and imports (%)

	Exports	Imports
1950 - 81	34.6	22.1
1950 - 60	0.7	22.0
1960 - 70	66.3	16.8
1970 - 80	24.6	27.5
1970 - 74	33.5	51.5
1974 - 81	15.0	22.5
1976 - 77	19.5	17.5
1977 - 78	13.3	22.0
1978 - 79	62.4	15.4
1979 - 80	37.6	28.7
1980 - 81	29.2	126.2

Source: UNCTAD, 1983, Handbook of International Trade and Development Statistics.

Before oil, the foreign trade sector was very small indeed. But the jumps in exports, as given, reflect the basic changes in the importance of the foreign trade sector.

AN OPEN ECONOMY

It is relevant here to consider the openness of the Libyan economy. As the economy grows, the degree to which an economy is open is modified. This will be a crucial factor later on in discussing the economic policies of Libya, on both theoretical and practical levels. Two measures are used to test the degree of openness of the economy. The first is the average propensity to import and the second is the relative importance of traded goods.

Traded goods are not an easy concept to define. Due to transportation costs one can classify goods on the basis of those that can enter international trade and those that cannot.[4] The ratio of traded to non-traded goods are those produced domestically against those in part exported. This does not pose any difficulty since the range of domestically produced goods in Libya is quite small. Importables are those goods produced domestically <u>and</u> imported; again the number of goods produced domestically and competing with imports is quite small. The ratio of traded goods to non-traded goods is very high. This is approximated by dividing total foreign trade by GDP. It can be seen from Table 4.3 that 80 per cent of GDP is passing through international trade.

The marginal propensity to import is, by definition, the

growth in imports as the national income increases. By relating the increase in GDP to the increase in imports, it is obvious that, for the period with which this study is concerned the propensity to import was considerable. It fluctuates within very small limits due to temporary factors. In the years 1974-75 and 1978-81 it reached a very high level as the GDP in these two periods experienced an exceptional rate of growth due to rises in oil prices. Imports, as a percentage of national expenditure, were quite high. The nature of expenditure on imports is shown in Table 4.3. Both the average and marginal propensities to import increased during the 1970's. The implications of the openness of the Libyan economy will be considered later.

However, the openness of the economy, according to the rhetoric of development in Libya, is taken as a sign of weakness for which efforts should be directed towards reducing the implied dependency. Those who are eating from overseas cannot be truly independent. Therefore, if one followed the rhetoric of development, one could easily conclude that self-sufficiency was the ultimate objective of economic development efforts.

Table 4.3 Trade and GDP at current prices, (millions of US $)

Year	GDP	Imports	Exports	Total	Trade/GDP
1965	1,401	320	790	1,210	0.86
1970	3,618	554	2,357	2,911	0.80
1975	12,768	3,542	6,834	10,376	0.81
1980	38,961	6,777	21,910	28,687	0.74

Source: UNCTAD, 1983, '<u>Handbook of International Trade and Development Statistics</u>.

Neither the first plan of economic transformation (1976-80) nor the second plan for economic and social transformation (1981-85) reflected the rhetoric of development. To reduce the dependency of the economy on foreign trade is not to eliminate the foreign trade sector, however to narrow the openness of the economy would obviously necessitate an inward-looking development policy. Furthermore, a planned concentration of investment would be needed to expand those sectors which provide substitutes for imported goods, so as to reduce and eventually eliminate their importation. Imports, however, include capital goods and consumer goods. Capital goods would require a higher stage of development in the economy, a highly-trained labour-force, technical know-how and large markets. It has been said that domestic production requires the existence of a local market as a prerequisite for an export drive at a later stage[5] however the debate over export promotion versus import substitution as a development strategy has not yet been definitely concluded. The right strategy would be decided on the basis of many conditions, such as the size of the internal market, the balance of payments position and the stage of the economy's development.

Water places serious limitations on both agricultural and industrial development. Experience has shown that water needed for industrial projects is no less important than water for agriculture. A textile complex in Janzur experienced serious problems as the water it needed was not given adequate consideration. The quantity of water needed for the regular use of the textile complex did, in fact, affect the level of production costs. Expanding available water resources should be a primary objective of any long-term planning in the economy. The tapping of known reservoirs in the desert is one way of providing solutions to this problem.

Agricultural production did not respond adequately to the concentrated efforts in the development plan. The constraints on the development of the agricultural sector are too great. Poor land, creeping deserts, meagre and unpredictable rainfall and very hot weather are only some of the many problems that limit the development of agriculture. Furthermore shortage of labour skilled or otherwise, should not be ignored. The use on non-Libyan labour is not a long-term solution, although Tunisians and Egyptians have provided valuable labour for agriculture. A long-term solution needs to be considered in the light of the development of the economy as a whole. If agricultural production cannot be raised to the standard prevailing in the Mediterranean region, one must ask whether it would be worthwhile to pursue an agricultural development policy which would divert necessary resources, both capital and human, from other sectors of the economy.

Inward-looking policy, however, is not a rational path for the development of the Libyan economy. We have seen that it is an open economy and that its domestic market is not very large. No thorough import substitution strategy could succeed. High-cost, heavily-protected industries could survive on subsidies, substituting for imports, as long as income from oil continues to flow. It is not feasible to continue supporting inefficient industries indefinitely.

SOCIO-ECONOMIC TRANSFORMATION PLANS

The thrust of the plan for the industrial development of Libya has been concentrated on heavy industries. These industries are not regarded as import-substituting since their products could not replace quality imports. It must be asked how these industries can promote the creation of further industries in the country. Iron, steel aluminium, cement and petro-chemical complexes make no immediate contribution to limiting imports or reducing the dependency of the economy on foreign trade. On the contrary, such industries would certainly need foreign markets as the national market is limited. As such, the importance of foreign trade is going to increase and with it economic dependency.

Only in agriculture is there a trend to enforce self-sufficiency, in food. Even before the first plan for economic and social transformation, expenditure on agricultural projects was unlimited. Food production was to be accelerated at all costs to reduce dependence on imports. As the resources basis of agriculture is very fragile, agricultural development efforts have not responded to these intensified efforts. It was realised that the higher percentage of financial resources devoted to agriculture harmed, rather than aided, that sector[6]. This came about because of the precarious nature of Libyan agriculture and the availability of water resources. In the Jifarah Plain, in particular, the depth of water in wells sank below sea-level, leading to a crisis in the availability of water for agriculture.

COMMERCIAL POLICY

Trade in Libya has always been state-controlled. All the traditional measures of controlling foreign trade have been applied. Tariff and non-tariff barriers have been erected and quantitative controls through licences, quotas and foreign exchange control were necessary measures in the early years when the Libyan economy shared a deficit. The newly-independent Libya could not finance the necessary imports. Exports were limited and consisted of scrap-metal and some agricultural products. These exports, limited in both value and volume, could not gain enough foreign currency to meet the cost of the country's meagre imports. Furthermore the balance of trade registered persistent deficits which had to be financed by foreign aid and other foreign financial resources[7]. It seemed necessary to control trade so as to cope with this chronic deficit in the balance of payments.

The discovery and export of oil drastically changed the economy of the country. By 1964-65, the balance of payments registered a surplus and both exports and imports had increased. In spite of the favourable trade balance and the surplus in the balance of payments, no serious step was taken to reduce controls and regulations in order to liberate foreign trade. Tariff and non-tariff barriers continued to exist, though their strict implementation was not observed. Tariffs were not used as an economic policy tool, but rather as a means of securing finance for the budget. Unequitable as they were, import tariffs continued to serve this financial objective. The new income-tax law for 1967 introduced, for the first time, the concept of progressiveness in the tax system. Progressive taxation was even more spectacular in the income-tax law of 1973. Direct taxes were not introduced until the late 1960's. Indirect taxes continued to serve as the sources of finance for the budget, even though it was not needed as income from oil started to flow in.

The stated objective of this law was the redistribution of wealth in favour of low-income groups. However, low-income groups continued to suffer from the incidence of indirect taxation. The government support of basic commodities had not redressed the tax burden since basic goods were not limited to high-income groups.

With the dramatic changes in trade practice after 1977, private sector trading was abolished completely. The decision was taken by the People's Congress in 1978 and implemented by the High Popular Committee in 1980. Trade became a part of the economy as a whole under the supervision of state trading organisations. New institutions were developed and expanded. The Ministry of Economy which had originally implemented commercial policy continued to do so up to the time when Ministries were changed into Secretariats. As trade organisations undertook the import of goods and services, the power of the Secretariats to enforce laws and regulations became weaker and weaker. Trade organisations were under pressure to prove the efficiency of the new system.

DEVELOPMENT POLICY OBJECTIVES

I suggest that, instead of trying to deduce the trends of foreign trade and development policy, we look at the objectives stated in the three development plans. In comparing them. care must be taken not to confuse the stated objectives and the practical policy-orientation of allocating resources to each sector since they may not be consistent. Conditions changed dramatically after the three-year plan and the first five-year transformation plan. Internal and external trade has been completely taken over by Popular Committees. There was no change in the importance of trade or the way in which it was directed and conducted. However, new institutions developed as Popular Committees took over the running of private concerns and extended their control to some government-run organisations.

Trade is part and parcel of the economic and social development plan. In a socialist, planned economy, objectives have to be stated and targets set. What are the objectives of the development policy as stated in the transformation plan and what are the results compared to the stated objective? The intention here is to trace the thinking of the planners in the last decade and to see how development policy progressed.

In all the plans, the main stated objective in foreign trade has been the diversification of the economy. Diversification may be considered as the objective of the development policy in general. As far as foreign trade is concerned, the interpret-

Table 4.4 Realised and planned GDP growth

		1976–80		1981–85
	Activities	Planned %	Realised	Planned %
1	Agriculture, Forest & Fisheries	15.8	3.9	7.4
2	Oil & Gas	7.8	4.1	5.9
3	Mining & Quarrying	10.3	9.3	9.0
4	Manufacturing Industries	30.7	21.5	22.4
5	Electricity & Water	23.0	21.5	14.8
6	Construction	12.5	7.8	12.5
7	Trade, Restaurants & Hotels	11.0	8.6	8.0
8	Transport, Storage & Communications	18.7	6.7	8.0
9	Finance, Insurance	14.0	13.0	10.0
10	Ownership of Houses	10.9	6.4	7.1
11	Public Services	8.8	16.2	5.0
12	Education Services	14.0	13.7	8.1
13	Health Services	12.0	19.8	10.0
14	Other Services	10.0	7.1	8.0

Source: Secretariat of Planning, Transformation Plan 1981 - 85, Central Bank of Libya Bulletin.

ation of diversification is a reduction in imports and an increase in non-oil exports.

SUMMARY OF THE SOCIO-ECONOMIC TRANSFORMATION PLAN

As stated, the objectives of the plan were:

1. To achieve a high degree of self-sufficiency and self-reliance as well as to give priority to increasing productivity.
2. To reduce crude-oil production to the level necessary for financing the transformation programmes and projects.
3. To intensify development of human resources and increase the contribution of Libyans to the transformation process.
4. To improve the pattern of individual consumption further, raising the standard of living, distributing wealth more fairly and achieving more balanced regional development.
5. To adopt an effective policy for the development of science and technology in the future, together with the protection and improvement of the environment.

It should be noted that the social and economic plans are called 'transformation' plans. However, the value-system of any society is not easy to transform. So transformation is taken here to mean an improvement in the social and economic well-being of the population of the country. This would include unquantifiable measures, such as security, national pride and social status of individuals. Only economic aspects of these objectives are to be examined here and only those relating to Libyan foreign trade are to be particularly looked at in the context of the development policy.

EXPORTS

As stated in the current economic and social transformation plan for 1981-85, the main aim is the diversification of exports. The plan high-lights the importance of locating suitable markets for the new Libyan products, emphasising the shift from exporting crude-oil to exporting refined products. The estimates for the re-estructured export sector are given in the following table:

Table 4.5 Projected exports 1980-85, (in LD millions at 1980 constant prices)

	1980	1985	Growth-rate
Crude-oil and gas	6,544.3	4,303.0	(-) 7.5
Oil refining products	296.1	845.4	23.3
Petro-chemicals	22.2	114.0	38.3
Chemicals	- -	18.8	- -
Re-exporting	2.2	4.0	12.7
Total export of goods	6,864.8	5,285.2	(-) 4.2

Source: Secretariat of Planning, Summary of Economic Transformation Plan 1981-85

The failure to achieve the planned level of exports for the first transformation plan was explained by the fact that most of the important industrial projects were large and tended to be biased towards heavy industry. The gestation period for these projects and industrialising industries is very long. The estimated time for their completion tends to be pushed back by the complicated nature of industrial complexes. They demand advanced technology and intensive capital investment. This delay is a familiar case in developing countries. However, petro-chemicals, where the real comparative advantage of the country lies, are reaching a stage where production and export can begin. Expansion of petro-chemicals and planned new phases are already at an advanced stage. The real challenge now is in meeting the complicated task of securing markets for the finished products of these industries.

The natural market for Libyan petro-chemicals is the EEC. As the EEC countries are Libya's most important trade partners, export of Libyan petro-chemicals needs secure access to the European market. However, export to other markets ought not to be forgotten, such as developing countries, the Americas and Eastern Europe. The EEC would, however, remain the major outlet for petro-chemical products. Steps should be taken as early as possible to enter the European market since it is close to Libya, with minimum transportation costs. Industries in Europe can depend on a secure supply from Libyan petro-chemicals. Arrangements of long and medium-term contracts negotiated at an early stage could help advance the marketing process. Obviously the Libyan internal market cannot absorb the products of the industrial complexes now under construction. A good part of these products have to be exported. An export drive and a well-conceived strategy for opening up new markets should be the next step in the planning process.

It is astonishing that no formal agreement to regulate trade has been negotiated with the EEC. Out of all the Mediterranean countries, only Libya has failed to conclude any formal arrangement with Europe.

OIL EXPORT AND THE DEVELOPMENT OF THE OIL INDUSTRY

The development of the Libyan oil industry is one of the success stories of recent times and an important consideration in the context of trade and development. The exceedingly favourable concessions given to the international oil companies whetted their appetite for oil discoveries and accelerated the interest in further exploration. This, in turn, quickened the pace of their development. The 1955 petroleum law served this policy by providing the legal framework within which oil companies worked for oil discovery in the late 1950's. Concessions were granted to all types of companies; independent, government-owned and private companies alike. By 1970, the list of oil-exploring companies covered all interested parties of different nationalities. With the discovery of oil in the late fifties and the beginning of exports in early 1960's oil law regulations witnessed a gradual but persistent trend of change. However, oil companies immediately realised that the generosity of the oil law could not continue.

It has been observed by commentators that the acceleration in the production of Libyan oil was not only to meet the expanding demand world-wide, especially after the closure of the Suez Canal, but also to recover costs and capital invested by oil companies in the industry.

In fact, the period 1960-73 could be described as a period of continuous conflict between the Libyan Government and the oil companies. The first major amendment of the petroleum law was in 1961, accompanied by regulation number 6, to bridge the obvious need to oblige oil companies to publish their crude posted prices. There was no mention of how crude prices came to be formed in the original law. Posted prices became not only obligatory, but a detailed and well-defined way of negotiating between the government on one side and oil companies on the other, to reach an agreement on posted prices. In 1965, OPEC negotiated the royalty expensing agreement a 12.5 per cent royalty that was paid to the government and later deducted from government income. This was embodied in another amendment of the petroleum law in 1965 which improved the government bargaining position and tightened rules defining taxable income.

Table 4.6 Crude-oil production and export, (1,000 barrels)

Year	Production	Exports
1965	445,252	442,388
1970	1,225,436	1,206,839
1975	540,129	522,345
1976	707,335	675,862
1977	753,130	709,198
1978	314,497	188,092
1979	763,556	182,016
1980	668,133	619,781
1981	429,859	387,794

Source: 1982, Central Bank of Libya Bulletin Vol.23, No.1-6

In 1968, the Ministry of Petroleum issued regulation number 8, which embodied the decisions taken by the OPEC Conference in Baghdad in the same year[8]. Petroleum regulation number 8 proved to be important in later negotiations between the new revolutionary government and oil companies[9].

The enforcement of this regulation by the revolutionary government substantially reduced the power of oil companies and set the scene for serious negotiations following limitations on the volume of production in a move aimed at conservation. The pressure put on independent oil companies, who relied heavily on Libyan crude, succeeded in creating the right conditions for a domino theory. The fall of independent companies paved the way for the major companies' acceptance of adjusting the prices of crude and the enforcement of the new, rigorous conservation policy. Thus the Libyan revolution's first important and immediate contribution was to revolutionise the oil industry. As prices were adjusted under Libyan pressure , further changes in the structure of the petroleum industry followed. Serious world-wide, re-structuring of the oil industry came as the culmination of a decade of persistent Libyan pressure on oil companies.

The Libyan revolution succeeded in changing the basic structure of the world petroleum industry. Libya was the first to reap the abundant financial returns of this change. Oil prices soared and with them the income of oil-producing countries. The fall of production in Libya from a record high of 3.2 to 1.7 million barrels a day did not affect the foreign exchange earnings. In fact, after 1973, foreign exchange earnings from oil reached new heights, in spite of falling production levels, but the fall in Libyan production later reduced the importance of Libya's role in the industry. Firm negotiating tactics as well as the high level of Libyan production gave the revolutionary government a unique opportunity to upset the monopoly of the major oil companies.

Having succeeded in dismantling the multi-national companies' control over crude-oil production and pricing, Libya continued to push for higher prices during the 1970's. This, however, lost steam as prices reached quite a high level and the production of Libya dwindled into fourth place (See Table 4.6). The persistent policy of higher prices proved to be harmful as the demand for Libyan oil weakened and the traditional markets were lost to other producers. The high level of exports and nominal higher prices that surged during the seventies increased the government's ability to finance ambitious development programmes dramatically and raised the country's reserves to a new high level. The balance of payment surplus enabled the country to venture into exporting capital and increasing aid to other developing countries. As the absorption capacity became manifestly limited for the potential expenditure on development programmes, foreign outlets were used for capital investment.

The development policy objective is: To reduce crude oil production to the level necessary for financing the transformation programmes and projects. The difficulty with this objective, as stated here, is that the reduction of oil exports is tied to the level of financing the programmes and projects of the plan.

The level of production reached in 1969-1970 was simply too high and beyond the optimum level of oil-production. The conservation move of the early 1970's was not simply a negotiating tactic, but rather a genuine desire on the part of the Libyan authorities to rationalise oil exploitation. The finiteness of oil resources and the limited absorptive capacity of the economy justify the ceiling on production. There must be an optimum rate of oil extraction in the context of the economy's capacity to absorb. This optimum rate of oil extraction is a dynamic concept. It may not be easy to determine, as the changes experienced by oil-producing countries are so fast and so profound, both economically and socially. Obviously if there is an agreement on an optimum rate of oil extraction, then there would be no problem for OPEC in imposing discipline on its members in enforcing production ceilings and market sharing.

There is, however, a broad agreement among economists that the value of natural resources is closely connected with economic rent. The economic rent of natural resources is the difference between the market value of the resource and the cost of its production - it is measurable [10]. On the basis of production cost, GDP should be adjusted so as to reduce rent, or the difference between market value and the cost of manufacturing from the resource. Professor Stauffer estimated that the GDP of oil-producing countries as a whole is overstated by at least one half, and more likely by a factor of two. The reproducible value added in oil-production, after rent deductions, represents the contribution of oil to national income. The rent is a transformation of national capital from its natural resource state into liquid capital in a Central Bank portfolio. There is an element of risk as the erosion of the purchasing power of the new form of national capital is real. In deciding on the optimum rate of oil extraction these elements ought to be taken into consideration.

The contribution of other sectors of the economy is very limited. Oil will continue to be the foreign exchange earner of the country over the coming decades. Diversification of the economy is an important target that must be pursued vigorously. It would lead to the expansion of tradable goods sectors, both importables and exportables. Importables would substitute for imports in the first stage with the potential to export in the future. Exportables would replace crude-oil as the country's foreign exchange earner. If this is not done, the registered rates of growth of the national economy will reflect only the transformation of national capital from one state to another and no development will be achieved.

IMPORTS

The growth-rate of imports increased drastically in both value and volume. This is not extraordinary in such circumstances, especially where no balance of payments constraint exists, but is contrary to the stated objective of the development plan: that imports must be reduced to the absolute minimum.

There are two ways to achieve this goal. Firstly, to expand domestic production so that local production will be substituted for imports. Secondly, to reduce the level of consumption so as to reduce the need for more imports. These two ways have been tried and vigorously pursued during the last fifteen years.

Trade is under the control of the state, even with the existence of substantial private sector activities as in the early 1970's. Tariffs, import licensing, advance payment and exchange control are the familiar tools of controlling private sector imports. When the Popular Committees took over from the private sector, advising them on how to run the new companies was less problematic.

There are no detailed explanations of how to achieve the objective of reducing imports. It is assumed that this could be secured by the expansion of internal production. Import substitutes, both in agricultural products and in manufacturing, are to replace imports. The second possibility is to reduce consumption. The welfare implications of reducing consumption are not socially or politically acceptable. The stated objective is to increase, rather than reduce, consumption. However, the drive to reduce consumption has been incessantly emphasised. Under the pretext of fighting conspicuous consumption and the limitation of luxury goods, high tarrif walls and outright prevention of the importation of certain types of goods have been enforced.

There has also been a drive to promote a simple life-style - an undeclared campaign against what might be considered a luxury and bourgeois pattern of consumption. However, this campaign was not effective and did not contribute to a reduction in imports. The level of imports surged to higher levels as the income from oil increased. As moral persuasion was not effective in reducing consumption, more direct ways of achieving this aim were applied. The most spectacular and direct way was the reduction of take-home income via the changes in salary scales and the demonetisation of currency notes. This, combined with the direct control of imports of consumer goods through state organisations, proved to be effective. Rationalising consumption is an honourable under-taking. In a newly-rich society with fast-changing patterns of consumption, waste must be controlled. Educational campaigns to advise households of how to improve their standard of living without wasting valuable resources should be organised.

With the huge increase in income from oil, plans for the economic development of the country became more ambitious. Capital was not a constraint. The labour-force was assumed to be infinitely elastic. Simply by producing a list of all possible and desirable projects, a blue-print for a five-year plan is formulated. This is true when comparing the first and the second transformation plans. With the failure of the agriculture sector to respond to stimuli and the rigidity of import-substituting industries, conditions are set for a shift to new ambitious, long-term heavy industries such as iron, steel, aluminium, tractor-assembly and petro-chemicals. Although this trend has existed since the early 1970's, it became more apparent with the increase in income from oil as a result of price adjustments in 1974 and 1979. In meeting the rising demand of the new, planned economic development for labour in the mid-1970's, immigration increased. The percentage of non-Libyans to Libyans was particularly high, setting-up social, economic and cultural tensions within Libya. It is true that most of the labourers came from other Arab countries particularly Egypt, Tunisia and Sudan, with minimum linguistic and cultural differences, but it is also true that increasing numbers of African workers came from Chad, Niger and Nigeria as well as from South-East Asia.

The problem of how to implement an ambitious development plan in a large country, with a very limited labour supply and abundant capital is challenging. This is the question that the planners faced and tried to solve. The problem of labour-supply was first looked at in the context of wider Arab unity. Encouraging the movement of Arab labour en masse into the country would not affect the social and economic structure of the country. It might even serve to further Arab unity. This view was reluctantly abandoned in the late 1970's. The traditional sources of labour have been South-East Asia and sub-Saharan Africa. However, the social problems created by this foreign labour-force obliged the planners to reconsider the real political and social costs involved. The choice was between reducing the rate of implementation of the development plan or reducing the foreign labour-force. The decision was a middle-of-the-road one: not to abandon the ambitious rate at which the transformation plan was being implemented, nor to reduce drastically the foreign labour-force. This was a good decision.

But what about the Libyan labour-force? Economic development of the country is of concern to the population of Libya. In the absence of popular participation in development efforts, economic development is no more than a colonial undertaking. This would mean that particular projects would be implanted in the midst of an apathetic and non-participating population. This is not to say that the contribution of a foreign labour-force is to to be denied or rejected completely.

In the face of the shortage of labour, and particularly skilled labour, augmenting a domestic labour-force is necessary. This has been the experience of many developed, as well as developing, countries. Filling the gaps caused by labour-shortages is difficult; however, depending almost completely on foreign labour for the implementation of the development plan is considerably worse. However, it cannot be denied that foreign labour has often been essential. Foreign labour is effective in building roads, harbours and housing projects, but technical know-how and skills are needed in the early stages of development in agriculture and industry.

We have seen that one of the objectives of the transformation plan is to intensify the development of human resources and increase the contribution of Libyans to the transformation process. This has not been a tenable objective, as social and economic tension was over-riding. The labour-force was decidedly reduced by this tension and as Popular Committees kept changing, more workers changed their positions to become managers. This trend was also obvious in the government-run sector, only in the last two years do things seem to have changed. The labour-force has been increasing as more members who left in the seventies are coming back to work, especially in agriculture. This trend is reflected in the noticeable increase in the supply of vegetables, fruit and agricultural produce in the big population centres.

The position of the balance of payments is very precarious. The trade balance, however, is favourable and responsible for the surplus. But the crude market is anything but secure; it depends on the demand for energy and fast-developing substitutes for oil are already reducing the share of oil in international energy markets; thus reducing not only the volume of oil exports, but also the price per barrel. I am not speculating on the future of oil-production and prices, but trying to look at things as they have developed during the last decade.

Trade played an important role in the expansion and development of the Libyan economy. Oil and gas exports more than paid for the expanding rate of imports. Although the high level of reserves gives a margin of security, it does not do so to a great degree as it has the side-effect of accelerating inflation through its effect on the money supply[11]. One way to reduce reserves is to tailor oil-production to the absorptive capacity of the economy. This is possible since the experiences of the first and second development plans revealed the reasonable level of expenditure possible.

Development policy in Libya is not stable as stated in the strategy of the transformation plan, there was a shift from industry to agriculture in the first three-year plan. That plan replaced the second five-year plan 1968-72. The shift in emphasis in resource allocation followed a period of heavy expenditure on agriculture in the pre-plan period, that is in the period 1970-73. As the agricultural sector did not respond, there has been a shift back to industrial development[12].

Industrial development policy tilted towards heavy industries. In fact, a careful examination of the current plan would reveal how strong is the bias towards them. A Secretariat for heavy industry was created - as separate from light industry. The Secretariat of Light Industry was finally cancelled and administratively annexed to the Secretariat of the Economy. The expectation of the plan is to raise the contribution of heavy industries to the GDP from 2.4 to 6.3 per cent in 1985, hoping for an annual growth-rate as high as 24.6 per cent.

Industrial development, especially of heavy industries, would require a continuous flow of capital goods, intermediate goods and some raw materials from outside the country. Light industries that would serve for import-substitution are not being favoured in the development plan. And the agricultural sector is not giving the expected returns on investment. The contribution of heavy industry to exports is not certain. What is certain is the need to increase imports for these industries. What transpires then, is an intensification of Libya's dependency of foreign trade. That seems to contradict one of the basic objectives of the transformation plan. However, this is a short- and medium-term problem. In the long-term things may look different, as heavy industries will be 'industrialising' in the sense that they will supply the necessary materials for industries to be developed. This is a conscious choice of strategy.

REFERENCES

1. Kindleberger C.P., 1958, *Economic Development*, McGraw Hill, p.234.

2. Little I.M., Scitowsky T. and Scott M., 1970, *Industry and Trade in some Developing Countries. A Comparative Study.*

3. Higgins B., 1959, *'Economic Development'*, Constable.

4. McKinnon R.M., 1963, *The Optimum Currency Areas*, A.E.R.

5. Linder S.B., 1961, *An Essay on Trade and Transformation, Stockholm.*

6. Allan J.A. (ed.), 1981, *Libya the Experience of Oil*, Croom Helm, London.

7. Higgins B., 1959, *op.cit.*

8. Waddams F.C., 1970, *The Libyan Oil Industry*, Croom Helm, London.

9. Barker P. and McLachlan K.S., in Allan J.A. (ed), 1981, *op.cit.*

10. Stauffer T., September 1983, *OPEC Fund Newsletter*, Vol.1, No.3.

11. Bhalla, 1982.

12. Allan J.A., 1981, *op.cit.*

Chapter 5

THE IMPACT OF RECENT ECONOMIC CHANGES IN LIBYA ON MONETARY AGGREGATES

Ali A. Abdussalam

INTRODUCTION

Since the early days of the revolution that took place in Libya in September 1969 there have been steady and systematic changes in the economy, as well as in other aspects of life. The economic changes were aimed at transforming the Libyan economy from being market-orientated to being socialist. It is natural that behavioural and institutional changes should follow the structural changes in the economy. Some of these changes were introduced in the mid-1970's in order to speed up the transformation of the economic system. This paper will attempt to analyse the impact of such changes on money, credit and banking in Libya. The main economic changes will be briefly surveyed in the first section. In the second section, a general theoretical framework will be presented. In the third section, the impact of these changes on monetary aggregates will be analysed.

1. Recent Economic Changes

From 1969 until now (1984), numerous measures have been taken in order to re-shape the Libyan economy and to re-structure it on a socialist basis. Some of the measures which have bearing on this study will be summarised in this section.

NATIONALISATION OF BANKS

One of the first steps to be taken by the revolutionary regime in 1969 was to Libyanise the remaining branches of foreign banks in the country, namely Barclays Bank D.C.O., Banco di Roma, Banco di Napoli, and the Arab Bank, thereby completing the process which had started in 1964. In the following year, these banks were nationalised and subsequently some of them merged to form new banks[1]. The banking system was composed of five banks, three of which were completely owned by the Central Bank. But, following the introduction of more socialist measures in 1977, all banks became completely state-owned.

ABOLITION OF PRIVATE TRADE

In September 1975, the Libyan government started the process of nationalising foreign trade. Government agencies and corporations replaced the private sector in importing and trading a wide range of goods and services[2]. This was followed two years later by the abolition of private wholesale and retail trading. This type of activity was confined to government corporations[3]. A new economic system was envisaged by the 'Green Book'[4]. According to the new outlook, private trade was considered an unproductive activity, as well as being a form of exploitation. Therefore, it had to be abolished.

RESTRICTION OF PRIVATE OWNERSHIP

In the new economic system outlined by the 'Green Book', private ownership was severely restricted. It was argued that unrestricted ownership would lead to exploitation through wages, rent and profit and that it would give rise to income disparity and inequality[5]. Consequently, a law was promulgated in 1977[6] which restricted housing and real-estate ownership to one per family. Land was considered a public domain and could not, therefore, be privately owned. Each individual was entitled, however, to use land for production purposes in order to satisfy his material needs. This was intended to break up tribal land-ownership and to prevent the exploitation and income disparity that might ensue.

In the new economic set-up, small ventures could be carried out as long as they involved self-employment or family undertakings. But if somebody outside the family had to be employed, he was to be treated as a partner, sharing labour and revenues.

CURRENCY RESTRICTIONS

Two actions were taken by the monetary authorities in 1980; one was to replace the old 5 and 10 Libyan dinar notes with new ones and the other was to restrict cash withdrawal from any one account to 500 dinars per month. These measures were intended to force the currency held by the public back into the banking system. The impact of these decisions on money and credit will be discussed later. We turn now to the general theoretical framework that will be followed in this paper.

2. General Theoretical Framework

The money-supply and bank credit are the outcome of interaction between the banks, the public and the monetary authorities. Monetary economics postulates that there is a close and stable relationship between the money stock and the monetary base[7]. This relationship is usually expressed in the following manner: $M = m.B$

Where M is the money stock whether narrowly or broadly defined; m is the money multiplier and B the monetary base., The monetary base can be defined as the net monetary liabilities of the government held by the public and commerical banks. The monetary authorities supply base-money to satisfy the public's demand for currency (C^P) and the banks' demand for liquid assets (L). $B = L + C^P$

Liquid assets include reserves (R), vault cash (V), interbank deposits (N) and net foreign deposits of banks (NF). $L = R + V + N + NF$

On the other hand, the sources of the monetary base consist of gold stock (U), foreign assets (F), treasury securities (S), bank borrowing from the Central Bank (A), other credit (OC), government deposits (G) and the net value of other items (O). $B = U + F + S + A + OC - G - O$

The monetary base is obtained by consolidating the balance sheets of both the Banking and Issue Departments of the Central Bank of Libya[8].

By defining money to include currency and demand deposits held by the public and performing a few mathematical manipulations on the system of equations, we can derive the money multiplier. The narrow money multiplier can be expressed in the following manner[9]:

$$m_1 = \frac{1 + k}{(1-b)\ (1+t) + k}$$

Where k is the ratio of currency held by the public (C^P) to demand deposits of the public (D^P); l is the ratio of bank liquid assets to their local deposit liabilities ($D^P + T$); t is the ratio of public time deposits (T) to demand ceposit and b is the ratio of bank borrowing from the Central Bank to their total deposits liabilities. The liquidity ratio (l) can be expanded futher to show its major components. That is:

$l = r^w + e + v + n + f$

Where r is the weighted average required reserve ratio; e is the excess reserve ratio; v vault cash ratio; n inter-bank deposit ratio and f the bank net foreign asset ratio. They represent the ratio of their respective magnitudes to the total deposit liabilities of banks.

The bank credit can be expressed in a similar fashion. $E = (m_2 - 1)\ .B^a$ Where E is the bank credit; m is the inclusive money multiplier and B is the net source base. That is the sources base minus bank borrowing. The bank credit is obtained by consolidating the balance sheets of the commercial banks and the Central Bank.

It is evident that through this reduced model-form, we can account for the institutional set-up as well as the behavioural pattern of banks and the public on money and credit. The banks can influence money and credit through the management of their reserves, especially excess reserves. The public, on the other hand, can influence these magnitudes by their preference for holding currency relative to demand deposits. The monetary authorities can affect the monetary aggregates by influencing the base and manipulating the reserve requirement ratios. The interaction of the banks, the public and the monetary authorities to influence money and credit in changing economic conditions will be investigated in the next section.

3. The Impact of Recent Economic Changes on Money and Credit

To analyse the impact of economic changes on the monetary aggregates, we need to look closely at the behaviour of the banks, the public and the monetary authorities.

THE BANKS

The banks can influence money and credit through the multiplier by the management of their excess reserves. Excess reserves are the difference between actual and legal reserves. Like other economic units, banks try to use their resources in an optimal manner. In other words, given the institutional framework and investment opportunities, banks try to minimise their excess reserves without running the risk of illiquidity or reserve deficiency. As can be readily seen from the previous equations, there exists an inverse relationship between the multiplier, and hence money and credit, and the excess reserve ratio. The lower the excess reserve ratio the greater the expansion in money and credit. It can be seen from empirical investigation of bank data that excess reserves, especially excess liquid reserves, are relatively high. The annual average excess reserve ratio and excess liquidty ratio are 17 per cent and 28 per cent respectively. The rates are even higher if quarterly or monthly data are used. The annual excess reserve ratios are shown in Table 5.1 below.

The liquidity position of banks resembles a cycle trend movement with peaks in 1963, 1971 and 1980 and troughs in 1960, 1969 and 1975. In the early 1960's excess reserves were climbing because of the robust economic activities which had accompanied the discovery and export of oil. Other sectors were growing rapidly and oil companies were holding accounts with commercial banks. Moreover, during that period the first

Table 5.1 The annual excess reserve ratios and excess liquidity ratios for the period 1958-81

Year	Exc.Res. Ratio* (e)	Exc.Liq.Ratio** (l^e)
1958	-	0.225
1959	-	0.243
1960	-	0.152
1961	-	0.340
1962	-	0.371
1963	0.558	0.663
1964	0.113	0.155
1965	0.309	0.339
1966	0.156	0.117
1967	0.215	0.159
1968	0.169	0.087
1969	0.080	-0.007
1970	0.108	0.198
1971	0.342	0.391
1972	0.344	0.384
1973	0.086	0.277
1974	0.098	0.181
1975	0.106	0.163
1976	0.068	0.240
1977	0.038	0.272
1978	0.062	0.268
1979	0.037	0.454
1980	0.211	0.680
1981	0.066	0.456

* Legal reserve requirements on demand deposits and time deposits were introduced for the first time in July 1963. The ratios were 10 per cent on demand deposits and 5 per cent on time deposits. These ratios were raised in July 1966 to 15 per cent and 7.5 per cent respectively.

** In 1958 banks were required to hold liquid assets at the rate of 20 per cent of their total deposit liabilities. The rate was raised in July 1966 to 25 per cent. But since November 1970 it has been reduced to 15 per cent.

development plan (1963-1968) was launched. These conditions contributed to the strong liquidity position in the banking system. But in 1969, the banks were in a tight liquidity position. This was caused by the run on banks which was triggered by the prevailing uncertainty following the political change during that year. However, the liquidity situation improved in the early 1970's, especially after the launching of the three-year plan

Fig. 5.1 Major annual components of the liquidity ratio, 1956-81

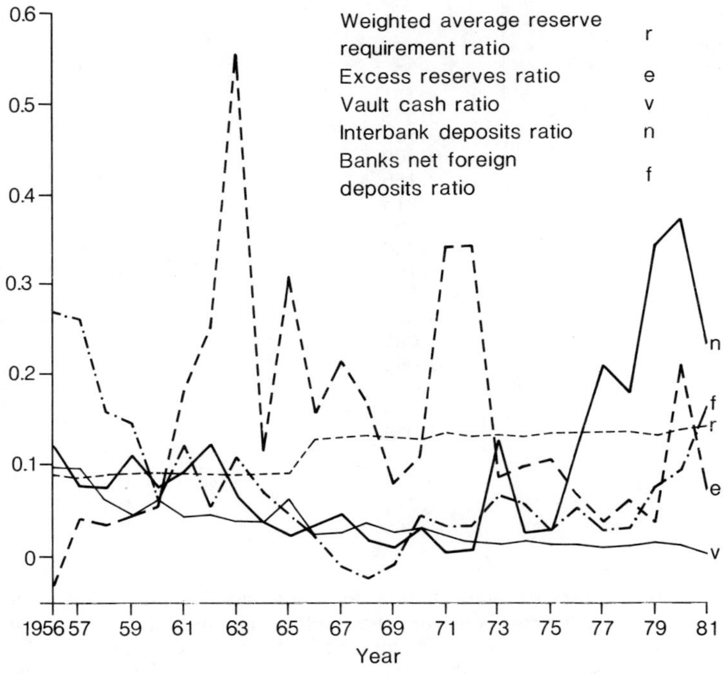

(1973-1975). Those were the years of high economic growth and the banks participated actively in this process by financing trade and real-estate business. Furthermore, the banks were encouraged to grant loans for housing and urban development projects. Whenever the banks experienced a liquidity squeeze, they could discount these loans in the Central Bank. This led the banks to manage their resources more aggressively, a fact which could account for the low liquidity position they experienced in 1975. But after 1977 and following the socialist measures, there was another run on banks and their liquidity position deteriorated. It was not until 1980 that the situation seemingly improved again. This was brought about by coerced channelling of currency held by the public into the banking system. (see Fig. 5.1).

When analysing bank performance, we have to consider that several factors have constrained the efficient use of bank resources as demonstrated by the relatively high liquidity ratios. Firstly, bank management is characteristically conservative if not cautious in conducting bank business. The bulk of bank activities were directed towards relatively-secure, short-term credit, especially in the trade sector. When they moved reluctantly into the real-estate business, it was with the inducement and backing of the monetary authorities, which did not in any event, last long. Secondly, the lack of a developed financial market has limited the scope of bank portfolio management. Moreover, banks were restricted in making short-term investment at home or abroad. They were also instructed, from time to time, to adopt more stringent measures in granting credit. More recently, banks were not allowed to make personal, or consumer, loans. Thirdly, the monetary authorities' paternalistic attitude towards the banking system has limited the bank performance. Since 1958, the monetary authorities have stipulated a certain liquidity measure. At that time there were no reserve requirements and the banking system lacked domestic managerial skills. Therefore some operational guidelines had to be devised in order to ensure a sound banking environment. But with the growth of the banking system, this has constrained banks from seeking their optimum portfolio position independently.

The position of the commercial banks was made even more difficult by the actions of the monetary authorities and the changing economic environment over the last few years. The sudden and erratic actions of the monetary authorities have created uncertainty and consequently an unstable banking environment. In the mid-1970's the banks were first induced to grant loans for housing, real-estate and construction, but this situation was later abruptly reversed[10]. Then in 1980 there was the induced currency influx into the banking system and the ensuing restriction on cash withdrawal. All these actions added to the uncertainty of the banking business and adversely affected bank credit. Finally, the increasing control of the banking system by the monetary authorities has, to all intents and purposes, made the banking system into a monopoly. The banks can no longer take the initiative, they have to wait for instructions from the monetary authorities. In effect, they have become financial agents for public (government) and semi-public corporations.

THE PUBLIC

The behaviour of the non-bank public also influences the growth of money and credit through the currency ratio (k) and the time deposit ratio. The non-bank public allocates its money balances between currency and demand deposits and its deposits between demand and time deposits. So both currency and time deposits can be expressed as ratios of demand deposits. That is:

$k = C^p/D^p$

$t = T/D^p$

Given the socio-economic conditions that prevail in the economy, the public usually decides to hold a certain portion of its monetary assets in the form of currency. The desired level of curency with the public, relative to its demand deposits, is expressed by the currency ratio (k), whereas the desired level of time deposits that the public want to hold, relative to demand deposits, is expressed by the (t) ratio.

The currency ratio (k) represents a leakage in the multiplier; for an increase in this ratio tends to have an inverse effect on the multiplier and hence on money and credit. The currency ratio has averaged about 1.0 for the period 1956-81. This means that the public tends, on average, to divide its balances about evenly between currency and demand deposits. A summary of the annual currency and time deposit ratio is shown in Table 4.2. The currency ratio (k) is relatively high compared with similar ratios in advanced economies[11]. This ratio shows a declining trend although, at times, it fluctuates sharply.

Several factors affect the growth or decline of the currency ratio. Among these factors are the cost of holding currency, bank services, seasonal variations, population mobility, income level, the public's tax liabilities and uncertainty. The public tends to weigh the advantages of holding currency against the benefits of using the demand deposits. In the early 1960's the majority of people, especially in rural areas, tended to hold most, if not all, of their money balances in currency. The inacessibility of banks and the inconvenience that might accompany checking deposits raised the currency ratio during that period. But with the growth of the banking system and urbanisation, the currency ratio started to decline in 1965 only rising again in 1969. The increase of the currency ratio in 1969 was caused by the uncertainty that followed the revolution. But in 1970, the currency ratio resumed its downward trend

Fig 5.2 Major annual components of the money multiplier, 1956-81

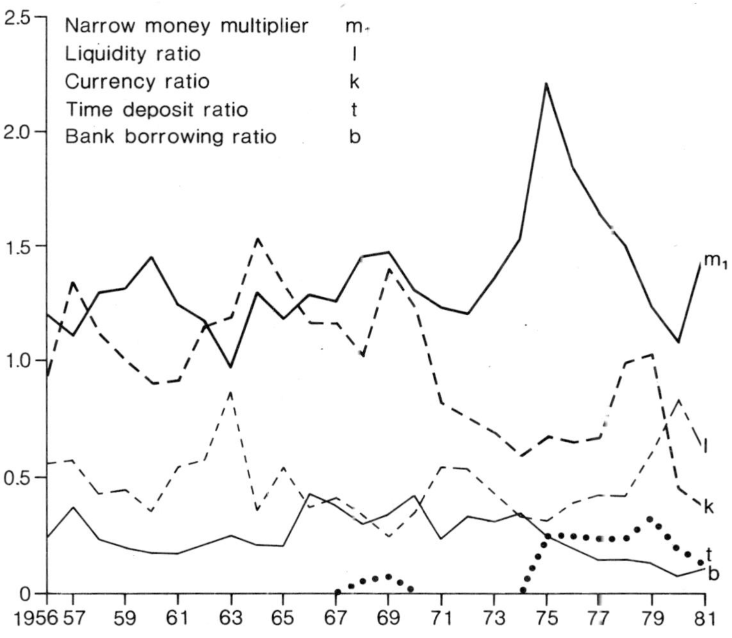

Table 5.2 Currency and time deposit ratios 1956-1981

Year	Currency Ratio (k)	Time Deposit Ratio (t)
1956	0.921	0.242
1957	1.346	0.372
1958	1.112	0.232
1959	0.993	0.194
1960	0.897	0.173
1961	0.908	0.171
1962	1.144	0.206
1963	1.183	0.251
1964	1.531	0.210
1965	1.321	0.201
1966	1.159	0.425
1967	1.157	0.377
1968	1.016	0.296
1969	1.399	0.340
1970	1.232	0.423
1971	0.817	0.234
1972	0.751	0.331
1973	0.690	0.311
1974	0.591	0.345
1975	0.671	0.249
1976	0.644	0.247
1977	0.664	0.234
1978	0.990	0.236
1979	1.026	0.326
1980	0.446	0.192
1981	0.362	0.126

until the middle of that decade. Then the currency ratio started climbing again in 1977. It appears that the introduction of the new socialist measures caused a run on banks and raised the liquidity ratio. With uncertainty clouding the future of economic activities and with no adequate explanation about the place and future of savings in the new system, the people preferred to hold more currency (see Fig.5.2).

The increase in the amount of currency outside banks does not change the size of the money supply but it alters the composition of the money stock. Since it constitutes a leakage outside the banking system, it does however, affect the expansion of bank credit adversely. This is probably one of the reasons that led the monetary authorities to intervene in order to stem the flow of currency out of the banks. Thus it was announced on May 15 1980 that within a week all the

5 and 10 Libyan dinar notes would be recalled and replaced by new ones. During that year the amount of currency ouside banks was reduced by half [12]. The monetary authorities introduced another measure restricting cash withdrawal to 500 dinars per month. Other measures were taken to encourage the use of cheques in settling business transactions [13]. These actions account for the decline in the currency ratio over the last three years. Some of these drastic actions, together with other economic measures, have created uncertainty and triggered expectations that other events might be waiting in the wind. Therefore, the currency ratio can be expected to rise again. Most people do not want currency as such, but to use it to acquire other assets such as real-estate, gold, livestock or foreign currency. That is, to use it as a hedge against unexpected changes.

The time deposit ratio (t), on the other hand, reflects the manner in which the public allocates its money between demand deposits and time deposits. The time deposit ratio (t) depends on the magnitude of each of these deposits and/or the proportional change in their magnitudes. The time deposit ratio is relatively low and stable; it averaged about 0.27 during the twenty-six year period from 1956 to 1981 (see Table 5.2).

Among the major factors which have contributed to the slow growth and ultimately the decline in the time deposit ratio (t) are the interest rate on time deposits, the rate of return on other assets and uncertainty. Since many people consider interest rates to be the equivalent of usury, they hesitate to put their money in interest-paying deposits. Moreoever, the rate of return on other ventures such as real-estate, trade (before its abolition) and agriculture were higher than what the banks would offer to attract time deposits. In the prevailing economic conditions and the vague interpretation of savings, it was not expected that the time deposit ratio (t) would show any significant increase. Thus, despite the noticeable growth in the banking system [14] and the increased awareness of banking services, many people find it more convenient to hold currency rather than deposit with banks. They tend to perceive banks as mere safe-boxes and, in many cases, compulsory safe-boxes. This attitude towards the banking system can be attributed to the actions of the monetary authorities.

THE MONETARY AUTHORITIES [15]

The monetary authorities can affect money and credit through both the monetary base and the multiplier. Most of the sources of the base such as gold, bank borrowing, government securities and other credit, are controlled by the monetary authorities. Other exogenous sources such as foreign assets are known to them. In addition, the monetary authorities determine the required liquidity ratio and the legal reserve ratios on both

Table 5.3 Money and bank credit for the period 1956-81 (LD millions)

Year	Narrow Money (M_2)	Broad Money (M_2)	Bank Credit (E)
1956	10.805	12.167	3.127
1957	11.080	12.836	2.797
1958	13.655	15.152	4.575
1959	17.969	19.716	5.993
1960	21.887	23.884	8.778
1961	26.923	29.341	7.606
1962	28.330	31.053	6.829
1963	32.924	36.709	2.582
1964	40.625	44.000	12.537
1965	59.098	64.224	14.113
1966	88.858	106.332	37.148
1967	113.720	133.578	43.117
1968	139.711	160.236	64.239
1969	175.553	200.404	81.439
1970	203.447	242.011	85.379
1971	268.328	302.939	83.643
1972	343.560	408.446	121.597
1973	496.112	587.440	220.487
1974	705.709	859.097	399.170
1975	861.596	990.003	600.127
1976	1113.377	1280.727	676.813
1977	1466.483	1672.998	784.626
1978	1746.193	1953.522	792.151
1979	2080.808	2416.087	720.530
1980	2794.052	3165.163	572.966
1981	3012.498	3289.383	1249.797

Fig. 5.3 Annual money and credit

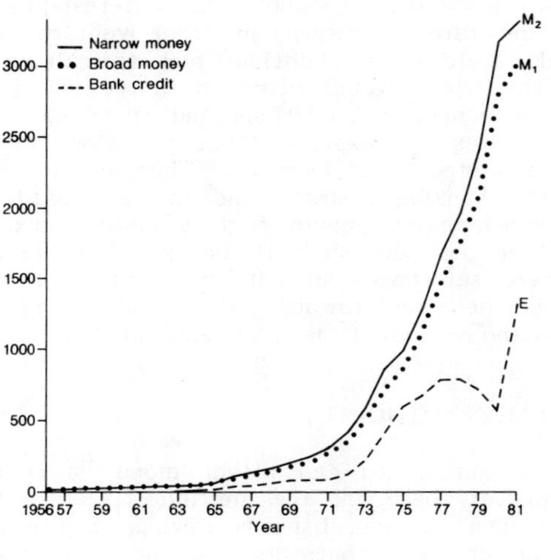

demand deposits and time deposits. Above all, the monetary authorities own and control the whole banking system in Libya. The question is not whether the monetary authorities can greatly influence money and credit, but how the monetary measures can be implemented when they have been introduced, and to what extent these powers would be exercised.

Although it is difficult to separate monetary actions from other economic measures, because they are inter-related, it could be pointed out that some of the measures introduced by the monetary authorities are counter-productive. The very measures which are intended to mitigate the currency drain outside banks lead, when ill-timed or improperly conducted, to the opposite result. When the actions of the monetary authorities are frustrated by the defensive counter-measures of the public, they blame their failure on the public's irrational behaviour. The monetary authorities should not expect unorthodox methods to work in changing circumstances.

The impact of the economic changes and the actions of the monetary authorities might not be significant in the short-run, but will deeply affect money and credit in the long-run. The situation of the monetary aggregates is shown in Table 5.3 and Fig. 5.3.

CONCLUSION

In the last few years, the Libyan economy has undergone several drastic changes. These changes were intended to transform the liberal posture of the economy to a socialist one. The structure of the economy and the methods used to carry out the transformation process have created uncertainty with regard to the future of economic activities. This is reflected in the behaviour of both the banks and the public in the monetary sector. The monetary authorities have resorted to some drastic measures in conducting monetary policy, in order to influence money and credit. Some results might be achieved in the short-run. But this approach might be destabilising in the long-run. Traditional methods would not often work in a changing environment, nor would the traditional set-up conform to new changes. Short-term policies, if not properly conceived or implemented, will hamper the attainment of long-term goals.

REFERENCES

1. Central Bank of Libya, *14th Annual Report of the Board of Directors, Financial Year 1969-70*, pp.54-58.

2. Central Bank of Libya, *20th Annual Report 1976*, p.103.

3. Central Bank of Libya, *21st Annual Report 1978*, p.64.

4. Muammar Al Qathafi, *The Green Book, Part Two, The Solution of Economic Problem 'Socialism'*. The Public Establishment for Publishing, Advertising and Distribution, Tripoli.

5. *Ibid.*, pp.19-ff.

6. Law No.4 for 1977.

7. Albert E. Burger, 1971, *The Money Supply Process*, Belmont: Wadsworth Publishing Company, Inc.

8. For the derivation of the monetary base and a detailed analysis of its sources, the reader is referred to Ali A. Abdussalam, 1976, *Money Supply in a Small Open Economy: The Case of Libya*. (Unpublished Ph.D. Dissertation), University of Cincinnati, Cincinnati, pp.54-70.

9. *Ibid.*, pp.70-100.

10. Central Bank of Libya, *18th Annual Report, 1974*, pp.58-59.

11. Robert E., Weintraub, 1970, *Introduction to Monetary Economics*, The Ronald Press Company, New York, p.185

12. Central Bank of Libya, *Economic Bulletin, Arabic Edition July-December 1980*, p.41.

13. *Ibid.*

14. In the 1950's there were less than 20 bank branches in the country and most of them were in Tripoli and Binghazi. But by 1980 there were 116 branches distributed all over the country.

15. 'The monetary authorities' usually means the Central Bank. In some cases it includes the Treasury also. But, in the case of Libya, includes the Central Bank, the Treasury and the political leadership.

Chapter 6

FEZZAN: POPULATION, DEVELOPMENT AND ECONOMIC CHANGE

Mohamed Alawar

INTRODUCTION

The Fezzan region, stretching over 640-770 square kilometres of arid land, is situated in the south western corner of Libya and encompasses about one-third of the country's territory. A large proportion of the region consists of uninhabitable sand dunes, gravel table-land (serirs) and hill ranges; it is partially water-less and plant-less. Rainfall is scanty and seldom experienced. However, the tiny settled portion of the region corresponds to the three main sub-regions of: Wadi Ash Shati, Wadi Al Amal (Al Ajal), and the Murzuq basin, where water is easily obtainable to support palm growing and small cultivated gardens. Historically, the most important elements in establishing and observing the settlement pattern were sub-surface water and traditional trade routes to Central Africa. Currently, however, agriculture is the only means of supporting socio-economic welfare and might be the only factor able to stabilise the population and sustain the pattern of key settlements. At present, the most serious constraints on the transformation and development of the region are the limited man-power resources. Hence, there is an urgency for a well-organised educational programme, particularly at the level of vocational training, to reduce the sizeable youth migration and secure an adequate living for rural populations.

Demographic transition of higher population growth which Fezzan is now experiencing appear to demonstrate the classic development of reduced mortality and high fertility rates. According to the 1964 population census, Fezzan registered the highest growth-rates in Libya, 3.7 per cent, and the second-highest fertility-rate after the sub-region of El-Khalij[1]. A rough measure of the regional fertility is expressed by the ratio of children under five years of age to women between the ages of 15 and 49, which is calculated to be 680 children per 1,000 women. In addition birth-rates have continued to climb steadily and remain above the national average, while the mortality-rate has been decreasing appreciably 34 per thousand in 1954 and 9

Fig. 6.1 Population distribution in the Fezzan in 1964

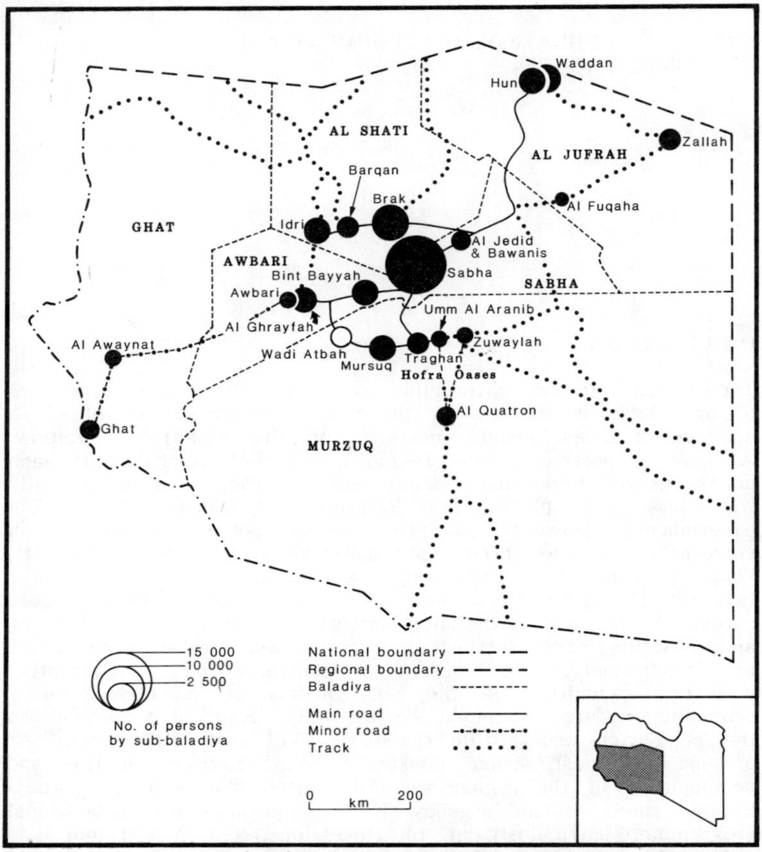

Source: Clarke, J.I.& FISHER, W. B., (ed.), 1972, POPULATION OF THE MIDDLE EAST AND NORTH AFRICA, N. Y., p322

POPULATION GROWTH AND DISTRIBUTION

Table 6.1 Population in the Fezzan region according to Government surveys

1954	Population Census	59,313
1964	Population Census	79,329
1973	Population Census	110,318
1980	Population Estimated	161,960
1985	Population Estimated	206,000
1970	Birth Rate (per thousand)	58
1970	Death Rate (per thousand)	9

per thousand in 1973. Although the region is characterised by fast growth, the rapid increase is almost matched by the balance of extra and intra-regional migration resulting from the deterioration of the sub-regional economic structure. Similarly, the increase population has exceeded the rate of expansion of agricultural land [2]. To a certain extent, agriculture which is limited to oases, has developed as the main element in the concentration of population (Fig. 6.2) and there has been a demographic adjustment in the location of economic opportunities. Thus, population distribution depends largely on traditional agricultural activities; 91 per cent of the population is identified with such under-takings and the density of occupation is influenced by the degree of land fragmentation.

This suggests that a decline in agriculture-orientated centres was the product of rural migration to more economically attractive areas. The region's annual growth-rate of 4.5 per cent stands in marked contrast to the regional distribution, and the increase of Awbari, Brak and Sabha urban areas seems hardly possible without heavy migration from surrounding agricultural settlements.

From 1964 to 1973, the regional rate of population growth did not change much, being about 4.5 per cent (Table 6.2). The rate for urban centres was clearly different. Sabha, for example, which was a source of migration during the 1954-64 period, grew by 137 per cent to double its population in a ten-year period (1964-73) [3]. By contrast, the agriculturally-orientated centres of Wadi Al Ajal and the Murzuq basin experienced a modest annual growth of less than 2 per cent, which through natural increase should have been at least 4 per cent annually. This supports the afore mentioned idea that settlement growth does not correspond evenly with the regional rate of increase. By far the fastest population growth took place in the administrative centres of Awbari, 93 per cent, Brak, 125 per cent and Sabha,

Fig. 6.2 Town size and growth in Fezzan in 1973 & 1980

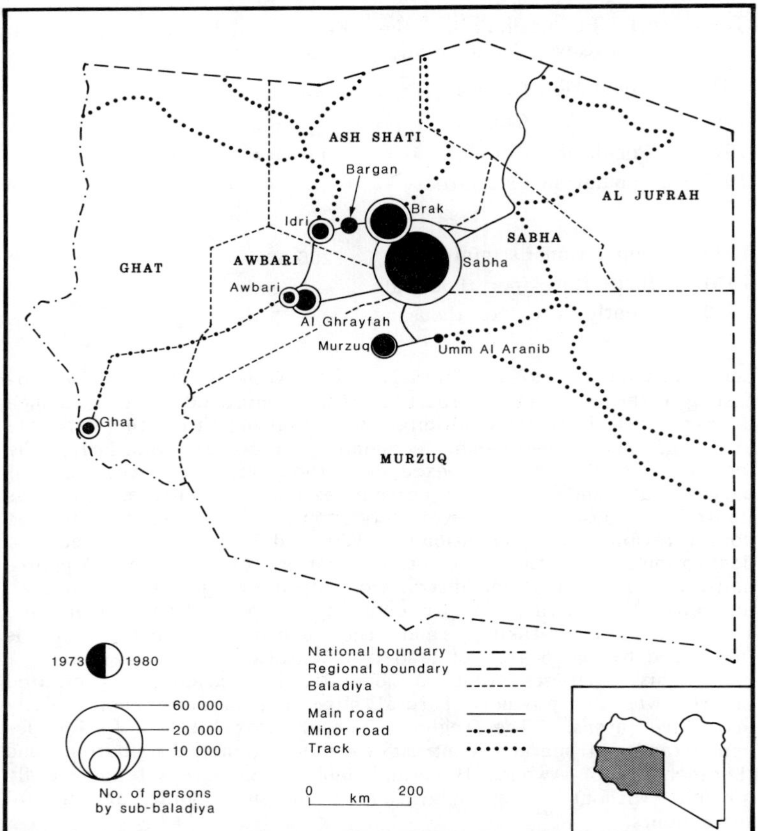

Source: Ministry of Planning, 1972, PRELIMINARY REPORT OF POPULATION CENSUS 1973, Tripoli. Ministry of Planning, February 1974, SETTLEMENT P9 PATTERN STUDY: SABHA REGION, Rome
*1980 projection based on author's estimation

Table 6.2 Estimated annual population growth for Fezzan, 1954-85

Period	Fezzan	Wadi Ash Shati	Al Ajal	Murzuq
1945–65	3.7	3.2	3.8	3.5
1964–73	4.5	4.1	4.8	4.0
1975–85	4.1	3.6	3.2	3.9

Source: 1964 Population Census
1973 Population Census
Ministry of Planning 1970, Southern Muhafadahs Regional Study, Tripoli.

137 per cent. The super-imposition of commercial and government services on present agricultural activities contributed to the dominance of these centres. It appears likely that the trend of future growth will follow the same course; the administrative centres will attract migrants and show sustained growth, while other towns will remain comparatively stagnant (Fig 6.2). It should be recognised, however, that small towns will have definite limitations on their growth and in the future will be a source of migration because of the disequilibrium between the economic opportunities in urban and rural areas. The lack of water, roads and economic stagnation have limited potential growth in these communities.

Significantly, however, the distribution and growth of the population of Fezzan set quantitative and qualitative limitations on the nature of economic growth. The changes in occupational structure and the redistribution of the population have been demographic responses to the new economic demand. Nevertheless, the structure and growth of regional human resources will dictate the shape of future economic growth and thus determine both the distribution and structural growth of the population.

POPULATION STRUCTURE

Consideration of the Fezzan population's sex ratio and age structure variations will be limited to the statistical information provided by the 1964 census. Fezzan's population is very youthful, with nearly 74 per cent below the age of 45 years, 30 per cent aged 10 years or less, and only 4 per cent aged 65 or over. With its tendency towards rapid growth, the rising population will affect those young groups highly receptive to

Table 6.3 Regional growth of the Fezzan population 1964-80

	1964				1973				1980**			
		Project				Project				Project		
	Total	Urban	Rural	Town	Total	Urban	Rural	Town	Total	Urban	Rüral	Town
Wadi Ash Shati (Brak)	18,876	9,380	9,496	2,550	27,196	13,915	13,281	40,40	32,985	16,937	15,394	7,546
Percentage of the region	28	25	33	14	25	20	32	21	25	20	31	19
Wadi Al Ajal (Awbari)	12,452	5,740	6,712	1,060	19,002	8,405	10,596	3,000	24,249	10,332	12,888	7,105
Percentage of the region	19	15	12	9	17	12	26	16	18	12	26	18
Murzuq (Umm Al Aranib)	15,000	7,620	7,380	1,020	21,305	10,703	10,602	1,892	24,460	13,020	12,898	2,963
Percentage of the region	22	20	26	7	19	15	26	7	18	15	26	7

Source: 1. Ministry of Planning, 1974, Settlement Pattern Study: Sabha Region, Italconsult, Rome.

2. Ministry of Planning, Preliminary Report of the National Census, Tripoli.

3. Ministry of Economics and Commerce, 1964, The National Population Census: Sabha and Awbari Districts, Tripoli.

**1980 based on estimated annual growth rates of 1964-1973: 4% Wadi Shati, 5% Awbari, 4% Murzuq.

migration. The main age variations are clearly distinguishable between urban and agricultural centres, the former showing an above-average proportion of adults (52.9 per cent as against 43.5 per cent), and a rather low proportion of children (44.3 per cent against 46.5 per cent)[4]. Urban Sabha shows a distinctly less youthful structure, with 35.2 per cent below 15 years of age and an adult male proportion above the regional average. These factors reflect the significance of rural migration. Regionally, the most youthful population is found in the predominantly agricultural centres, particularly those of Wadi Al Amal (Al Ajal) and Murzuq sub-regions where agriculture has been least modernised and human fertility is above average.

The 1964 census suggests a predominance of females in the agriculturally-orientated centres of Traghan, Murzuq and Awbari with an average sex ratio of 100 males to 107 females. This holds true for the regional ratio as a whole which indicates a steady decrease since the 1954 census. The actual values for Fezzan are 106.4, 106.7, and 105.5 for the three censuses, while the national average has been increased from 107.6 in 1954 to 113 in 1973[5]. However, the positive association between sex ratio and population increase does not apply to Fezzan or its sub-regions during the 1964-73 period, when population growth was quite high. This regional decrease may be attributed to the in-migration of families returning from Chad and Niger and to the movement of rural families as in the case of the migrants from lower Wadi Ash Shati.

The population structure, according to the 1964 and 1973 censuses, shares the characteristics of wide-base variations associated with the demographic transition from high birth and death-rates to declining mortality rates[6]. Umm Al Aranib, for example, shows the highest proportion of old people and Sabha the lowest; a fact which supports the greater mobility of younger people and the differences in standards of living. In Awbari, on the other hand, there is an abrupt decrease starting at twenty years. Sabha and Brak show overwhelming in-migration, especially in the age-groupes of 20-25, 30-35, and 35-40. Males outnumber females in each age chart.

The data on the economic activites was characterised by a low percentage of male workers, who were 52.6 of the entire labour-force in rural areas engaged in agriculture, a fact which suggests that the great majority of the un-enumerated were female workers. This is especially true in Murzuq and Awbari where 54 and 69 per cent, respectively, of the traditional farmers were female workers. If the number of female agricultural workers is at least equal to that of males, the proportion of the agricultural labour force is raised to a much more realistic figure of about 68 per cent. These changes in female agricultural activities have been partly responsible for the recent occupational redistribution of the region's population.

INTERNAL MIGRATION

Table 6.4 Net internal migration by district in 1964

District	Number of Changes
Sabha	+ 3.568
Ash Shati	- 3.155
Murzuq	- 2.645
Ajal	- 1.257

Source : Ministry of Economy and Commerce, 1966, General Population Census: 1964, Tripoli

During the last two decades, the regional population has been characterised by a high rate of natural increase and low socio-economic stagnation in the small towns. However, despite the disruptive forces and inequalities between sub-regional populations, initiated by wide-spread movement, internal migration acted as an instrument of education, cultural diffusion, and social integration. The lack of economic and educational opportunities in the agricultural centres with highly traditional ways of life has produced a classic response to migration in and out of the Fezzan region, both temporary and permanent. The remarkable influx of migrants was also a response to the rapid expansion of government employment which offered new openings to rural migrants who, without formal education, were able to take up unskilled and profitable occupations.

The migration from rural to urban areas was a result of deteriorating agricultural activities and disruption of the work-force. It is estimated that in 1985 the work-force will consist of 50,000 persons or 26 per cent of the total population. It is further assumed that at least 80 per cent of this work-force will be engaged in non-agricultural sectors[7]. This will create a substantial surplus of males of working age in the rural areas and so contribute to the constant migration to the Sabha and/or sub-regional urban centres.

In view of the region's small total population, the scale of migration is particularly significant. In contrast to the high rates of regional growth during the 1954-64 decade, the over-all yearly population growth in rural locations did not exceed two per cent annually[8]. Considering a natural increase of about four per cent, the gap between rural population and natural increase indicates an actual rural migration of approximately 16,000 persons during the 1954-64 period. According to both the 1964 and 1973 censuses, rural population growth was below the registered average, strong evidence of a population loss which involved the younger age group searching for wage-earning jobs or educational opportunities.

In the 1973 census nearly 36 per cent of the region's total population had changed residence during their lifetime, and over 56 per cent in Sabha had arrived from elsewhere. This census showed a regional population loss of 9,000 persons to the two northern cities of Tripoli and Binghazi and a net gain of 137 per cent for Sabha from the rural districts of Awbari, Murzuq and upper Wadi Ash Shati. This apparent pattern of influx has been directed to Sabha, which showed a heavy concentration of young males particularly when compared with the regional population as a whole. Sabha received as much as 65 per cent of internal regional movement, whereas the urban centres of Brak, Awbari and Murzuq received migrants mainly from local areas.

EMPLOYMENT AND INCOME

Agriculture is still considered as the dominant sector providing employment for the majority of the population of Fezzan. In the general manpower survey of 1973, the regional work-force was estimated at 25.4 per cent of the total population, and at least 80 per cent was classified as unskilled agricultural labour. This yielded a total of about 11,800 jobs for less than one per cent of the region's cultivated land, and created a high man-land ratio of 4.6 per hectare per head of family[9]. Non-agricultural jobs have been dominated by the public sector since industrial employment is limited and traditional handicrafts are female-orientated activities offering few full-time jobs.

It appears that professional and technical work-forces account for 13.2 per cent of the region's employment and are dominated by foreign technicians in the private sector of the economy. The majority of unskilled labour is employed by the government and the agricultural sector. Due to the traditional organisation of the region's economy, trade and commerce are often part-time activities. Except for public services, no other sector contributed more than 8 per cent of the total employment (Table 6.5). Government jobs have become the major source of employment, providing part-time and double employment for the majority of urban centres and rural areas. Although government employment plays a marginal role in job structure, it encompasses an extremely high proportion of unskilled labour. In fact, nearly 45 per cent of the 8,000 government employees are unskilled workers attracted by higher-paid, part-time jobs[10]. This suggests that there has been a considerable flow of rural population into other activities.

Results of the survey conducted by the Italconsult team in 1973 indicated that 75 per cent of traditional farmers were holding second jobs. This labour shift and structural change

Table 6.5 Sectorial distribution of employment within Fezzan 1964-73

Sector	1964	1973	Annual Growth %	1964	1973	Annual Growth %	1964	1973	Annual Growth %	1964	1973	Annual Growth %
Agriculture	6513	11793	8.4	1407	3450	14.0	2034	2800	3.7	1750	3000	7.1
Manufacturing and mining	1929	2614	3.5	311	360	1.6	193	290	5.0	814	830	0.2
Construction	1505	3820	15.0	290	337	1.6	323	492	5.2	276	391	4.2
Trade	630	1251	10.0	153	186	2.1	82	115	4.0	170	215	2.6
Communications & utilities	559	1657	19.6	91	168	8.4	97	193	9.2	54	106	9.6
Government Service	4517	5829	2.9	1041	1190	1.4	492	629	2.7	621	798	2.9
Other Services	2558	1307	4.8	1124	271	-32.0	304	189	-3.8	510	215	-5.8
Total	18211	28281	5.5	4418	5942	3.4	3525	4703	3.4	4195	5525	3.2
Work-force/ Population Ratio			27.8			23.4			28.3			27.9

Sources : 1. Ministry of Planning, 1973, Settlement Pattern Study: Sabha Region, Italconsult, Rome.
2. Ministry of Planning, 1968, Statistical data on the important economic sectors, Tripoli
3. C.A.D. General Programme for Agricultural Development of Fezzan region, Jaroslov Cernl, Beograd.

have had a significant impact on the regional work-force, both quantitatively and qualitatively. Within the ten-year period, 1964-73, the total labour-force decreased from 37.5 per cent to 25.4 per cent of the total population, while the population itself increased by almost 44 per cent during the same period. This decline may be attributed to the increase in the young age-group (0 to 15 years), the decrease of female labour from 25 to 10 per cent and the out-migration of males. Relative high-productivity in agriculture, higher part-time government wages, and a more valuable agricultural product have certainly made new demands on double employment. These socio-economic systems have increased the out-migration of working age-groups, especially unskilled and better-educated workers who leave in search of more profitable non-agricultural jobs. Accordingly, this is a significant reduction in the labour-force, and a substantial shift in employment to more financially rewarding professions (Table 6.6).

Table 6.6 National average daily wage in the main sectors, (L.D.)

Sector	1968	1976
Agriculture	1.00	1.35
Oil and mining	0.75	1.00
Government	0.70	1.45
Construction	1.20	2.00

Source: J.A. Allan, K.S. McLachlan and E.T. Penrose, 1973, Libya: Agriculture and Economic Development, London, p.21.
Ministry of Planning, 1976, Statistical Data on the Important Economic Sector, Tripoli

There appear to be early signs of the gradual breaking-away from subsistence conditions to more functional structures of income and employment. Because of the higher value of farming products and the increase in purchasing power, part-time gardening activities and higher involvement in land-holding have become the main characteristics of traditional farming. Non-agricultural job opportunities are growing rapidly at an average of 11.5 per cent annually, while full-time agricultural employment has been decreasing. Surprisingly, statistical information in the 1973 census indicates a different situation [11]. However, the data provided in the census did not recognise the overlapping elements of part-time or double employment which were clearly identified in the survey conducted for the traditional farmers in the region. This strengthens the assumption that some structural variations in employment functions exist, especially with the growth of school enrolment by almost 50 per cent which, in the future, will provide people considerably more skilled than exist today.

The increased proportion of the youthful population will lead to an expansion of the average household size and a surplus of young males of working age, highly receptive to migration. If no appropriate jobs are created to absorb the surplus labour-force, a dangerous economic and political situation may develop.

TRADITIONAL AGRICULTURE

Because the majority of farmers do not possess sufficient capital to operate large farms, most of them produce fruit, vegetables, cereals and dairy products in small agricultural lots of less than two hectares. The over-grazed sandy loam or clay soil, the shallow water-table, and the fragmentation of land have limited the extent of agriculture. Farm production is not carried out commercially, but a high percentage of the area is under intensive cultivation. Crop production and land-use (Table 6.7) were characterised by a very high percentage of cereals (95.6 per cent), a very small percentage of industrial crops (1.5 per cent), and vegetables (2.3 per cent); only 3.8 per cent of the total land is of a commercial nature. The low percentage of fodder crops (1.6 per cent) shows the limited development in animal husbandry as well as the unfavourable relationship between crops and livestock production.

Since 1960, agriculture production has been decreasing steadily and has not been able to provide sufficient food to meet the region's nutritional requirements. The conditions of farm life for the majority of farmers have remained much the same, with the net annual income per family actively involved in agriculture at 400 Libyan dinars, about one-sixth of the average regional income[12]. Traditional farmers under these conditions were influenced in their agricultural land-use and crop production practices, disbelieving that they had security of stability and failing to profit from farming. They tried to extract the utmost from the land without renewing the fertility of the soil and were therefore more like part-time tenants than farmers. Secondly, production under part-time farming was concentrated on crops that were consumed on the farm such as wheat, barley, and vegetables (Table 6.8). Since imported farm products were available at much lower prices, local farmers were in no position to compete successfully even in local markets.

By 1964, the government had established an agricultural bank to encourage modern farming in the region and to provide farmers with loans for farm improvements. However, the bank was only partially successful in lending money and eliminating

Table 6.7 Traditional types of crops and percentage land-use in Fezzan

	Awbari	Brak	Murzuq
Wheat, barley, oats, millet, maize and sorghum	16.5	16.5	18.6
Alfalfa	3.1	8.3	5.5
Carrot, radish, turnip and potatoes	3.7	8.6	10.8
Cabbage, lettuce, onion, cauliflower	5.7	5.5	6.7
Fallow	58.6	46.6	46.1
Palm trees	12.9	9.1	7.1
Beans, tomatoes and peas	2.4	2.1	0
Abandoned	4.7	2.8	2.9
Non-agricultural and built-up areas	0.2	0.6	0.3

Sources: Ministry of Planning, Summer 1978, *Survey of Traditional Farmers*, Tripoli.
Ministry of Agriculture, 1972, *Agriculture Survey Report*, Tripoli

high interest rates and was incapable of increasing agricultural output to provide sufficient food even for the minimum consumption. The conditions of farm life for the majority of farmers either remained much the same as they had been in 1960, or even deteriorated. The wide-spread poverty and ignorance among farmers contributed to the mis-use of the money borrowed for non-agricultural purposes. Therefore, farmers were unable to develop their farms or improve their living conditions. This led to continuous migration, increases in food prices, complete dependency on imported agricultural products and a decrease in the limited cultivated area.

It has been demonstrated that no investment in agriculture can be directed towards the redevelopment of traditional farming.

The present farming practices have resulted in a further decline in productivity and stagnation in agricultural land expansion[13]. The provisions intended to improve agricultural production or the social level of farm populations have failed to provide farmers with stable incomes. However, the government settlement programmes, established in 1973 with full implementation and control, were intended for those who will farm the land and thereby improve their standard of living. This may improve the socio-economic conditions and enhance the stability of rural people.

NON-AGRICULTURAL EMPLOYMENT

Fezzan's regional economy depends largely on public and construction activities, the most significant features of the economic growth pattern. In recent years, the government has provided most of the salaried jobs for the unskilled rural workers. After independence, the public sector expansion began to increase the government's contribution to the regional economy. In fact, all other economic sectors in the region would have been unable to survive without the increasing expansion of public services. The growth of the construction industry, handicrafts, and commercial activities was a direct response to government involvement. Employment by the government has been increasing steadily and was estimated in 1978 at 7,000 workers, expanding nearly as fast as the population itself. Government employment is alarming and certainly more than is needed by the local authorities. [14]

The construction industry is second in terms of employment, the result of growing demands in both the private and the public sectors. It has accommodated a significant number of unskilled rural labourers who had restricted access to jobs in the public services due to their lack of qualifications. Although participation in employment by the construction industry appears to be significant because of the region's fast-growing demand (Table 6.9), its future role will depend on the fluctuating size of public programmes. The present size of construction employment is alarming even though it is a characteristic of the early stages of economic development in which high priority must be given to the creation of an efficient infrastructure [15]. The employment of unskilled and rural migrant workers has adversely affected the agricultural activities and drained the rural population since more than 50 per cent of the total work-force is engaged in construction activities. This situation could create welfare problems with little contribution to the regional economy.

Other sectors have not grown equally in importance. Manufacturing is still a handicraft occupation contributing less than five per cent to regional employment. The government's

Table 6.8 Planted and cultivated areas and agricultural production in Fezzan in 1973

SUB-REGION	WHEAT Area planted (ha)	WHEAT Area cultivated (ha)	WHEAT Production (tons)	BARLEY Area planted (ha)	BARLEY Area cultivated (ha)	BARLEY Production (tons)
Sabha	585	578	6,480	87	85	656
Ash Shati	725	623	3,483	991	858	4,972
Al Amal (Al Ajal)	1,728	1,708	14,974	288	284	3,068
Murzuq	704	670	8,136	93	86	1,186
Total	3,742	3,579	33,073	1,459	1,313	9,882

Sources : Ministry of Planning, 1974, *Preliminary report on the agricultural resources, Sabha region* Tripoli, p.51
Ministry of Agriculture

Table 6.9 Total work-force structure in Fezzan in 1980

	Agriculture	Industry	Trade	Services
Sabha	10.6	32.8	5.0	51.6
Libya	6.8	27.4	7.5	58.3

Source: Secretariat of Utilities, May 1982, Sabha Region, SPLAJ, p.20

industrial establishment depends largely on the reorganisation and perseverance of local handicrafts. These considerations are partly implemented in the rug and weaving factory, the tomato processing plant in Sabha and the palm tree furniture centre in Traghan. The productive capacity and employment contributions of these establishments are negligible to both the regional economy and work-force infrastructure.

The difficulties of utilising the regional mineral resources have directed production, in most cases, to local consumption rather than market-orientated products. The rapid increase in employment, accompanied by vast expansion in educational and health services, have caused the regional economy to become dependent on government services with little effort made to utilise the region's potential resources.

AGRICULTURAL DEVELOPMENT PROJECTS

In 1973 the Fezzan Council of Agricultural Development was established in order to: (a) proclaim a new farmland policy, (b) produce marketable quantities of cereal, meat, and vegetables, (c) improve the productivity of the farm population, (d) preserve the areas threatened by depopulation, and (e) suggest the need and direction of investment in items that increase agricultural output and reduce production costs. The objectives of the programme included economic, as well as social and political, elements. The economic objectives attempted to raise the level of income through the acceleration of agricultural development. The social aims were the abolition of social injustice that had resulted from the unequal distribution of wealth. The political objectives were implicit in the formulation of economic and social goals with which to stabilise the depopulated areas. Measures for implementing the improvement plan were considered within the framework of technical, resources and human potential. Considering the inter-relationship of the various objectives, the programme has to consider equally agricultural improvements and the stability of potential work-forces within the region. The development plan called for vertical expansion, land-reclamation in order to stabilise the rural-urban migration and improvements in the standard of living for a large proportion of the rural area.

The plan will promote agricultural settlements near those major towns highly vulnerable to population movement. This plan involves intensification of farming by dividing reclaimed land into individual farm units of ten hectares. Each farm is to be further divided into three sections, and each unit will be sown with a single crop or set of related crops. Rotation is compulsory and is supervised by the project management to prevent soil exhaustion and to regulate the use of weather resources. The major crops suitable to the climatic conditions, soil and water potential have been determined to be wheat, barley and alfalfa.

In addition to the farmland and water resources, farmers are entitled to a house, farm machinery, and irrigation equipment in the early stages of development. Moreover, the farmers were asked to join the co-operative societies established for the purpose of organising cultivation, land-use, marketing and all those agricultural and social services required by the members. The co-operative organisation formed in each project to reduce the cost of production and improve farming efficiency will also collectively market the major crops in order to secure a higher price than could be obtained by individual farmers.

The organisational service structure was to provide farmers with seeds, loans, fertilisers and farm machinery, and to supervise farming activities within its local jursidiction. The co-operative units are under the supervision of officials appointed by the High Council of Agricultural Development; later they will be elected - as seems to be appropriate, given general tendencies - by the project beneficiaries. These elected committees will perform the High Council duties of distributing new farms, determining the socio-economic conditions of those eligible to acquire farmland, and forecasting the technical, economic and social needs of their project. It will also administer and initiate the future development of the project service centre which generally includes: primary schools, kindergartens, the post office, the suque (market), the mosque, banks and hotels, fire and police stations, the administrative centre, houses for community workers, and medical clinics.

The improvement of animal husbandry is another agricultural service of the co-operatives. Each project has a veterinary centre which offers medical treatment for sick animals to the project beneficiaries. However, these projects are to be considered as an initial stage and are being carried out on an experimental basis in the Awbari, Traghan and Brak districts.

There is no doubt that the project's co-operative structure

has succeeded in stimulating agricultural productivity and has enabled the new owners to receive higher prices for their products. These achievements have resulted in a considerable increase in crop production. The average yield of wheat per hectare increased by 24.2 per cent on the project farm during 1976 compared with the preceding year when only 5.3 per cent was realised on the traditional farms[16]. This increase can be attributed to modernisation producing greater efficiency in production.

CONCLUSION

The scanty population, shortage of skills, work-force potential, and high rates of intra-regional migration within the Fezzan region are serious problems and are likely to remain so for years to come. The high fertility-rates, and decreasing mortality, attributed to improvement of health and education, are matched by high mobility amongst educated and skilled youths especially to Tripoli and Binghazi to fill professional and technical posts, or to enrol in the northern universities. However, even with the major improvements in agriculture over the last ten years and social and economic development, the region still suffers from demographic push factors due to poor utilisation of the potential physical resources. Equally the shortage of labour and orientation towards non-agricultural activities has become a major constraint on development. Little has been done to deal with these problems, especially by way of diversification of economic activities and expansion of vocational training in order to increase the standard of living, reduce sub-regional imbalance and consequently stabilise the rural population.

REFERENCES

1. The Council of Agricultural Development, 1975, *Wadi Ash Shati Agricultural Scheme*, p.4

2. Ministry of Agricultural Development, 1973, *Agricultural Development Programme: Fezzan Area, Preliminary Report by the German Consul*, Tripoli, p.42

3. Nijim B.K., 1975, *Sex Ratio and Landholding Pattern in Libya*, Iowa, p.6.

4. Ministry of Economics and Commerce, 1964, *General Population Census: Sabha and Awbari Districts*, Tripoli.

5. Nijim B.K., *op.cit.*, p.6

6. Pan C.L., 1949, 'Population of Libya', in *Population Studies*, p.105

7. The Council of Agricultural Development, *op.cit.*, p.33

8. Ministry of Planning, 1974, *Settlement Pattern*

Study: SabhaRegion, Rome, p.20.

9. The Council of Agricultural Development, Holzman P., 1974, Morzog Project: Regional Survey, Wakut, p.42

10. *Ibid.*,

11. Ministry of Planning, 1973, *Preliminary Report of Population Census*.

12. The Council of Agricultural Development, 1974, *op.cit.*,

13. Allan J.A., 1976, 'Drought in Libya: Some Solutions Available to an Oil-Rich Government', in *African Affairs*, pp.154-155

14. Ministry of Planning, 1974, *op.cit.*, p.41

15. *Ibid.*

16. Ministry of Planning, 1976, *Statistical Data on the Important Economic Sectors*, Tripoli.

PART THREE: WATER AND LAND RESOURCES

Chapter 7

THE TRIPOLI AGGLOMERATION LAND-USE CHANGES AND LAND-USE OPTIONS

M.M. Buru

ABSTRACT

This study examines the changes in land-use since the early 1950's, especially the development of agriculture, the reclamation of dune areas, the extension of woodland and the intensification of urban land-use close to Tripoli. The method used was the interpretation of aerial photographs available for 1953, 1976-77, 1968 and 1980. In addition, satellite imagery for 1972 and 1979 provided the basis for additional estimates of land cover changes. The analysis revealed a five-fold increase in the area covered by urban developments between 1953 and 1976-77, an increase in woodland, and a dramatic fall in the area of dunes from 25 to only 2 per cent of the region as a result of dune reclamation, tree planting and the extension of irrigated land.

The second part of this study is a brief review of the land and water resources of the region and a comparison of the land-use options which should be considered in future development strategies.

INTRODUCTION

The physical national perspective plan (1980-2000) prepared by the Secretariat of Utilities divided the country into four regions: Tripoli, Sabha, Al-Khalij and Binghazi. The region of Tripoli with which this article is concerned is sub-divided into five sub-regions: Tripoli, Zuwarah, Al Khums, Misratah and Gharyan.

The boundary of the Tarabulus or Tripoli agglomeration contains all the sub-baladiyas of Tarabulus and the sub-baladiyas of Janzur, As Sawani Bin Ghashir and Tajura. The agglomeration takes in all the principal centres of activity of the sub-baladiyas and its territory all lies within 45 minutes travelling time of the central business district.

A surface area of 1,253 square kilometres is inhabited by 994,000 persons (1980 figure), with an average density of population of 793 persons per square kilometre. Tarabulus also

7.1 The Tripoli agglomeration - hydrological features

THE TRIPOLI AGGLOMERATION - HYDROLOGICAL FEATURES

Rainfall - mean annual in mm

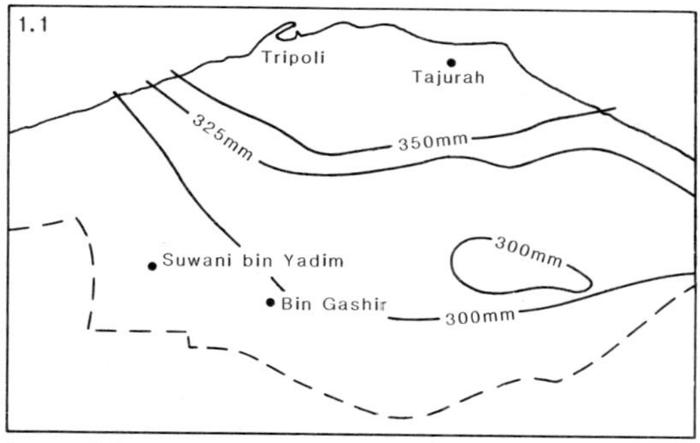

Source: Polservice - Wadeco, 1980, Map 2

Water-level declines in the upper aquifer - 1949-78

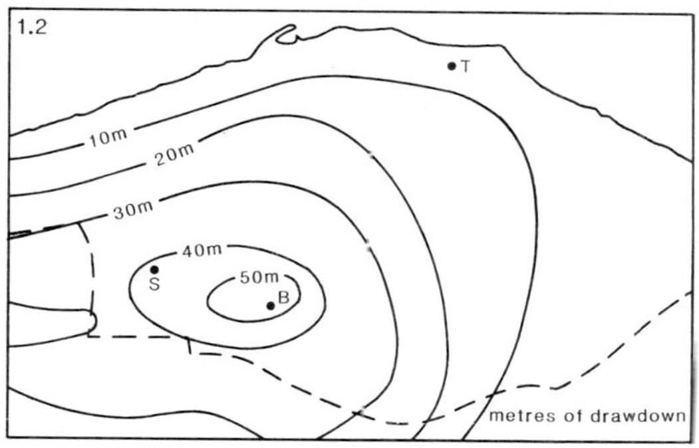

Source: Secretariat of Agricultural Reclamation and Land Development, 1981, p 29

Sea-water intrusion

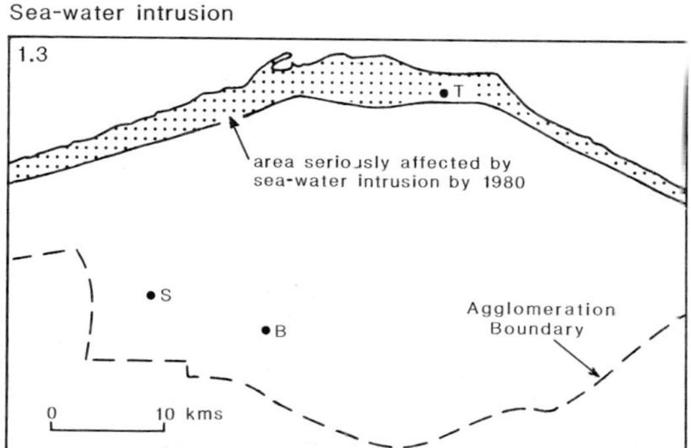

Source: SCET, 1981, Vol 1

functions as the capital of a country of 1,775,500 square kilometres. Tripoli agglomeration comprises a relatively small area (0.6 per cent) of the total but includes 49.3 per cent of the regional population and 30.6 per cent of the national population. Tripoli agglomeration takes in 30.4 per cent of the non-Libyans in the country.

The growth-rates and structure of employment in Tripoli agglomeration enhance its importance. It is responsible for 51.1 per cent of employment in the region and for 30.4 per cent of those actively employed thoughout the country. No less than 36.3 per cent of the nation's service functions, 33.0 per cent of industrial activities and 13.0 per cent of value added in agriculture are to be found in the agglomeration. The critical role played by Tarabulus region scarcely needs further emphasis. In order to sustain rapid rates of growth in population numbers and in economy, there has been an increasing demand for all factor inputs. It is a paradox that the economic boom that has been supported by development of oil exports has put growing pressures on a commodity more precious for the long term than oil itself - water. This chapter will examine the changing pattern of water use in the Tripoli agglomeration to identify problems and suggest possible solutions.

1. The Study Area

The Tripoli agglomeration is unique in Libya in that most of the region enjoys a favouable rainfall, between 250 and 350 millimetres per year (with some annual variation) and soils which, while not rich in organic matter, are responsive to dryland and irrigated systems of farming. Furthermore, until recently the groundwater resources of the area close to Tripoli were substantial. In no other part of Libya were land and water resources so favourably arranged.

RENEWABLE RESOURCES

Renewable resources, such as soil, water and vegetation, are best regarded as complex ecological systems, sustainable where they are not being down-graded by activities such as agriculture and livestock rearing. The usefulness of natural resources is dependent on man's ability to exploit them. This ability in turn, depends on the availability of capital to purchase agricultural and irrigation equipment, and upon a demand for livestock products to provide the incentive to rear them. The availability of funds to invest in the agricultural sector can, equally, lead to changes which tend to enhance renewable natural resources: for example the reclamation of unused land, such as dunes, by afforestation.

Renewable natural resources may either be robust and

Fig. 7.2 Soil map of the Tripoli agglomeration

SOIL MAP OF THE TRIPOLI AGGLOMERATION

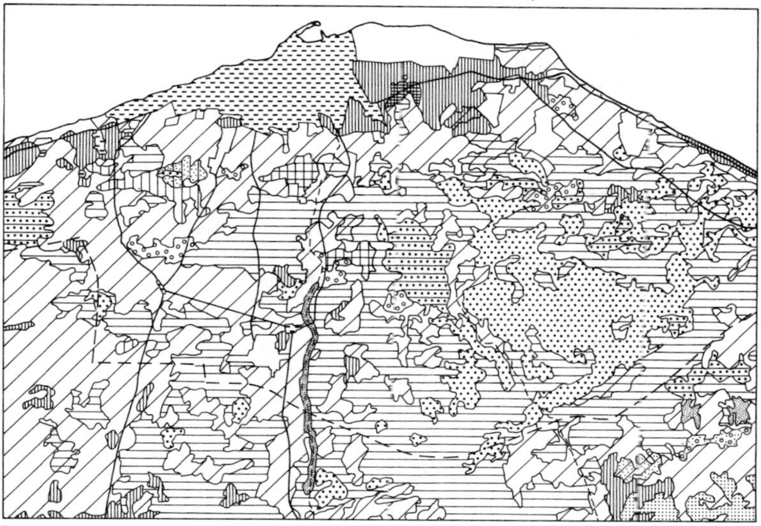

Source: Soviet Soil - Ecological Expedition, 1980

0 10 kms

LEGEND

- FBd-Reddish brown arid differentiated soils
- FBdcr-Reddish brown arid differentiated crust soils
- FBsd-Reddish brown arid slightly differentiated soils
- FBsdcr-Reddish brown arid slightly differentiated crust soils
- FBnd-Reddish brown arid non-differentiated soils
- FBndcr-Reddish brown arid non-differentiated crust soils
- Asd-Alluvial slightly differentiated soils
- LCs-Cinnamonic lithosols
- Lfb-Reddish brown lithosols
- CRnm-Non-monolithic soils
- SC-Continental sands
- Urban and built-up areas
- Areas excluded from survey
- - - - - Wadis
- ——— Roads
- — — — Agglomeration Boundary

Fig. 7.3 Coverage of aerial photography and Landsat imagery

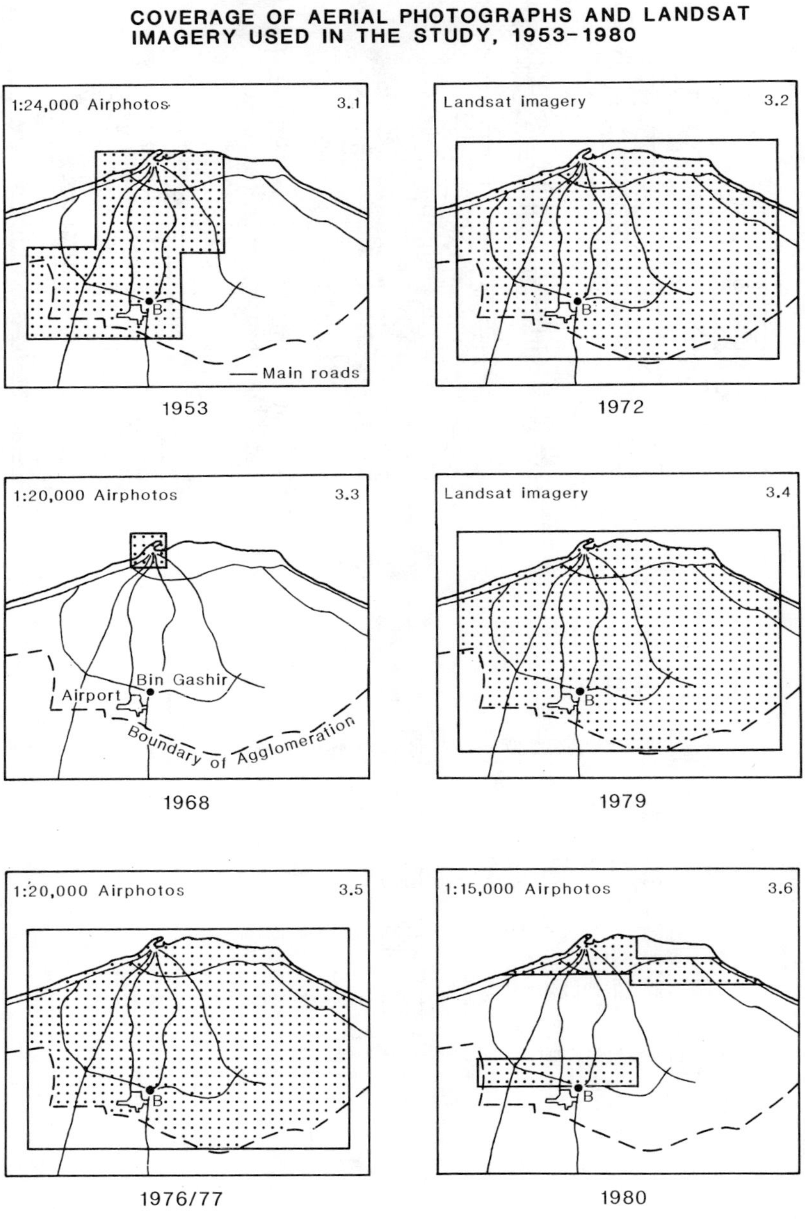

able to sustain an intensification of agricultural and pastoral practices, or marginal and vulnerable to over-use, such as those in the Tripoli agglomeration, particularly water. If the whole of the Tripoli agglomeration were to be irrigated for two seasons, the water requirement would be two billion cubic metres of water per year, which is almost ten times the current estimated level of use for the whole of the Jifarah Plain. This figure represents a vast demand on resources. This assumes 1.5 metres depth of water per year for 1,400 km^2 of the whole agglomeration). As the aquifer cannot sustain even the 50 per cent of the agglomeration partially irrigated in 1983, requiring about 200 million cubic metres of water per year, a level of use which was causing the water table to drop at the unacceptable rate of between 1 and 5 metres per year, depending on the location, expansion of irrigated agriculture is undesirable.

The soils of the Tripoli agglomeration are not easily degraded. They are generally light, sandy and well-drained without any significant profile development or organic accumulation. In good rainfall years they can produce reasonable dryland grain yields of 0.5 tonnes per hectare or more and with irrigation a wide range of vegetables and fruit. The surface has always been vulnerable to sand erosion reducing the possibilities of extending the cultivated area and reclaiming more land.

THE ECONOMIC CONTEXT AND PHASES OF DEVELOPMENT

Libya has experienced dramatic changes in its factor mix since the 1950's, and has been able to experiment in its development policy and see to what extent capital can substitute for land and water resources and labour.

In the 1950's, Libya was extremely short of capital resources, but during the 1960's oil revenue changed the shape of the economy and by 1965 it was enabling significant development budget allocations. In the late 1960's, it is estimated that the cultivated area of the Jifarah Plain was extended at the rate of 2 per cent per year, especially for citrus fruit and tomatoes [1]. The 1970's witnessed a continuation of this trend until 1976 when it was realised that ecological disaster was imminent in the Jifarah Plain unless the use of groundwater was reduced. The planting of tomatoes and citrus was officially proscribed, although continued by farmers where they could escape detection.

The other major change in land-use brought about by increased national wealth was the growth of Tripoli and other settlements, as well as improvements in communications including roads, airports and ports. The rates of extension accorded with the progressive improvements in oil revenue. The extension of Tripoli occurred in two forms. Firstly in the building of new residential areas on all sides of the city through the investment of public and private funds, and secondly in the

Fig. 7.4 Changes in land use in the Tripoli agglomeration

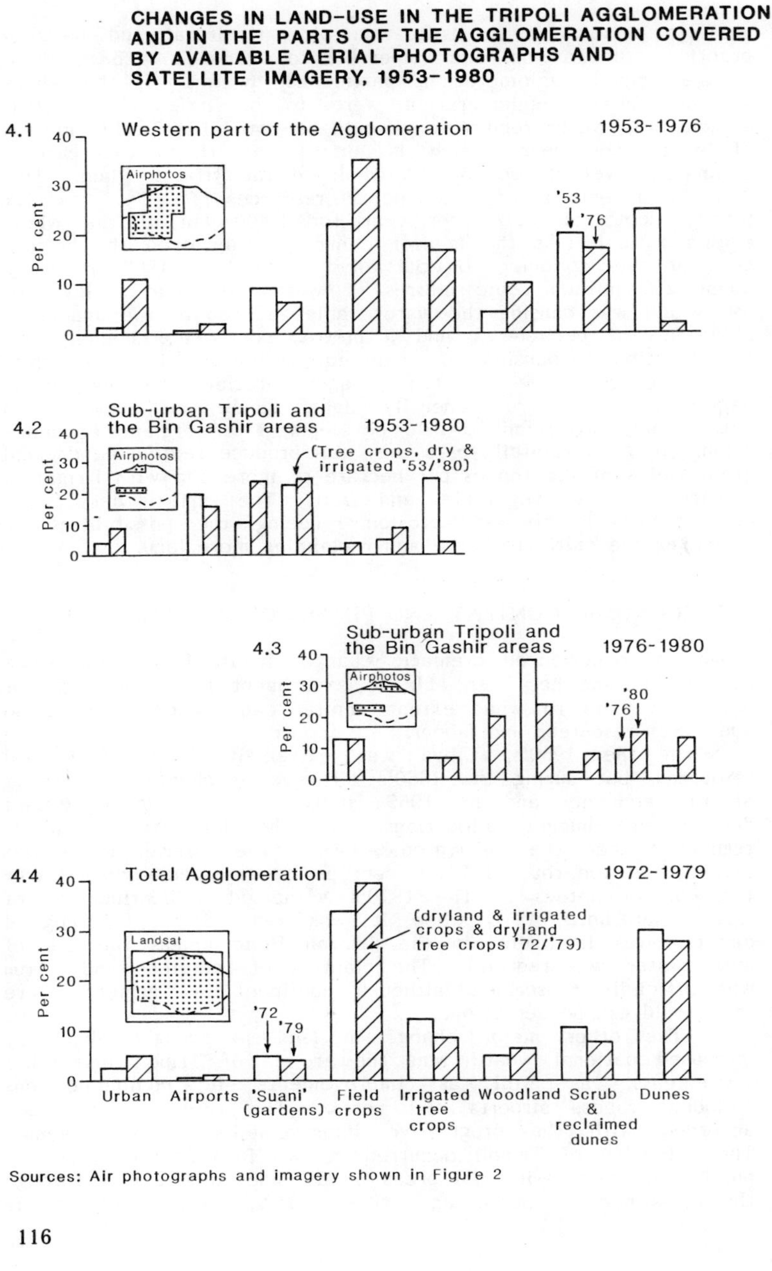

Sources: Air photographs and imagery shown in Figure 2

'suani', the gardens which extended from Suq al Jumah to Tajura. These became desirable residential areas, especially with the improvement of the road network and the acquisition of motor vehicles by the vast majority of Libyan families. Tripoli's boundary was now difficult to define, since the traditionally agricultural areas took on the function of a dormitory for the town.
Other major changes in land-use resulted from two initiatives. Firstly uncultivated land was settled by families who had previously farmed in the 'suani', but also by Libyan families who had come from outside Libya in the 1960's and 1970's especially from Tunisia. Secondly, from the government reclamation of of dune areas by planting retaining grasses and appropriate shrubs and trees, increasing wooded areas.

2. Evidence of Change

RESEARCH METHODS

The series of air photographs and two satellite images shown in Table 7.1 were used to estimate the areas of major land-use types in the Tripoli agglomeration. The photographs were viewed by stereoscope and as mosaics, and interpretations were effected according to the classifications shown in Table 7.2. The satellite imagery was acquired by the Landsat multi-spectral scanner sensors and processed digitally to enable classification of the spectral data. Extensive fieldwork was also carried out to check and modify the classification in order to improve it as a basis for extending the areas of the various land-use types. The initial classification for the satellite imagery was more detailed than the land-use classes for the interpretation of the aerial photographs (see Table 7.3). These classes were therefore aggregated to accord as nearly as possible with those used for the airphoto interpretation. Fieldwork was of course not possible in association with the interpretation of the old photographs, but it was considered that the value of the data derived from them far outweighed their inevitable inaccuracies.

Area measurements were completed by means of a digitiser. Unfortunately, the aerial imagery did not in all cases cover the whole of the study area. As a result the only significant comparison was between the results for 1953 and 1976.

RESULTS OF THE AERIAL PHOTOGRAPH AND SATELLITE IMAGE INTERPRETATION

The results bring a number of surprises although all the changes in land-use are, simultaneously, consistent with the economic analysis outlined in the previous section.

Table 7.1 Air photographs and images used in the study

Date	Area	Scale	Type of Product
<u>Air photos</u>			
May/June 1953	Tripoli and Bin Ghashir	1:24,000	Air photo mosaic - Fairey Surveys Ltd.
Feb. (7) 1968	Tripoli urban area	1:25,000	Air photos - small strip of the urban area - Hunting Surveys Ltd.
Dec-Feb. 1976-77	Agglomeration	1:20,000	Air photos - KLM
1980	Strips only	1:15,000	Air photos - Polservice
<u>Satellite Images</u>			
Feb. 1973	Agglomeration	1:250,000	Landsat MS5 - computer classified
Feb. 1979	Agglomeration	1:250,000	Landsat MS5 - computer classified

Table 7.2 Land-use classification - aerial photography study 1953/1976-77

Built-up area	- urban land - airports
Suani (gardens)	- former palm gardens mainly used for residential purposes by 1980
Cultivated land	- including mixed dryland and irrigated land
Tree crops	- olives but including some citrus
Woodland	- old woods but especially newly-planted woodland after 1965
Scrub and reclaimed land	- former scrub which was used for grazing but also including the large reclaimed areas after 1965
Sand dunes	- uncultivated dune areas

Table 7.3 Land-use classification - satellite image study 1972-79

Built-up area	- urban land - airports
Suani	- former palm gardens mainly used for residential purposes
Irrigated field cultivation	- all irrigated field crops (winter) including small plots detectable by the imagery (1 ha.)
Unirrigated field cultivation	- dryland field crops
Fallow land	- bare soil within areas mainly under cultivation
Irrigated agriculture with arboriculture including olives	- irrigated inter-cropping within the extensive olive plantations including citrus areas; citrus could be interplanted in the olives.

Fig. 7.5 Land use units in the Tripoli agglomeration

LAND UNITS IN THE TRIPOLI AGGLOMERATION

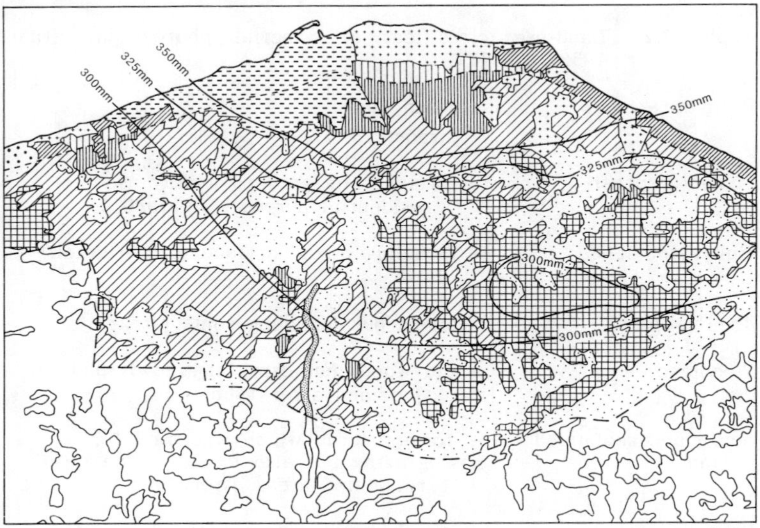

Based on Figures 1.3 and 2

0 10 kms

LEGEND

Tracts with contaminated groundwater

- Reddish-brown; differentiated
- Reddish-brown; slightly differentiated
- Reddish-brown; non-differentiated

Tracts south of the contaminated groundwater

- Reddish-brown; differentiated
- Reddish-brown; slightly differentiated
- Reddish-brown; non-differentiated
- Continental sands (dunes)
- Alluvial slightly differentiated

- Built-up area
- Areas excluded from the survey
- Isohyets
- Southern position of sea-water intrusion in 1980
- Agglomeration Boundary

Continuation of Table 7.3

Woodland	- old woodland and newly-planted trees (older than five years)
Bare soil	- including dunes

Table 7.4 shows the results of the area measurements completed on the photographs and imagery available. The most obvious changes are the increase in the built-up area, the increase in the cultivated area and the dramatic fall in the area of sand dunes. These changes have been made possible partly by the energy of the Libyan community, and after 1965 by the capacity of both the public and the private sectors to invest in housing, public works, agriculture and land reclamation[2].

THE IMPACT OF LAND-USE CHANGES ON RENEWABLE NATURAL RESOURCES

There are three renewable natural resources in the Tripoli agglomeration, of which water is of over-riding importance. The other two are soil and vegetation. The changes in land-use have increased demand for water, affecting groundwater reserves. The urban population of Tripoli increased from less than 100,000 in the 1950's, and 300,000 in the 1960's, to almost 1 million by 1980. Natural increases of over 3 per cent per annum plus immigration from rural areas after 1965, of between 100,000 and 200,000 aliens involved in development projects, accounted for the increase. The Tripoli agglomeration accommodated additional population outside the city bringing the total to almost half of the Libyan population. This large population, with a high standard of living, increased the urban and domestic demand for water by a factor of at least twenty.

Meanwhile the expansion of irrigated agriculture went ahead after 1953 and especially in the 1960's. Exact figures for this expansion are difficult to determine because the changes were unsystematic, inconsistent and not always sustained. It is estimated that the rural demand for water increased 500 per cent in the period 1953-76. At the same time industrial enterprises started to use water, especially after 1969, and these requirements became a heavy burden on the limited water resources.

The demand for water has reached a level of at least six times the rate of recharge in the agglomeration itself and in the whole Jifarah hydrological system it has been estimated to be four times the rate of recharge; dramatically impairing the future availability of water. Another irreversible effect of the excessive use of water in agriculture is sea-water

Table 7.4 Land-use changes between 1953 and 1976-77 based on aerial photography intepretation (%)

Built-up area - urban	1.5	11.0
- airports	0.5	2.0
Suani	9.0	6.5
Cultivated land - mixed dry and irrigated land	22.0	35.0
Tree crops	18.0	16.5
Woodland	4.0	10.0
Scrub and reclaimed land	20.0	17.0
Dunes	25.0	2.0

Note: See Table 7.2 for a more detailed description of the land-use types.

intrusion resulting from the reduction in hydraulic head following over-pumping of groundwater. The salt water had reached points 6 kilometres inland by 1980 and seems likely to affect the whole of the Tripoli agglomeration by the end of the century unless water-conserving practices are implemented.

The impact of land-use changes in potentially productive soils has been less dramatic. The best soils lie close to Tripoli and the expansion of the city has reduced the area of soil of reasonable quality in direct proportion to that built upon. The expansion of Tripoli airport also covered good-quality soils, which could have been used to produce dryland crops economically. However, there could be no case for expanding irrigated agriculture near the airport after 1965, since the demand for water was already too high. Groundwater levels continued to fall at Bin Ghashir at the rate of over 5 metres per year by 1980.

Vegetation resources in the Tripoli agglomeration have been improved by the development activities of the 1960's and 1970's, such as afforestation and land-reclamation. The increase in green cover not only conserves the soil, but also provides recreation areas for the urban population and improves the appearance of the agglomeration. The economic value of the increased vegetation is not, however, great and the impact of the deep-rooting species which alone can colonise the dunes will be to place a further demand on soil moisture supplies. Less water will infiltrate the soil following periods of precipitation and trees and shrubs may, occasionally, even draw directly on groundwater.

Land-use in the Tripoli Agglomeration

Table 7.5 Land-use changes 1972-79 based on satellite imagery

Land-use	1972 (%)	1979 (%)
Urban	3.5	5.0
Airports	0.5	1.0
Suani	5.0	4.5
Sub-Total	(9.0)	(10.5)
Irrigated field cultivation	10.0	9.0
Unirrigated field cultivation	23.0	18.5
Fallow land	n.a	12.0
Irrigated agriculture with arboriculture including olives	12.5	8.5
Woodland	5.0	6.5
Sub-Total	(50.5)	(54.5)
High-density range	0.5	0.5
Medium-density range	5.5	4.5
Low-density range	4.5	2.5
Bare soil	30.0	27.5
Sub-Total	(40.5)	(35.0)
	100.0	100.0

Note: See Table 7.3 for a more detailed description of the land-use types.

It remains to examine the renewable natural resources of the Tripoli agglomeration in a systematic way which takes into account their current and future status on the basis of existing or alternative strategies for their use. The economic, social and political goals of the government and people of Libya must also be taken into account in the analysis. The approach taken will be that known as 'Land Evaluation'[3].

3. Renewable Natural Resources in the Agglomeration

CLIMATE, SOIL AND GROUNDWATER

The Tripoli agglomeration receives enough precipitation in three out of five years to support dryland field crops. Dryland tree crops, such as olives, can always be grown in most of the region.

The capability of the soils of the region lies mainly in classes III and IV[4]. Nevertheless, both dryland and irrigated crops can provide yields which are adequate by international standards; financial gross returns per hectare for dryland and irrigated crops were approximately 100 to 200 US dollars and 1,000 to 2,000 dollars per hectare respectively. It is clear that dryland financial returns are so small in the early 1980's that there can never be any economic case for impeding urban development in potential dryland agriculture areas.

The groundwater resources of the region were being recharged naturally at a rate of about 0.1 metres per unit of area in the agglomeration in 1980. The rate of withdrawal for the region as a whole was at least six times this figure. Groundwater cannot sustain the existing irrigated agriculture in the agglomeration and it would seem appropriate both to reduce the partially-irrigated area by at least 50 per cent and to improve water use and distribution in the remainder. This last would involve using drip and trickle systems of irrigation with a consequent reduction in the range of crops which could be raised.

In places near Tripoli the intrusion of sea-water inland has reached 6 kilometres and is still advancing. The result is that about one-third of the Tripoli agglomeration, the strip adjacent to the sea, can no longer be irrigated by *in situ* groundwater resources. Thus urban land-use and irrigated farming are not in competition.

LAND EVALUATION FOR URBAN AND INDUSTRIAL DEVELOPMENT, IRRIGATED FARMING, DRYLAND FARMING AND RECREATION

An assessment of the natural resources of the Tripoli agglomeration with a view to recommending future land-use must take into account:-

1. The status of soil, water and vegetation resources and the rainfall of the region.
2. The economic returns to be gained from each type of land-use in particular tracts of the region.
3. The economic, social and political goals of the Libyan Government.
4. The attitudes and perceptions of the Libyan farming

community.

The first group of factors has been discussed in the preceding section and Figures 7.2, 7.3 and 7.4 illustrate the resources in the study area. The question of economic returns has also been raised in the previous section, in comparing dryland and irrigated strategies. Gross returns on dryland and irrigated farming differ by as much as ten times (US $100 - 200 vs. US $1000 - 2000 per hectare) but returns on urban uses are more attractive than both. The use of land for recreation is much more attractive than for dryland farming and, in some circumstances, more economically attractive than for irrigated farming.

The analysis is best approached by examining the evaluation outlined in Table 7.6, which provides a semi-quantitative assessment of the relative suitability of various tracts in the agglomeration for the five land-use options considered. A fully-quantitative assessment would require much more physical and economic data based on carefully-directed field observation and surveys.

Implicit in the analysis are very important problems for the government and the local farming community. Firstly there is no area in which irrigated farming is the best option from the point of view of resource conservation. Only limited areas of units 2A and 2B should be used for irrigated farming. This situation does not accord with the wishes of the government to bring increases in agricultural production, or with the current perceptions of farmers who wish to maximise production per unit of land, failing to recognise the much more important measure, namely returns per unit of water.

The coastal strip, arbitarily defined here as the area affected by sea-water intrusion, should be limited to urban, industrial, residential, and recreational use according to soil type. New irrigated farming is not an option and existing irrigated farming should cease in the contaminated coastal strip as defined in Figure 7.5.

Finally, the issue of land tenure should be addressed. Since dryland farming is the agricultural practice viable over the majority of the agglomeration, and units of 100 hectares are needed to sustain a family, smaller units could only be part-time enterprises. Furthermore, if irrigated farming is to be carried out on only a small fraction of soil types 2A and 2B then this 'small proportion' (say 1,000 hectares) could either be fragmented on existing holdings, again providing only part-time activity for some of the farming community or consolidated into a few, centrally-managed schemes on which new high-technology farming could be effectively organised.

In the light of these observations, it is clearly inappropriate to cause a major change in land tenure for the purpose of managing irrigated farming. As for dryland farming, it could similarly either be run as a part-time activity on existing holdings, or holdings would have to be consolidated in order to

Table 7.6 An evaluation of land-use types in the Tripoli agglomeration

Land units	Land-use types: Urban and industrial	Residential	Irrigated farming	Dryland trees and crops	Recreation (including woodland)
1 6km coastal strip					
1A Suani	S_3	S_1	N_2	S2	N_1
1B Soil	S_2	S_2	N_2	S_2	S_1
1C Soil (Dunes)	S_3	S2	N_2	N_2	S_1
2 S of 6km coastal strip					
2A Soil	S_3	S_3	S_2*	S_1	S_3
2B Soil	S_3	S_3	S_2*	S_1	S_3
2C Soil (Dunes)	N_1	S_3	N_2	N_2	S_1

* limited by groundwater availability (economically S_1)

S_1 Suitable
S_2 Less suitable
S_3 Marginally suitable

N_1 Not suitable without considerable investment
N_2 Not suitable in any circumstances

Source: The suitability classes are based on: A Framework for Land Evaluation, 1976, Rome.

provide sufficient returns to support a family. However since, by its nature, dryland farming creates seasonally-concentrated work, activity even on large dryland farms could only be part-time.

Livestock rearing has not been addressed here. Animal products are very important elements in the current agricultural economy of the Tripoli area. The demand for them is an extremely potent force in the agricultural sector which has important consequences on land and water management. Livestock need fodder, and fodder requires irrigation, unless it comes from abroad via government schemes and associated subsidies. Much of the grain, and all of the alfalfa, in the Tripoli area is produced for animals which are kept by farms. As water is demonstrably not a reliable resource, the livestock rearing is not a sustainable activity.

Water is the beginning and end of all agriculture in northern Libya. *In situ* groundwater was effectively close to exhaustion by the early 1980's. Proposals to bring water from the south, Fezzan, to the Jifarah would transform the situation but economical use of expensive water from the south could only be justified if it were deployed on carefully-managed and efficient farms. It would be wise to limit the use of water to the 1,000 hectares suggested as the maximum irrigable area in the agglomeration.

ACKNOWLEDGEMENTS

The author wishes to thank Dr. J.A. Allan and his assistants, Mr. Nick Hutchings and Mr. Kenneth Wilson, for their help in preparation of this study. Assistance was also received from the Department of Geography in the University of London in the use of the digitising equipment for area measurement. Classification of the Landsat imagery for 1972 and 1979 was undertaken on the system originally devised by Mr. J. Latham at Erim Laboratories, Ann Arbor. The author would also like to express his gratitude to Milud Hilmi, Director of the Urban Development Unit of the Secretariat of Utilities, Tripoli, Dr. Bakhbakhi of the Secretariat of Agriculture and officials of the Survey Department at the Secretariat of Planning.

REFERENCES

1. Allan J.A. McLachlan K.S. and Penrose E.T., 1973, *Libya: Agriculture and Economic Development*, Frank Cass, London.

2. Allan J.A., 1981, *Libya: the Experience of Oil*, Croom Helm, London, pp.121-7 & pp.196ff.

3. FAO, 1976, A Framework for Land Evaluation, FAO, Rome.

4. Soviet Soil - Ecological Expedition, 1980, *Soil Maps and Report on the Soils of the Tripoli Region*, Moscow and Tripoli.

ANNEX

LAND CAPABILITY AND OPTIMUM LAND-USE IN LIBYA

Russian Soil-Ecological Expedition

Class I. Best Lands

Small patches near towns of: Al Aziziyah Al Azizihah, Bin Ghashir

Reddish-brown and differentiated soils
Low relief
Good drainage
Often irrigated
No significant limitations

Class II. Good Land

Large tracts
Reddish-brown and differentiated or slightly-differentiated soils
Rolling plains and gentle slopes
Good drainage
Negative factors: slightly eroded, stony surface, some unfavourable chemical characteristics.
On the whole, suitable for intensive farming.

Class III Lands of Medium Quality

Divided into 4 sub-classes

Sub-class I Reddish-brown, arid, differentiated soils
Gentle gradients
Slightly saline
Nearly all used for agriculture

Sub-class II Reddish-brown and differentiated soils
Slanting slopes
Slightly alkaline
Mainly under cultivation

Sub-class III Largest tracts concentrated in littoral Jifarah Plain
South of Qasr al Qaradulli, Misratah, Al Aziziyah and the Jabal Nafusah uplands
Slanting slopes
Slightly alkaline
Good drainage

	Favourable physical qualities for irrigation, especially sprinkle and sub-surface irrigation
Subclass IV	More stony Smaller fine earth layer Limits on intensity of farming
Subclass V	Largest tracts in southern part of littoral Jifarah Plain and in Jabal Nafusah uplands More stony Small fine earth layer Recommended for pasture
Class VI	Land of Poor Quality Found near towns of: Al Zawiyah, Gharyan, Sabratah, Tarhunah, Al Khums, Jafrin, Zlitan Aeolian soils Rolling plains and dissected uplands Moderately saline Undeveloped soil profile Very stony Moderately eroded Substantial limitations on agriculture, some grazing and forestry.
Class VII	Land of a very poor quality Considerable tracts in Jabal Nafusah Uplands Limits include: high dissection of territory steepness of slopes very stony surface high salinity nutrient deficiency skeletal structure Some forest land
Class VIII	Worst land Jabal Nafusah Uplands Considerable limitations: very high salinity steep relief bare soil

Chapter 8

DEVELOPING TRENDS OF FARM/RANGELAND RESOURCES IN THE EASTERN ZONE OF LIBYA

Hosney A. Benzabih

The Eastern Zone, sometimes known as the Binghazi region, is the name given to five districts lying in an area roughly stretching between the Gulf of Sirt shoreline in the west to the Libyan frontier in the east. The area was traditionally known as Barquah, or Cyrenaica in Europe when early settlements occurred during the classical period. Geographically, the area forms a fairly coherent region. Its physical landscape is dominated by the Jabal Al-Akhdar, a multi-terraced plateau. The mean maximum rainfall can reach 500 to 600 millimetres per year, but only in the highlands. Its climatic conditions are better suited to grazing than to agriculture.

The region was subjected to more Italian colonial military action than elsewhere in the country. The Italians tried to undermine the political and economic independence of the tribal organisation which had prevailed in the region for centuries. The colonial policy, which was aimed at enhancing the Italian presence in the region came into effect in the early 1930's. It had a devastating impact on the indigenous way of life, as revealed in previous analysis[1]. Subsequently, the Italians were able to fulfil their objectives in establishing the 'quarta sponda' (Fourth Shore) after completing their demographic settlement in the northern districts of Cyrenaica. A para-state corporation, 'Ente per la Colonizazione della Cirenaica' (ECC), carried out the development and promotion of the demographic estates which totalled 1,772 households by the early 1940's. Simultaneously, the indigenous communities, deprived of their traditional site for cash-crops and animal grazing, became entrenched in the marginal area of the interior[2]. Accordingly, a dualistic land-use emerged in the region, a dichotomy between a modern sector managed by aliens in the northern districts and a traditional land-use pattern carried out by the indigenous communities in the interior. This gradually created regional dualism, the legacy of which has been deeply imprinted on the area ever since.

The legacy of the demographic estates, although based on family-farm patterns with an alien context super-imposed at the expense of community-managed,traditional land-use, has inspired all subsequent policy-makers to decide to adopt the ECC approach in developing agricultural resources since the discovery of oil.

Fig. 8.1 Eastern Zone land use

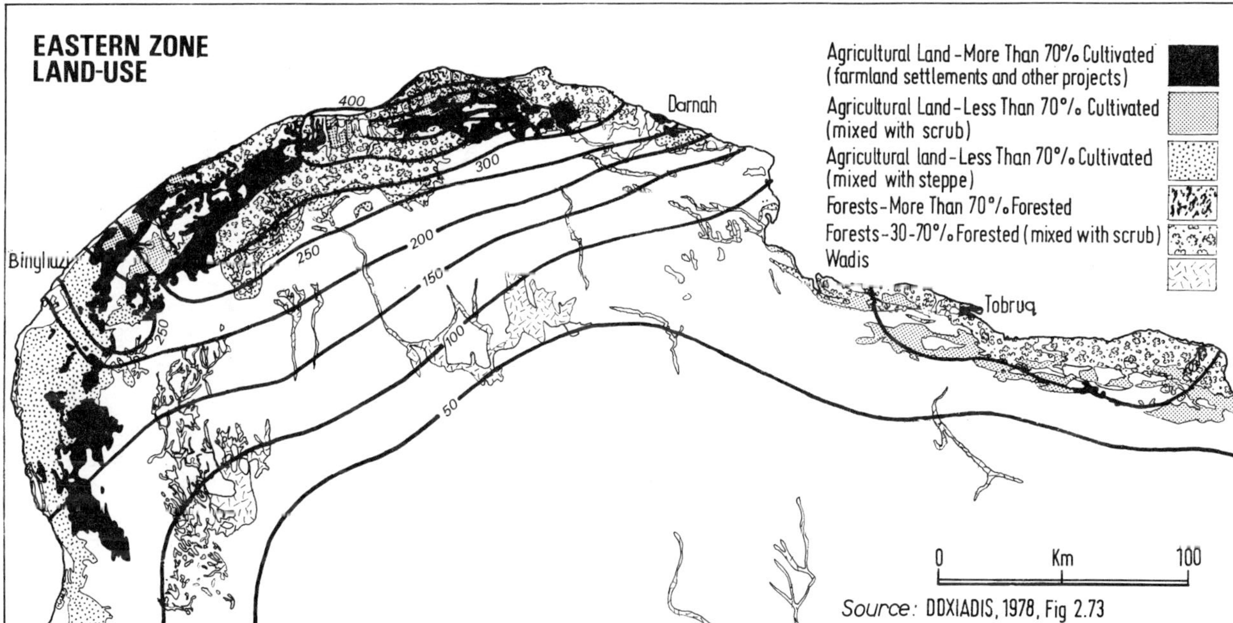

The National Agricultural Settlement Authority (NASA) was the first state body initiated in the early sixties to renovate and promote the legacy of the Ente settlements. Apart from a complex environment of tribal lands in the region, which overshadowed the process of rehabilitation of the settlements, NASA failed to bring about any positive achievements. As a consequence, the pre-1969 planning authorities were uncertain of the absorptive capacity of the agricultural sectors, as observers have noted:-

> The experience of the generation of planners and politicians responsible for Libya's affairs in the 1963-69 period appears, however, to have led them to conclude that the agricultural sector should not necessarily attract such a high proportion of development funds since agriculture was only allowed to absorb 12.7 per cent of the resources actually allocated[3].

Moreover, the planning authorities went so far as to consider that outlays for the agricultural sector would be wasted until an adequate level of social and economic infrastructure could be secured[4]. Nevertheless, such views were overthrown in 1969 and they were replaced by radical perspectives.

Substantial oil revenues in the post-revolution era enabled successive planning bodies to initiate ambitious socio-economic development strategies, which the country urgently required. However, the wisdom of very high allocation and expenditure of funds, especially on the country's renewable and non-renewable resources, had been recognised[5]. As anticipated, priority in the subsequent development plans in the 1970's was given to the agricultural sector. However, although the pre-1969 agricultural strategies were reviewed, an endorsement of the small-farm, land-settlement approach adopted in the 1960's finally emerged, but this time on a larger scale[6].

On a regional level the redevelopment of farmlands and the creation of a modern sector of dryland farming in the eastern zone has been taken over by the Jabal Al Akhdar Authority, which replaced NASA. The Jabal Al Akhdar Project (JAP) speeded up the process of developing farms, and the acreage of agricultural land has increased substantially. By 1980 the physical landscape of the old settlement site changed dramatically and the essential infrastructure, such as farm houses, road networks and other affiliated facilities, was well developed. By 1978, 1,809 farms were distributed, out of an anticipated total of 1,842 serving a total of around 3,651 households. Geographically, the overwhelming majority of the farms are based on dryland farming and are grouped inconsistently in an area beyond the 250 millimetre isohyet of the northern slope of the Jabal Al Akhdar and its adjacent areas. At the Al Marj Basin (Barce Plain), which has fertile alluvial soil, more than one-third of farms have been allocated. Land-use patterns were laid down by the Project Authority. The farmers have, however, to a greater or lesser extent, made decisions based on a compromise between the economic and physical realities and their own personal preferences. Yet, in the absence of a comprehensive ex-post evaluation of the region's farmland, the economic viability of the farms is difficult to establish. Nonetheless, the farmland settlements benefit from the government's benevolent policy towards agriculture in general. Agricultural inputs are heavy; subsidised in Libya by as much as fifty per cent and including seeds, fertilizers, pesticides, agricultural machinery and fuel as well as fodder. Equally, interest-free agricultural credit facilities are officially provided for those in need[7].

The size and space of the settlement farmlands vis-à-vis the region's total usable surface, is revealed in the attached figure. The settlements are projected to sustain 3,651 households in the near future. This is about thirteen per cent of the 31,000 households who, according to 1973 census classification of households, live in rural areas. The scope for transferring substantially more rural households to the modern sector of dry farming is unpredictable. Regrettably, further land reclamation is unlikely because of the nature of the region's broken terrain and the shallowness of the soil. Arable land within the 300 millimetre rainfall isohyet has become increasingly confined (see figure attached). The problems of expanding land reclamation are clearly evident when cropping takes place in poorer areas around the settlement periphery, as observed in recent years[8]. The physical constraints are a major drawback to any prolonged transformation programme of the rural population into a modern dry farming sector. Consequently, the bulk of rural households who are outside the settlement farmlands remain diffused in the traditional sector, which manages to continue in more ragged enclaves both on and off the settlement domain. In addition, a large segment of rural households have embarked on non-agricultural activities in the urban centres of the coastal district.

Against the region's hinterland, the settlement spacial domain, despite being relatively small-scale, has a disproportionate impact on the region's agrarian structure. Land in the eastern zone was traditionally perceived as a single grazing/cash-crop unit. It was exploited on a nomadic mode whereby seasonal patterns of movement were devised to make maximum use of distant pasture that flourished at particular times of the year. The ecological rationality of the complex network of linkages between often subtly-defined environmental belts, is well documented[9]. A significant area in the coastal district which was customarily considered as the best watered rangeland in the region, was important to the nomadic herds for spring/summer grazing resources and nomadic cash-crops. Since these areas are part of the settlement programme, pastoralists have been deprived of access to seasonal grazing and pastoral engagements have primarily been confined to the interior (i.e. the traditional site for winter grazing). Consequently, pastoralism over the years, has gradually lost its ecological astuteness.

Disequilibrium in managing the region's grazing resources

has had severe environmental repercussions. The early entrenchment of the Bedouin communities in the interior during the colonial period put pressure on the interior range, making it more liable to overgrazing [10]. Apart from short intervals, this disequilibrium has been maintained over the years without fundamental change. Simultaneously, over-stocking continues and consequently the vegetation cover is reduced by persistent over-grazing [11]. The increasing demand for livestock products, particularly mutton and lamb, in the years following oil discovery, encouraged the market-orientated tendencies of livestock-breeding enterprises. For example, between 1960 and 1974 although the number of goats remained fairly stable, the number of sheep more than doubled. This exerted pressure on the rangeland to an alarming extent.

Some interior communities, anxious to secure their livelihood, have shown a certain dynamism in managing range resouces:

> The Fuakher (tribe)...have financed fifty water tanks in the richest part of their territory, and have reduced the mobility of their flocks...by the use of vehicles to transport fodder and water to the herds... [12]

Nonetheless, the management of rangeland is still far from being adequately controlled. Range production in the eastern zone (the forest and rangeland area, above the 50 millimetre isohyet in the eastern zone, estimated at 4.5 million hectares) has been estimated at about 358 million Scandinavian Feed Units per year (SFU is equivalent to 0.7 starch equivalent or one kilogramme of barley grain) [13]. It was also suggested that the actual feed equivalent of the 1974 livestock population in the eastern zone was 471 million SFU's per year and assumed that 25 per cent of the livestock feed requirements would be provided from outside the actual range [14]. That still left total livestock fed consumption on the range closer to the total range production. In this sense, livestock were taking perhaps twice as much as they would have been under proper management, which would have allowed for the regeneration of the pasture. The pressure on rangeland is evident and the tendency towards desertification is ominous. In this regard, more than 3.5 million hectares of soil erosion potential were recorded in the eastern zone [15].

The Forest and Rangeland Project is the body responsible for developing the rangeland resources of the periphery. Environmental conservation and the security of pastoralists' livelihoods are the two main objectives of the project. The surface-area destined to be developed is about 200,000 hectares, which covers most of the wadis in the steppe zone on the southern slope of the Jabal Al Akhdar below the 250 millimetre rainfall isohyet. The project is currently only active in 75,000 hectares where 60 cereal-fodder-irrigated farms and a number of cisterns were completed. Twenty-three wells were drilled and 4,000 kilometres of range fences were extended. (The ambitious programme of the FRP is well illustrated in JAP public-

Table 8 .1: Oil Revenues, allocations and expenditures in Libya in 1973-75 and 1976-80 - Development plans with reference to the agricultural sector on regional and national levels, (in LD millions).

	1973-1975		1976-1980	
	allocations	expenditure	allocations	expenditure
Oil Revenues [1]	5,664.7		20,381.6	
Development Plans	2,585.9	2,204.8 [2]	8,813.1	7,606.4 [3]
Agricultural Sector	595.4	554.8 [2]	1,817.8	1,604.3 [3]
<u>The Eastern Zone</u>				
Farmland Settlement Project [4]	n/a	78.4	189.5	n/a
Rangeland Development Project [4]	n/a	3.9	29.8	n/a

Sources: 1) Census and Statistics Department, Secretariat of Planning, Dec. 1981, <u>External Trade Statistics for the Calendar Year 1980</u>, Tripoli

2) Auditing Department, Secretariat of Planning, 1978, <u>Follow-up Report on Three-Year Development Plan 1973-75</u>, Tripoli, p.17

3) Secretariat of Planning, (undated), <u>The Plan of Economic and Social Transformation, 1981-85</u>, Part 1, Tripoli, p.40

4) The Executive Authority of the Jabal Al Akhdar Project, March 1978, <u>Reconstruction and Development in the Jabal Al Akhdar Region</u>, Binghazi, p.141.

ations)[16]. Paradoxically, the FRP which is engaged in developing a remote, large-scale area, and has high costs, was allocated under 16 per cent of the budget for the farmland settlement project during the 1976-80 development plan, (see Table attached).

In conclusion, the different objectives of the region's agrarian development projects are exemplified by the conflict between the Forest and Rangeland Project. The unbalanced allocation funds for developing these different environments has also reinforced the patterns of polarisation, which were originally a creation of colonial upheaval. The dichotomy between the greener farmland settlement enclaves in the coastal district and the vast pastoral but lower quality hinterland, continues to characterise the eastern zone. Since development in Libya in general is closely related to oil and as the life-span of oil revenues becomes shorter[17], orientation towards a coherent inter-regional policy for integrating farmland and rangeland which will ensure access to the region's resources in a meaningful and equitable way is urgently required.

REFERENCES

1. Benzabih H.A., 1982, 'The Jabal Al Akhdar:- A Half Century of Nomadic Livelihood', in Joffé E.G.H. and McLachlan K.S. (eds.) *Social and Economic Development of Libya*, Menas Press Ltd., Wisbech, p.192.

2. Evans-Pritchard E.E., 1949, *The Sanusi of Cyrenaica*, Clarendon Press, Oxford,, p.229.

3. Allan J.A. and McLachlan K.S., 1976, 'Agricultural Development in Libya after Oil', in *African Affairs, the Quarterly Journal of the Royal African Society*, Vol.75, No.300, London.

4. Parks T.C., 1974, *The Impact of the Petroleum Industry on the Economic Development of Libya*, University of Illinois at Urbana Champaign, Urbana, (unpublished thesis).

5. Allan J.A., 1981, *Libya: The Experience of Oil*, Croom Helm, London, pp.25-35.

6. McLachlan K.S., 1982, 'Strategies for Agricultural Development in Libya', in Allan J.A. (ed.), *Libya since Independence*, Croom Helm, London, pp.9-34.

7. Agricultural Bank, December 1980, *The Twenty-Fourth Report of the Director Board on the Financial Year of 1980*, Tripoli.

8. Terratest, 1978, *Aerial Photography Survey of Cultivable Areas: Jabal Al Akhdar Region*, Scale 1:20,000, Sweden.

9. Evans-Pritchard E.E., *op.cit.*

Johnson D.L., 1973, *Jabal Al Akhdar, Cyrenaica: An Historical Geography of Settlement and Livelihood*, the University of Chicago, Dept. of Geography, Research Paper No.148, Chicago, p.215.

Kikhia M.M., 1968, *Le* Nomadisme *Pastoral en*

Cyrenaique Septentional, *La Pensée Universitaire*, (unpublished thesis), Aix en Provence.

10. Allan J.A., 1981, *op.cit.*, p.44.

11. Le Hoverov H.N., 1965, *Report to the Government of Libya on Improvement of Natural Pastures and Fodder Resources*, FAO. No.1973, Rome, p.43.

12. Albergoni G. and Vignet-Zunz J., 1982, 'Aspects of Modernisation among the Bedouin of Barqah' in Joffé E.G.H. and McLachlan K.S. (eds.) *op.cit.*, p.192.

13. Gintzburger G. and Bayoumi M., June 1977, *Survey of the Present Situation and Production of the Libyan Rangelands*, Natural Resources Unit, Agricultural Research Centre, Tripoli, p.27.

14. *Ibid.*

15. Doxiadis Associate International, (Rec. 1978), *Binghazi Region: Physical Development Plan, Existing Conditions and Alternative Strategies*, Report No.2, Vol.II, Prepared by DAI Consultants on Development and Ekistics, Athens, Fig.2.18.

16. e.g., 1978, *Harvests in all Seasons in Jabal Al Akhdar*.

17. Barker P. and McLachlan K.S., 1982, 'Development of the Libyan Oil Industry', in Allan J.A. (ed.), *op.cit.*, 37-69

Chapter 9

A RATIONALE FOR A 'GREEN RIVER' TO SUPPLY THE JIFARAH PLAIN OF NORTH WEST LIBYA

J.S. Latham

INTRODUCTION

In view of the growing population of the Jifarah Plain and of the authorities' desire to raise the standard of living, the general political orientation has been towards an integrated and sustained development of the region, the accent being placed upon self-sufficiency in food.

Certain constraints, however, tend to make these objectives difficult to attain. The major physical constraint is the water supply for the region, which must be of good quality for human consumption and available in large quantities for agriculture. During the past few years the groundwater reservoir of the Plain has been subjected to over-pumping and as a result of the low rate of recharge, associated with the aridity of the climate, there is a tendency towards depletion of this resource. The consequential sea-water intrusion would cause deterioration of the water quality which could eventually become unfit for both urban and agricultural use.

Additional water resources will therefore be required in the foreseeable future and there is a range of technically feasible solutions available to meet this requirement. The final choice will, however, depend upon the ability of the solution to resolve the problem durably, its compatibility with the social environment and its economic cost on a national basis.

THE WATER BALANCE SITUATION

Under natural conditions, long-term water recharge equalled disposal, the aquifer system was essentially full and there was no long-term change in storage. This condition existed until the early 1950's. As shown in the tabulation of historic water use, (Table 9.1), net water consumption in 1948 was about 19 million cubic metres per year. Discharge of excess water was through marshes, oases, sebkhas, springs and changes in sub-surface outflow to the sea controlled by fluctuating seaward hydraulic gradients. Based on hydrologic conditions prevailing then, sub-surface outflow to the sea was about 85 million cubic metres per year and the hydraulic head in both aquifers was everywhere sufficient to prevent intrusion of sea-water.

During 1953, net water consumption had increased to about 30 million cubic metres. At that time there was still sufficient hydraulic head at the coast to provide enough positive outflow, about 85 million cubic metres, to prevent sea-water intrusion. By 1958, net water consumption had increased to about 90 million cubic metres per year. The main impact of this was a reduction in storage in the Bin Ghashir area where pumping had increased. Any sub-surface outflow reduction was not yet reflected by observed sea-water intrusion. However, by 1973, net water consumption had increased to over 350 million cubic metres per year and in most significant fresh water areas there was a net negative outflow ie. while it is estimated there was still about 30 cubic metres of fresh water outflow, there was a far greater influx of sea-water, mixing with fresh water in storage, and damaging the aquifer system. For 1973, the annual decrease in storage of usable water was estimated to be 300 million cubic metres increasing to 400 by 1978.

From 1953 to 1978, the reduction in usable water stored in the Jifarah Plain groundwater basin has totalled 4.1 billion cubic metres or over 20 per cent of the total usable water stored in the system. Over 40 per cent of this reduction has occurred in the last five years. Usable water in storage is now being reduced by both de-watering of the aquifers and invasion of sea-water, which renders useless fresh water in storage. This is illustrated dramatically in the eastern part of Tripoli where fifteen municipal wells have been abandoned because of intrusion and the quality of water from the remaining wells exceeds 2,000 parts per million salinity.

If future water demands are to be supplied from groundwater, it is estimated that by 1990 much of the usable water in storage in the areas of major pumping will be exhausted; including supplies at Tripoli and Bin Ghashir which will either have been destroyed by sea-water intrusion or de-watered below economic limits. If the annual reduction in usable water in storage could be cut to half its present level by 1990, the total basin would yield usable water for at least 40 years, although progressive de-watering and adverse quality effects would begin much earlier. This would also require re-regulation of pumping patterns and transfer of groundwater. However, sea-water intrusion is now advancing rapidly in the Tripoli area and by 1985 the majority of Tripoli's existing supply wells, including Suani field, can be expected to be out of service because of salt intrusion.

To date, Jifarah Plain is using enormous quantities of water to irrigate its agriculture and to supply the requirements of its urban centres and industries. It has been estimated (see Table 9.2) that in 1978 alone some 563 million cubic metres

Table 9.1 Water use in the Jifarah Plain 1948-78, (m^3 millions per year)

Year	Agricultural water pumpage	Urban water pumpage	Total pumpage	Net water consumption
1948	12	12	24	19
1953	16	23	39	30
1963	80	25	105	90
1973	343	75	418	316
1978	463	95	563	483

Source: Welsh J.L., 1979, Critical Water Problems of the Jifarah Plain and Suggested Immediate Actions, FAO, p.16.

of water were being pumped from the region's aquifers and that this annual amount is still increasing every year. Some 85 per cent of this water is being used for agriculture. The long-term trend predicted for this water consumption is of further substantial increases in yearly water extraction - probably doubling the current extraction rate within the next twenty to thirty years - with urban centres increasing consumption rates at a faster rate than agriculture.

Table 9.2 Future water use in the Jifarah Plain 1978-2000, (m^3millions, per year)

Year	Agricultural water Application	Urban water use	Total water use	Net water consumption
1978	463	95	563	483
1985	580	170	750	640
1990	685	250	935	790
2000	845	330	1175	990

Source: Welsh J.L., June 1979, Critical Water Problems of the Jifarah Plain and Suggested Immediate Actions, FAO, p.16

Under these circumstances, it becomes quite apparent that in the long-run the Jifarah Plain aquifers are going to be depleted of extractable water; that the heavy saline intrusions from the Mediterranean Sea will penetrate deeply into the depleted aquifers; and that as a final result the capability of the aquifers both to store water and, indirectly, to collect and transport underground water from the southern part of the Plain to its agricultural area in the north and north-east will be severely impaired. In the future, not only will water have to be procured from other sources at very high cost but, an expensive system of water-distribution will have to be established throughout to deliver these immense amounts of water to their final points of consumption (i.e cities, villages, factories and widely-scattered farms which are now getting their water from local wells; from their undepleted aquifers) when required and in the quantities needed. The time the aquifers will take to become depleted will depend mostly on how much water will continue to be extracted each year from the aquifers; .on how efficiently it will be extracted and from which locations; the barriers that may have to be built against sea-water intrusion; the rate of deterioration of water quality; and many other factors.

Given this situation, a decision had to be made as to whether Libya wishes to destroy irreversibly its national resource and, if so, whether it wants to soften the impact of this disaster by maximising the benefits it will derive from it. Alternatively it could accept some strong constraints on its exploitation of the Jifarah Plain aquifers and treat this resource as a permanent patrimony for the benefit of the future Libyan generations.

THE ECONOMIC COSTS

Thirty to fifty years from now, Libya will base its standard of living principally on the level of productivity of its people, the efficiency of its industry and agriculture and only to a minor degree on its oil resources. Since the standard of living that the Libyan nation will expect to enjoy will be equivalent to that of any other developed nation, the productivity of the Libyan population, of its industries and agriculture, will also have to be on a par with that of the other developed countries of the world. Any substantial difference, either in the productivity of its people or in the efficiency of its industries and agriculture, will result inevitably in a lowering of the standard of living of the Libyan people. It must be noted that even today the Libyan standard of living is amongst the highest in the world even if we measure it in non-consumeristic terms. Libyans today enjoy better housing, food, medical-services, and working conditions than most Mediterranean nations, all of Eastern Europe, Russia, China, the rest of Asia, Africa and Latin America. Libyans will have to work very hard just to keep the standard of living they already have, not to mention eventual future improvements. In the short run, it may be possible to support a high standard of living even though national labour productivity, industrial and agricultural efficiency are much below the standard of other developed countries. But this condition may only last as long as foreign loans, accumulated savings and national resources, such as oil, coal or minerals, can make up the difference between what the nation is able to produce and what it wishes to consume. The low efficiency, instead of showing its normal consequence of higher costs for national products and, or, services available to the community, is masked by subsidies which either lower production costs artificially by absorbing the cost of its principal components (water, for example) or increase the workers' income artificially by paying them fully for services performed only partially. To some degree, both of these subsidy approaches are being used in Libya today.

Yet it can be argued in defence of subsidies that, in the short run, they may be necessary and justifiable if they are used to allow a nation to draw level with the productivity of the other developed countries of the world, and not as a temporary relief to create an artificial sensation of prosperity for its people. In fact, subsidies are necessary and useful when they are used to make it more bearable for a society to live through its painful transitional period - witness the eighteenth century's transformation of England into an industrial society, and that of most other Western countries shortly after - while a society completes the process of up-grading and re-allocating its labour-force in order to service both its newly-created industries and its modernised agriculture efficiently. In the case of Libya, for example, its agriculture will have to be transformed rapidly from subsistence and pastoral to highly-professional, intensive agriculture, heavily dependent on sophisticated irrigation practices and the ample availability of inexpensive, good-quality water.

Libya is currently experiencing a rather radical process of transformation which involves its productive processes, the individual motivations that stimulate productivity and the very objectives or productivity itself - be those lower production costs or greater national self-sufficiency, or a combination of both. Certainly, these factors are related to the actual cost of water to the end-user. In each case some of the components making up the final cost of water will be different, especially the components concerned with the costs of distribution and delivery; yet, the major component will remain the cost of producing water by pumping it from the local aquifers, by transporting it from outside the region, or by producing it through the desalinisation of sea-water.

The largest amount of water will continue to be used by the agricultural sector (given the goals of self-sufficiency). Furthermore, the agricultural sector is the one most vulnerable to increases in the cost of water. This is because the value of the water used to produce a given value in agricultural commodities is some ten to a hundred times larger than the value of the water needed to produce the same given value in industrial goods or urban services. Therefore, one must remain principally concerned with the cost of producing and delivering water to the agricultural sector. In fact, if sufficient water at an affordable cost can be produced for agriculture, it can be produced also for the other sectors of the economy, unless constraints of a socio-political nature are introduced to distort the relationship between water demand and water cost.

In terms of actual costs, extracting water from the Jifarah Plain aquifer is the least expensive solution for supplying water to consumers in that area. Present groundwater extraction costs are about 15 to 30 Libyan dinars per thousand cubic metres including both capital and operating costs. These are expected to increase as the water-level declines, both locally and throughout most of the Jifarah Plain, as a result of the massive quantities of water that are being extracted yearly from the aquifers (see Tables 9.1 and 9.2). The principal capital costs are the drilling of the well, the pump and the general installation; the principal operational costs will be the maintenance of the whole installation and the power required to operate the pumps. In addition, a combined capital and operational cost should be added to take into account the socio-economical effects of the depletion of the water reservoir of the aquifers. The capital costs will be a function of the depth of the well while the operational costs will be a function of the water-lift required to pump the water out of the well. The greater the water-lift, the larger the size of pump required (thus increasing its capital cost) and the more power will be required to lift the same quantity of water per unit of time (thus increasing the operational costs).

To tap the confined aquifer, wells up to several hundred metres deep are required; fortunately the water comes up the well by partial or total artesian effect and the actual water-lift is usually less than 50 metres. On the other hand, if very large quantities of water are extracted - as in the case in the Jifarah Plain - the artesian effect weakens, rapidly lowering the water - level within the well, and increasing the water extraction costs. After a while the water-level may have subsided to such an extent that it will start behaving as an unconfined aquifer. The rate of decline of the water-level decreases significantly per unit of water extracted, once the aquifer reaches its unconfined state; at that time much more water needs to be extracted to cause the same amount of water-level decline. There is a need for caution to prevent over-exploitation of the confined aquifers since substantial weakening of the artesian effect will cause a very large increase in the unit cost of extracting water due to the higher water-lift required and also the need to combat pollution from sea-water intrusion.

Forecasts of the estimated requirements are summarised in Table 9.3 together with the withdrawals from the Jifarah aquifer and the volume which must be transferred to satisfy the demand during the period ranging from 1985 to 2005. The data from this table show that:
mean annual growth rates of 3 and 7 per cent of the agricultural and urban water requirements respectively, are to be expected. These increases are acceptable within the framework of a sustained development policy. Nevertheless there is often a tendency to extend the areas of newly-developed irrigation

schemes to encourage increased water-use without seriously examining the other facets of agricultural production (inputs, extension work, agrarian reform, marketing etc) which are the economic justification for this water. Consequently, yields increase little in comparison with the large investments made by the authorities.

Extractions from the Jifarah aquifer are expected to increase with respect to the 1978 level (560 million cubic metres) until 1987 when they start to decrease and attain a constant value of 20.6 million cubic metres per year, which corresponds to the equilibrium of the aquifer. This rate of extraction is expected to occur by 2010 when the total demand will have attained the value of 1,409 million cubic metres per year[1].

Protection of the Jifarah aquifer from saline intrusion is of primary importance for the agricultural development of the region, since the presence of salt in irrigation water not only leads to a reduction of yields but can, in arid climates, give rise to an irreversible process of sterilisation of the soils.

Under these conditions of continously growing water costs Jifarah Plain agriculture will have to change radically, unless the Libyan nation is willing to lower its long-term standard of living and pay heavy subsidies in order to make 'cheap' water available for agriculture and also, perhaps allow the continuation of its inefficient agricultural practicies. If 'cheap' water is made available for agriculture, it may be possible to increase the areas under irrigation and Libya's total agricultural production even to the point of achieving total national food self-sufficiency. Yet by this policy, Libya may seriously weaken its current water self-sufficiency and make the nation too dependent on the good performance of very large desalinisation plants or extensive long-distance water transportation systems. Furthermore, 'cheap' water may easily encourage wastefulness and the perpetuation of inefficient agricultural practices.

In fact, a policy which minimises water prices to farmers will encouage extensive use of irrigation, expansion of the areas under irrigation and the growing of crops unconstrained by water costs. The resultant heavy consumption of water will soon exhaust the usable reserves of the Jifarah Plain aquifers and water scarcity, coupled with increased salinity of the little water available, will progressively cause the abandonment of areas formerly allocated to irrigated agriculture.

It may be possible, at this stage, to import water from other regions or to desalinise water from the Mediterranean Sea and build a capillary water-distribution system to deliver the water to the irrigated areas of Jifarah Plain. Yet the cost of subsidising this water in order to make it affordable to the local farmers would be severe enough to negatively influence the standard of living of the Libyan nation as a whole. Furthermore, the benefits of this policy of 'cheap' water would be questionable because even though Libya may, as a result of this policy, achieve agricultural self-sufficiency, it would lose water self-

Table 9.3 Forecasts of water supply and demand

N+ : reference level in Mm^3 (million cubic metres per year)
V++ : volume in Mm^3 in t and t+5

	DEMAND				SUPPLY			
Year	Agriculture	Urban	Total N	Total V++	Aquifer N	Aquifer V	New Sources N	New Sources V
1978	463	97	560		560			
1985	4580	170	750		608		142	
				4213		2823		1390
1990	685	250	935		521		414	
				4975		2372		2603
1995	765	290	1055		428		627	
				5575		1907		3668
2000	845	330	1175		335		840	
				6175		1303		4873
2005	925	370	1295		186		1109	
Total	-	-	-	20938	-	8405	-	12534

Source: Hamdane A., September 1979, Prospects for the Transfer of Water from the Fezzan to the Jifarah Plain, FAO, p.19

sufficiency greatly increasing its vulnerability to sudden disasters and foreign intervention.

Alternatively, if subsidies are re-orientated to encourage principally the increase of agricultural productivity, the Jifarah Plain may be able to substantially increase its total agricultural production while, at the same time, it will be able to effectively control, or, under some circumstances, even reduce its water consumption. Subsidies in this case should be orientated towards absorbing the costs of numerous and easily-accessible demonstration farms; effective agricultural extension services and educational campaigns; even, maybe, the temporary use of skilled farmers from other countries. Better seeds should be introduced as well as new cropping patterns and agricultural practices; farm-gate prices should be manipulated to reward farmers growing crops that fit into the pattern of high yields and low water consumption per unit of resultant production; water prices should also be allowed to increase and reflect actual water costs.

Under these circumstances the goal of national, total food self-sufficiency would have to be modified and re-orientated towards one of 'Emergency National Agricultural Self-Sufficiency', which may be defined as the level of national agriculture 'potential capacity' where minimum requirements for the entire country may be satisfied under emergency measures. Yet this 'potential capacity' is not fully utilised under normal circumstances while cheaper import substitutes are readily available. However, a policy of 'Emergency National Agricultural Self-Sufficiency' would be compatible with a policy of high water prices actually reflecting the unsubsidised cost of water, thus encouraging both a re-alignment of Jifarah Plain agriculture to reflect actual water costs and slowing down or even decreasing the total yearly water consumption by Jifarah Plain agriculture.

In actuality, a policy of allowing water costs to reach their true level will, over a number of years, produce radical changes not only in Libya's cultivation practices but also in the very crops the Libyan farmers will choose to produce. There will probably be a greater concentration of agriculture on intensive vegetable and orchard crops, with greater extended use of green houses and, perhaps, hydroponics cultures. Cultivation of cereals will probably be limited to rain-fed areas equipped with stand-by irrigation systems to be used during national food emergencies only. Large grazing areas will be set aside for the local meat industry complemented by feeding lots where locally-grown alfalfa and imported animal feeds will bring the local animals to optimum slaughtering weights: nevertheless, a substantial portion of the total meat requirement for the country will be satisfied through long-term contract imports; while active policies will further discourage meat consumption and encourage the use of protein-rich legumes. All crops and food products - especially meats - which, in order to be produced locally, would require a high consumption of water, will tend not to be produced in Libya unless the imports cost more or the reliability of the exporting sources make local cultivation mandatory.

Ultimately, a Jifarah Plain agricultural development policy based on the improvement of the agricultural productivity of its farms will soon be faced with the fact that the main constraints on the implementation of its development programmes are neither land resources nor water, but rather human resources.

More land, in fact, can still be reclaimed in Jifarah Plain; funds are available to improve this land with the infrastructure necessary to support settlers in the new areas, such as: roads, power-lines, houses, pipe-lines, wells and irrigation systems. Water is still available in large quantities, if only for a few decades more, but at an increasingly higher cost. The immediate problem lies in the very short supply of professional farmers to run these newly-developed farms efficiently. It requires a professional farmer capable of adopting the agricultural practices that ensure reasonable crop yields and skilled enough in the techniques of irrigation to know what can be expected from them. The objective, if agriculture is to continue, must be to ensure high water-productivity (high production of crops per unit of irrigation water used). Unfortunately, these farmers are in very short supply and their absence represents the principal constraint on the expansion of agricultural production in Jifarah Plain.

WATER SOURCE DIVERSIFICATION

Water resource depletion is a reality in the Jifarah Plain and one which cannot be ignored too long. So far the discussion has centred on the extraction of water from a confined aquifer which is being increasingly over-exploited, causing a substantial weakening of the artesian effect which is already starting to cause increases in the unit cost of extracting water.

Extracting water from other aquifers in Libya such as the Nubian sandstone at Al Kufrah-Tuzerbo or the Post-Eocene sandstone at Sarir or the Palaeozoic sandstone at Jabal Fezzan, will also have a local extraction cost probably camparable to that experienced in Jifarah Plain. The probable higher efficiency of larger pumps which could be used in the other aquifers will, in most cases, be more than compensated for by the higher costs of running these far away pumping installations. Some value must be added also to the cost of this water to compensate the region for the loss of revenues which might have been derived had the water, now extracted for transport to the Jifarah Plain, been used instead for its own agriculture and industry (which might eventually have been developed there, in the future, as a result of the large water supply available). The operational cost of transporting the water extracted from some other aquifer in another part of Libya across several hundred kilometres to some enormous water storage and distribution centre or centres in the Jifarah Plain, will be upwards of 100 Libyan dinars per 1,000 cubic metres of water per year. The capital cost of building the several hundred kilometres of pipe-line necessary to transport over one million cubic metres of water per day - almost an artificial river! - plus the cost of purchasing and installing the numerous pumping stations necessary to 'move' the water along this pipe-line, plus the cost of building the enormous storage and distribution centre or centres to receive the water will be staggering - probably several hundred million Libyan dinars. Once the water has arrived in the Jifarah Plain, it needs to be distributed throughout its tens of thousands of farms, its hundred cities and villages and its hundred factories and military installations. Some of this water may be injected into the aquifers and re-pumped out later in other locations but the vast majority must be pumped throughout the Plain across a capillary distribution system of pipe-lines. Initially, the cost of operating and building this system might equal that of the pipe-line built to transport the water to the coast. Current estimates for costs of long-distance water imports - but not including distribution costs - range between 250 and 300 Libyan dinars per 1,000 cubic metres about the same as the estimates for the cost of desalinised water.

Up to this point only the case of the transfer of water from a single source outside the plain has been examined. In the following section the possibility of having recourse to alternative technologies capable of creating new, local water resources obviating the need to turn to distant sources remote from the Plain, will be examined. Certainly, many choices for increasing the water resources of the Plain are available. Amongst these are:

DESALINATED SEA-WATER

Desalinated sea-water is a nearly inexhaustible source of fresh water. However, its exploitation has two serious limitations:

- the cost per unit volume is high
- it requires a high-level technological infrastructure

At present, there are two sea-water desalination plants in operation within the Jifarah Plain. One plant is located in Zuwarah and its purpose is to supply the municipal network. Its nominal capacity is 3.3 million cubic metres per year. However, since its completion in 1975 it has been plagued by break-downs.

The other plant is located in Janzur. Its purpose is to provide the textile plant with fresh water. Its nominal capacity is 8 million cubic metres per year. The desalination plants have not yet worked at full capacity for lack of demand.

WASTE WATER RECYCLING

Waste water treatment is at present only practised in Tripoli. The capacity is at the moment 30,000 cubic metres a day but the annual amount of treated water is 10 million cubic metres. The capacity of the plant will be double in the near future and further increase in the capacity is under study. The treated water is used in an agricultural project in southern Tripoli. The surplus of treated water is pumped into the sea. A treatment plant is also under study in Zawiah.

UP-GRADING OF THE QUALITY OF BRACKISH WATER IN STORAGE IN THE LOCAL AQUIFERS

This may be achieved through the use of the reverse osmosis process to plants located, when feasible, near the major points of consumption in the Jifarah Plain. Current costs of desalination by reverse osmosis are estimated to be between 80 and 120 Libyan dinars per 1,000 cubic metres depending on the concentration of the salts removed.

TRANSPORTING WATER BY OCEAN TANKER

While useful for emergency situations, this may prove even more costly than getting fresh water from desalinisation plants using sea-water. These costs, in fact, have been estimated at about 500 Libyan dinars per 1,000 cubic metres and do not include the cost of distributing their water throughout the Jifarah Plain. The costs of transporting water by under-sea pipe-line, by tanker, in icebergs or by other, more-exotic, means still need far more investigation before it will be possible even to come up with order-of-magnitude estimates.

It becomes quite evident that Jifarah Plain agriculture, under normal circumstances, will be able to afford only the water extracted from its local aquifers and that even this water will have to be used efficiently - ie. with high water-productivity rates and highly productive and selective agriculture - and sparingly, in order to avoid an excessive rate of decline in the water-level at the extraction points with resultant heavy increases in water costs. Agriculture in fact, will be able to afford water costs of over 30 Libyan dinars per 1,000 cubic metres only in exceptional circumstances of short duration, or under conditions of heavy government subsidies.

The true costs of alternative water sources potentially available to the consumers in the Jifarah Plain are as follows:-

(a) Water from local aquifers will cost between 15 and 30 dinars per 1,000 cubic metres, plus whatever cost will be attributed to the socio-economical effect resulting from the depletion of the water reservoirs of the Jifarah Plain aquifer.

(b) Water from other aquifers will cost almost ten times as much, betwen 250 and 300 dinars per 1,000 cubic metres, plus the cost of distributing this same water throughout the Plain to tens of thousands of local farms and the hundreds of villages, towns and industries.

(c) Water obtained from sea-water desalinisation will cost in the range of 250 to 300 dinars per 1,000 cubic metres, plus the cost of distributing this same water.

(d) Water obtained from brackish local aquifers, and up-graded through the reverse osmosis process, will cost between 80 and 120 dinars per 1,000 cubic metres plus distribution costs for delivering this water from its points of extraction to its points of consumption.

(e) Water imported into Libya by ocean tankers will cost around 500 dinars per 1,000 cubic metres plus the distribution costs.

(f) Cost of transporting water by under-sea pipe-line, by tanker in icebergs or by other, more exotic, means cannot yet be estimated.

From this list it is evident that, given the limitations of current technology, all factors point towards a logical decision to transport water from other aquifers despite the distances and complications involved. The cost of transported water from the Fezzan (approximately 78 dinars per 1,000 cubic metres) will certainly be high compared to the cost of water at present extracted from the Jifarah aquifer which varies from 15 to 30 dinars per 1,000 cubic metres. The lower cost is, however, obtained by exposing the aquifer to a very real risk as regards its future. It would be higher if suitable measures had been taken to ensure a moderate, but perennial, use of the aquifer.

To date, the programme for the transport of water has been initiated. It is planned to run for a ten-year period in a two-stage simultaneous development on both sides of the country. Current expectations for the duration of the water supply are a maximum of four hundred years. The major cause for concern, given the rationale outlined here, is whether this desperately-needed solution will produce the quantity of water required in time, or whether the decision to go ahead has come too late and additional large capital costs will be incurred for reclaiming the abandoned waste lands of the Jifarah Plain in the late 1990's. Indeed, one may wish to argue that the economic costs above should preclude such a consideration; that the era of independent agriculture in the north-west of Libya is at an end; and that the sector should be allowed to degenerate naturally, with financial resources being diverted to more long-term industrial projects which could create the required revenue to meet agricultural import demands in the future.

REFERENCE

1. December 1978, *A systems study for the water resources allocation and management plan of the Jifarah Plain Meta Systems*, FAO, p.266

Chapter 10

SHOULD LIBYAN AGRICULTURE ABSORB FURTHER INVESTMENT ?

J.A.Allan

ABSTRACT

In 1983, Libya embarked on another phase of agricultural development, a phase which followed the ecological disaster of the Jifarah Plain enacted during the 1960's and the early 1970's and then the ambitious and costly experiments in the south in the 1970's. Fossil water from the Sahara, located as much as 900 kilometres from the Mediterranean, is to be raised and pumped to planned agricultural projects in the North. This chapter examines the economic feasibility of such developments and the options foregone by taking this route to the establishment of secure, medium-term water resources for agriculture.

INTRODUCTION

Libya has a food deficit economy despite 5 billion US dollars (a conservative estimate) spent on the agricultural sector since oil revenues became significant in the mid-1960's. The Libyan environment and Libyan institutions have not, in general, been responsive to the investments made in agriculture, except for the remarkable and sadly misguided private sector flourish of the middle 1960's. Throughout, the limiting resource, water, has not proved to be readily substitutable by capital[1]. There have been shifts in the agricultural development strategy, reflecting the changes in the Libyan leadership's awareness of resource constraints. By the late 1960's, government commitment to agricultural spending had declined, as the water resource deficiencies of the Jifarah Plain were recognised by the cabinet of the time. The revolutionary regime had come to the same conclusion about the Jifarah by the mid-1970's and had by then commenced ambitious spending in the south at Al Kufrah and later at As Sarir and in Fezzan.

The newest shift in agricultural strategy is a consequence of the difficulties encountered in utilising the extensive, but remote water resources, of southern Libya economically. Good quality water is required in coastal Libya for urban and industrial uses as well as for agriculture; and this package of requirements could not be met by 1970, never mind by the early 1980's, from coastal groundwater. The huge volume of water required for agriculture (at least 12,000 cubic metres of water per year, per hectare) and the limited economic returns from agricultural enterprises, preclude the adoption of technology which could provide good-quality water for coastal Libya. The other technology is that of desalinisation which provides water too costly for use in agriculture. For Libya there remain the vast southern water resources, in some cases located inconveniently as much as 900 kilometres from the Mediterranean Sea, for which technology does exist to lift and then pump the water north. The purpose of the ensuing analysis is to evaluate the likely returns on capital and water if the southern water resources are used in the agricultural sector, and especially to draw attention to the costs, additional to the capital costs of the pipe-line, which should properly be borne by the agricultural sector for which the water is ostensibly being provided.

LIBYA'S REQUIREMENT OF ITS AGRICULTURAL SECTOR

Libya has a small, but rapidly increasing, population of 3.5 million in 1984, likely to approach 6 million by the end of the century. In 1984 a substantial proportion of the population of the workforce, about 50 per cent, were temporary residents. The proportion of the alien population will decline but the demand for water will rise steadily, although not necessarily in line with the increase in population. The level of water demand will depend on the extent to which water is allocated to the agricultural sector because in very rough terms it requires 20 times as much water to sustain an individual engaged in irrigated agriculture in the semi-arid environment of Libya as that required to sustain an individual residing in an urban area pursuing the activities associated with such residence, including a mix of industrial and service activities.

Despite much rhetoric and significant endeavour, Libya was still, in 1984, dependent on food imports. If Libya was to raise the staple foods for its 3.5 million people from its own land and water resources it would require about 300,000 hectares, 30 square kilometres, of very efficiently and perennially irrigated land. This is only a small area of the land referred to in another chapter as the Tripoli Agglomeration. This area would have to be irrigated mainly by new water as existing coastal groundwater is insufficient for the current level of irrigated farming, never mind new schemes. The amount of new water needed for the perennial irrigation of the sandy and free-draining 300,000 hectares envisaged above would be between three and five billion cubic metres, assuming the deployment of high-technology irrigation systems with which Libya's sandy soils are only economically irrigable. The range between three and five billion cubic metres arises because water can be used more or less efficiently in a variety of cropping regimes.

Making some very crude assumptions about the availability and likely patterns of use, the water required for a self-sufficient agriculture could be provided from resources in Jifaran and other coastal groundwater, plus contributions from the south. Safe yields on the Jifarah Plain were about 60-70 million cubic metres, sufficient to irrigate about 50,000 hectares, less than half its area of 120,000 hectares, according to studies in the early 1980's[2]. This figure of 50,000 hectares is unrealistic, however, as a progressively greater proportion of Jifaran water is destined for urban and industrial use. Thus new water for the additional 250,000 hectares, or 280,000 hectares if one is pessimistic about the outcome of the competition for Jifaran groundwater, would be required to ensure the irrigation of 300,000 hectares for self-sufficiency. Such water could only be supplied in the south or at the coast with water transported from the south.

The question emerges, to what extent can the water requirements for self-sufficient agriculture be supplied from the southern aquifers? Current wisdom has it that, very approximately, the quantities of water which the aquifers of the south-east and south-west could safely yield for upwards of fifty years would be 2 billion cubic metres respectively. Only the eastern pipe-line had been initiated at the time of writing.

Two billion cubic metres of water, if all of it were to be allocated to agricultural development, would effectively irrigate about 160,000 hectares at an ambitious 1.2 metres depth of water per hectare, per year; or 130,000 hectares if a more realistic 1.6 metres depth per year is assumed. The additional one cubic kilometre from the south-west could irrigate 80,000 hectares or 65,000 hectares according to the 1.2 and 1.6 depth assumptions. In short, even if all the water from the south were to be allocated to agriculture there would not be sufficient water to irrigate the 300,000 hectares needed for food self-sufficiency. And of course it is unrealistic to assume that all the water from the south will go to agriculture.

The proportion of southern water which could be allocated to agriculture could initially be high. In other arid regions where irrigation is essential for farming, such as Egypt, Arizona or southern California, the proportion of total utilised water consumed by agriculture is between 80 and 90 per cent. But in Libya, as in Arizona, the provision of high-cost water via expensive pipe-lines and considerable lifts of one hundred metres and more in the case of Arizona, will eventually be for urban use even if at the outset the water goes to farmers. The proportion of water allocated to Libyan agriculture will decline progressively during the coming decades and food self-sufficiency will accordingly become a progressive less realistic goal in the context of Libya's resource endowment and the current and envisaged technology with which to develop its land and water.

LIBYA'S WATER POLICY OPTIONS

The government of Libya can take a number of courses in developing and using its water resources although by 1983 it had opted for one particular policy, namely the pumping of finite fossile resources to the coast. Libya's policy options will be discussed in terms of the opportunities foregone in pursuing the water pipe-line project, and especially with respect to the down-stream expenses associated with the development of irrigation systems utilising the expensive high-technologies which alone make possible the productive use of Libya's sandy soils.

The decision to follow the pipe-line option involves the allocation of three billion US dollars to the construction of the first phase of the eastern pipe-line, on the assumption that half the water initially (1990), one-third eventually (2010), will be used for agriculture and one billion cubic metres initially, 700,000 cubic metres ultimately, will be utilised for irrigated farming. These quantities of water used in the east of the country and in the proposed tracts along the Gulf of Sirt would be sufficient to irrigate 83,000 hectares initially at 1.2 metres depth of irrigation water and 63,000 hectares at 1.6 metres depth.

A disturbing feature of the proposed development of high-technology agriculture in coastal eastern and central Libya is the cost of developing the tracts to which the water will be led. Recent experience in Libya and in Egypt indicates that even in farming systems which are technology rather than labour intensive the cost of developing a hectare would be between 5,000 and 10,000 US dollars, (these figures do not include the full costs of housing provision on Libyan farms). To develop the tracts mentioned above, 83,000 hectares or 63,000 hectares, would cost between 400 million and 600 million US dollars depending on the depth of water assumed to be necessary for effective irrigated farming. A proportionately larger sum would be required if water were to be pumped from the south-west to the Jifarah Plain. Existing irrigation systems on the Jifarah Plain would not be suitable for the expensive water coming from the south. Only the most water-conserving systems would be appropriate and by 1984 only some hundreds of hectares had been converted to such systems in the Jifarah. Very approximately an over-all investment in agronomically effective water-distribution systems at the farm level would require a further 2 to 3 billion dollar sum in due course, if the decision to pump water from the south-west were taken in addition to the decision already taken to pump water in the east. In 1980 when Libya's Gross Domestic Product (GDP) was approximatly 23 billion US dollars, allocating 3 billion dollars for the eastern pipe-line and about half that sum for the one in the west of the country was apparently financially feasible. Even the one billion US dollars initially required for water-distribution systems was conceivably within the scope of a ten-year development plan. But by 1984 with GDP at two-thirds (and at times less) of the 1980 level, the grand and comprehensive agricultural development option was no longer realistic.

So far we have assumed that the development of agriculture based on the new water would require 'down-stream' investment. Similar industrial and urban investments would also be inescapable to house the growing population and to provide value-adding activities in industry with consequences for employment. If half of the water is to go to agriculture then the national benefits of following such an option must be demonstrably more attractive than if the investment in the agricultural element of the programme (upwards of more than 5 billion US dollars seems a likely figure) were to go to urban and related developments.

In order to gain some notion of whether there could be a reasonable return on capital from using the southern water for highly specialised agriculture, we can switch the discussion to the farm level and consider the investment in terms of the costs of inputs and likely outputs. The eastern scheme capital costs alone would amount to over 2.2 billion US dollars (including half the pipe-line costs and say 0.7 billion dollars for the irrigation systems and land development - these are conservative estimates) which would bring the cost per hectare for the 83,000 hectares which could be irrigated to 27,000 US dollars per hectare and this before the cost of the water itself is considered.

If we look at wheat-raising as a possible way of recovering the capital investment, the result is disappointing. With yields of 5 tonnes per hectare, optimistic in the light of recent experience in irrigated Libya, then output would only amount to 1,500 US dollars per hectare. Against this would have to be put the cost of water, other inputs and labour. Even with a second crop in the summer of some other sort it would be an optimistic agricultural economist who would find more than a few hundred US dollars per year, per hectare, of benefit. Should the schemes go the disappointing way of earlier schemes in Libya, then the recovery of the investment would never be accomplished. In addition to the unpleasant economic significance of this conclusion there is the clear implication that wheat, the staple cereal, is not a cropping option and therefore food self-sufficiency is not possible. Only the production of high-value crops, taking advantage of the North African winter and spring temperatures makes any economic sense. Unfortunately the market for such products is already crowded in the short-term, but provided relative affluence gives Libya a development edge, in terms of its ability to capitalise projects, then in due course Libya could take over markets from established north Mediterranean competitors, as well as from others such as Egypt which are also striving to find a place in the winter vegetable and fruit markets of Europe and the Gulf.

So far it has been established firstly that there is not enough water for the irrigation of the area necessary to permit self-sufficiency and secondly that the cultivation of the major staples such as wheat is not economically viable. These are very important conclusions for those attempting to frame a national water policy. It remains to try to evaluate whether the billions which are destined for agriculture could be better deployed elsewhere.

Unfortunately it is even more difficult to estimate with any precision the likely returns on other types of investment in Libya. Investment in industry has been patchy in its success. Some petro-chemicals have been successfully marketed, but in the near-and medium-term, Libya's petro-chemicals and steel are unlikely to command viable prices by the time they come on stream in volume in the late 1980's. Undoubtedly the major success in Libyan economic development has been in the social returns resulting from investment in the nation's material and social infrastructures. There is still some scope for further investment in this area, and it could be argued that investment in the pipe-lines is a continuation of the pattern of investment started in the 1960's which has led to a progressive improvement in the standard of living of Libya's population. It could even be argued that the pipe-lines are essential, and investment in them is inevitable if the familiar way of life of the majority of Libya's people, living as they do in coastal areas, is to be sustained. Part of the investment in the pipe-lines could be considered as an insurance policy with respect to assured water supplies for Libya's coastal cities.

This last seems an eminently appropriate use for the water and one cannot help drawing parallels between the extraordinarily costly engineering of water for the relatively minor irrigated areas of Arizona (only 400,000 hectares in 1980) in the vicinities of the major and rapidly growing cities of Phoenix and Tucson. The shrewd political managers of these cities view the provision of water ostensibly for agriculture as only a first phase in ensuring a supply in the region. They intend ultimately to switch it to urban use for the communities engaged in a wide variety of specialised industrial, commercial, educational, scientific, leisure and other socially and economically viable activities, yielding a higher return than irrigated agriculture. Most importantly, the returns on water will be better in the urban uses than they would in agriculture. It goes without saying that the returns on capital will be more favourable in urban activities than in agriculture. It seems very likely that those managing coastal Libya will also find that there are economically and socially compelling reasons why it should adjust its policies with respect to the destination of its costly southern water. Water originally allocated to agriculture will undoubtedly find its way into uses with better returns on capital and, more important in the light of the high cost and scarcity of the southern water, with better returns on each precious cubic metre of water.

The question posed in the title of this chapter implies that the type and scale of investment in agriculture should be approached with the greatest care. The deserts of Libya have already proved well able to absorb capital investment, but often with no tangible return. The preceding discussion was steered to establish the idea that investment in irrigated farming based on southern water should be concentrated on one or a few, small tracts, totalling about 50,000 hectares in all. These tracts should be developed incrementally and not with ambitious speed. In the development of these tracts high-technology should be deployed for water-distribution so as to maximise Libya's comparative advantages, namely solar energy and relative affluence. Since such high-technology suits only a limited range of crops, and not food staples, food self-sufficiency should be abandoned as a national goal. Where the 50,000 hectares should be located would be the topic for another paper, but the advantages of the Jifarah Plain should not be overlocked. The Jifarah Plain is overwhelmingly the most favoured region for residence in Libya. In addition it has a climate and soils which have been shown to be favourable to the highly-motivated farmer with access to a supply of irrigation water. The case for redeveloping the Jifarah Plain is unanswerable; to experiment further in remote and untried environments would be irresponsible.

REFERENCES

1. Allan J.A., 1982, 'Capital Has Not Substituted for Water in Agriculture', in Allan J.A., *Libya Since Independence*, Croom Helm, London, pp.25-27.

2. Latham J.S., Allan J.A. and McLachlan K.S., 1981, *Monitoring Irrigated Land in the Jifarah Plain*, FAO, for the Secretariat of Agriculture, Tripoli.

PART FOUR: OIL, GAS AND HYDROCARBON RESOURCES

Chapter 11

THE LIBYAN ROLE WITHIN OPEC

Shukri Ghanem

CO-ORDINATION AND CONFLICT

Although oil posted prices in the Middle East were reduced several times during and after the Second World War, producing countries in the area were not directly affected since their income from oil was related to the volume of production and not the price of oil.

During the 1950's, the financial arrangement of the Oil Concession in the Middle East went through important changes whereby the principle of 50 per cent profit sharing was adopted instead of a fixed royalty on each barrel produced. This in fact gave importance to the price of oil and any cut in such prices by oil companies meant lower revenues for the producing countries. Consequently, when in February 1959 posted prices were reduced by about 8 per cent, the first Arab Petroleum Congress was organised in Cairo, April 1959. Besides Arab delegates, the conference was attended also by representatives from Iran and Venezuela. At that Congress, oil producing countries expressed their '...dissatisfaction and apprehension'[1] over posted price reductions. The Congress issued a resolution calling for oil companies not to reduce crude oil prices before consulting the producing countries.

In August 1960, oil companies again cut the crude oil posted price by 5 per cent. The oil companies claimed the need for such action was to meet the market realities which showed an increasing disparity between the posted prices because of the increase in the international oil supplies resulting from the new oil discoveries in Libya and the growth of Middle East crude production as well as the increasing competition from Soviet oil in the European market.

When the August price cut took place, General Qassim of Iraq invited oil-producing countries to discuss, 'the attitude of the host government towards the latest rounds of cuts in the posted price...'[2]. Iran, Kuwait, Saudi Arabia, Venezuela and Qatar accepted the invitation and met in Baghdad, September 10-14, 1960. Qassim's motives were not only the price cuts; he also wanted to curb the influence of his political rival, President Nasser, over oil. Nasser's influence was growing especially after the first Arab Petroleum Congress.

The Baghdad Conference issued a statement expressing the view that '...any fluctuation in the price of petroleum necessarily affects the implementation of the members' programme and results in dislocation detrimental not only to their own economies, but also to those of all consuming nations'[3]. The Conference issued three resolutions, the first laid a general principle that '...member countries can no longer remain indifferent to the attitude heretofore adopted by the oil companies in effecting price modifications'[4]. The countries also agreed to establish 'a permanent organisation called the organisation of petroleum exporting countries'. Egypt, which at that time was not producing enough oil to satisfy its needs, was kept out by the second resolution which limited the membership of the organisation to countries 'represented in this conference' and to 'any country with a substantial net export of crude petroleum'[5].

On September 24, 1960 the treaty establishing the Organisation of Petroleum Exporting Countries was published in Baghdad, Caracas, Kuwait, Riyadh and Tehran. Qatar attended the conference as an observer and became a member in 1961.

When OPEC was established its main aim was to '...raise the posted prices of crude or at any rate hold them to check further erosion of the revenues of member countries...'[6]. At the second meeting of the OPEC Conference, at Caracas in August 1961, a resolution was adopted stating that '...each member shall...compile and send to the board of governors a statement suported by texts of relevant agreements or correspondence, concerning its position in the matter of determination of prices at which its petroleum is paid for by exporting countries, and also concerning the appropriate procedure which regard to the settlement of disputes arising on that matter'. The resolution also stated '...that the board of governors shall refer the above-mentioned documentation to competent legal advisers for consideration and recommendation of steps which were to be taken in each case with the object of restoring prices to levels of which members consider justified and appropriate'[7]. At the same conference the board of governors was given the task of preparing a detailed study...' in order to arrive at a just pricing formula, supported by a study of international pro-ration, should that prove essential'.

Around that time, August 1961, Libya's first crude oil posted price was announced by Esso Standard, Libya: $2.21 per barrel of 39 degree API gravity from FOB Mersa Brega oil terminal. Esso claimed that the announced price reflected the Libyan crude's '...proper relationship to the posting of these crude oils with which it had to complete for market outlets.

In so doing, the character of the crude oil and its geographical location were taken into account[8]. Esso felt, according to its memorandum, that the 'fairest approach' to posting a price for the Libyan crude was to establish one which '...could bear a direct relationship without further quality adjustments' to the prices of the other Middle East crude oils which Zelten crude 'would seek to replace' in the market. The only adjustment the company considered was the freight, yet it chose to use the spot market rate which was law at that time compared to AFRA, the Average Freight Rate Assessment. The company chose four crudes exported from three countries as a base point for the Libyan oil price; these crudes were Saudi Arabian Light crude exported from Ras Tanura for the FOB price of $1.80 per barrel, Saudi crude exported from Sidon, Lebanon, in the Mediterranean for the FOB price of $2.17 per barrel, Iranian crude exported from Kharg Island for the FOB price of $1.73 and Iraqi oil exported from Banias, (Syria), for FOB $2.21 US per barrel.

The company added to the FOB prices of the four crudes the freight cost to Rotterdam and subtracted the freight cost from Rotterdam to Brega, taken to the nearest cent (see table). The Libyan Government protested to Esso[9] arguing that Esso should have calculated the posted price for the Libyan crude in accordance with clause 7, paragraph (2)a of the concession deed which states that the value of crude oil should be 'the average free competitive market price during the previous quarter FOB Libya Seaboard terminal...'. However, since there was no free competitive market for the Libyan crude, and since Esso was transferring the crude to its affiliates, the Commission requested the company to reconsider the price in accordance with paragraph (2)b of the same article which says that 'in the absence of a price FOB Libyan Seabord terminal under sub-paragraph (a) hereof, the average free competitive market price during the previous quarter FOB at the nearest seaboard terminal outside Libya for which such a price is published for petroleum of reasonably similar quality and gravity with such adjustments for quality, gravity and location as normally prevail in the oil industry...' The company refused to reconsider the price.

Consequently, when Libya joined the Organization of Petroleum Exporting Countries, it rightly felt its crude oil was under-priced, and therefore Libya's interests coincided with those of other members of OPEC. Libya was a special case. It was different from other OPEC countries in that it was the newest crude oil exporting state. Though it did not suffer price cuts (for it was not an exporter during the period of price cuts), it met with the consequences of the new low posted prices supposedly based on the prices of the Middle East crudes. At the same time, Libya did not want to discourage oil companies from continuing their activities; on the contrary, it wanted to induce them to carry out further

Table 11.1
Esso formula for the first Libya Crude Oil posted price

	SAUDI ARABIA		IRAN	IRAQ
	Ras Tanura	Sidon	Kharg Island	Banias
	34 API	34 API	34 API	36 API
Posted Price FOB	1.80	2.17	1.73	2.21
Freight to Rotterdam	0.58	0.26	0.69	0.26
CIF Rotterdam	2.38	2.43	2.42	2.47
MINUS:				
Freight Mersa Brega to Rotterdam	0.22	0.22	0.22	0.22
Parity Posting FOB Mersa Brega	2.16	2.21	2.20	2.25

Average Price Mersa Brega $\frac{2.16 + 2.21 + 2.20 + 2.25}{4} = 2.205$

activities and spend more money on exploration to develop its oil potential. Yet it did not want to neglect its rights or to miss the opportunity of gaining something from the collective effort which the Organisation of Petroleum Exporting Countries contemplated. Preservation of the Libyan national interests was not an easy thing to achieve in those circumstances, for the Libyan national interests were focussed on two areas which were hard to reconcile:

1. Not discouraging oil companies from continuing their vigorous exploration and heavy investment in the country. Such a goal could not be attained if a confrontation between oil companies and the government were to break out over any question in general and the question of oil price in particular. It was in the national interest of Libya to appease oil companies in order not to interrupt the flow of foreign capital and of the oil industry in Libya.

2. In the meantime, it was in the national interest to the country to reject the undervalued price of Libyan crude which was unilaterally declared by Esso. But for such a rejection to be effective, it would have meant a direct confrontation which could have escalated into an embargo on oil exports. Such a confrontation would have discouraged the oil companies operating in Libya.

The government chose a compromise and that was to protest at the prices, while receiving revenues calculated on these prices, and meanwhile to join OPEC. In the Organisation of Petroleum Exporting Countries, Libya was neither an active member nor a leading one; it was a follower. This was due to several reasons, one of which was not antagonizing oil companies. Another reason was the country's lack of educated people. At that time the Oil Ministry consisted of no more than ten people, none of whom was a college graduate. When several college graduates joined the Ministry in 1962 they were ignored, for they were politically suspected because of their loyalty to Nasser and because they represented too much of an administrative challenge to their conservative bosses.

OPEC failed during its first decade to control oil production or regulate its growth and consequently failed to restore prices to the levels which prevailed before its creation in 1960, yet the nominal posted prices of crude oil did not deteriorate further. This was considered as a success for OPEC when companies avoided confrontation with it and froze the posted prices at 1960 levels when OPEC was established. This should not be taken for granted since, in spite of the fact that nominal posted prices were left at the same level, their real value of course deteriorated as a result of the international inflation rate and the deterioration in the US dollar's purchasing power.

The end results for Libya, in the issue of posted price, were a freeze of the nominal posted prices at their level, which meant freezing the 1961 undervalued nominal posted price declared by Esso Oil Company and taken as a base price for other companies, and greater deterioration in their real value.

Libya continued receiving its income tax from oil companies according to the price they announced on the basis of Esso's first price of Libya oil, but meanwhile continued protesting against the basis of the price, challenging its legality and refusing to consider their payment as a final settlement of their accounts. Libya was also reserving its right to a retroactive claim for whenever this issue was settled.

Thus, although the Organisation of Petroleum Exporting Countries in fact did nothing positive for the Libyan oil price, one might say that indirectly it helped Libya by preventing oil companies from cutting the price further, but it is hard to prove or disprove such a claim. For what would have happened to crude oil posted prices in general and Libyan oil posted prices in particular had the OPEC not been created is a matter of speculation.

The fact remains that Libyan oil continued to be under-priced for the first decade, and that OPEC took no meaningful action to bring Libya in line with other producing countries in the Middle East.

But in its first decade of life, OPEC did affect Libyan oil policy and Libyan oil revenues outside the realm of pricing, mainly in royalty payments and income tax.

THE INCOME FROM OIL

When OPEC was created in 1960, individual member countries had different financial arrangements in dealings with oil companies. Some countries were levying a 50 per cent income tax on the oil companies' crude oil profits based on the posted prices; other countries were levying the same percentage, but based on the realised prices. Companies in the same country differed, majors mainly paying their income tax on the basis of posted prices, minus some discounts, independent oil companies paying their income tax on the basis of realised prices.

Furthermore, there was the problem of unrestricted discounts or marketing allowances. Oil companies were allowed, by law and practice, to give discounts. Libya was practically levying companies' income tax according to the realised prices, in spite of the fact that an amendment of the Libyan petroleum law took place in August, 1961, introducing for the first time a formula which used the posted prices as a base for calculating royalties [10]. Consequently, Libyan income per barrel fluctuated from company to company. Independent oil companies - the most important one being Oasis (a group of three American oil companies: Amerada, Continental and Marathon) - were giving discounts on the pretext of meeting competition in order to sell Libyan oil. In 1963, according to the Economist, '...unless the company exporting from Libya has, as Esso has, affiliate companies downstream to mop up most of its oil at posted prices, the prices a seller can get for Libyan oil are probably 50 cents per barrel lower than the posted price of $2.21 per barrel there'[11]. The Petrolem Intelligence Weekly reported that sales of Libyan oil to Greece were for $1.80 CIF[12].

Amerada Oil Company, as one of the owners of the Oasis Oil Company, sold Libyan oil for an average price of $1.47 per barrel[13], while for the Marathon Oil Company, another partner in the Oasis Oil Company, the average sale price of Libyan crude was $1.64 per barrel[14]. In 1965, the Petroleum Intelligence Weekly reported that the price of Libyan crude oil on the open market was between $1.60 and $1.65 per barrel[15]. The Economist pointed out that actual discounts were about 30 per cent of the posted prices (ie. 60 cents or more)[16]. Professor Adelman stated that 'Libyan crudes were said to be offered in the $1.30's...'[17].

The major oil companies - Esso, in the case of Libya - were also giving their affiliates discounts on the transferred crude oil. Although it is hard to know the size of such discounts to its affiliates, one may get an idea about them by noting the discounts Esso gave to non-affiliated companies. In 1982, Esso made a deal with the Italian state-owned company of ENI, to sell 50,000 barrels a day of Libyan and Kuwaiti crude oil for the posted price minus 20 per cent as a discount[18]. Realised oil prices in the Arabian Gulf were also sold at heavy discounts. According to Professor Adelman: 'In 1960, Soviet crudes were the most prominent low-priced sellers. In 1964 and 1965, North African, particularly Libyan, crudes were the most notable low-priced sellers[19].

Consequently, Libya's as well as other Middle Eastern countries' per barrel revenues were deteriorating and not identical. They deteriorated according to the average price each year, and was not identical among oil companies. While, according to Hartshorn, Esso Oil Company's average payment to the Libyan government was 90 cents per barrel for the years 1964 and 1965. The average payment per barrel to the government was 90 cents per barrel for the years 1964 and 1965 and the average payment per barrel to the government by Oasis Oil Company was about 50 cents per barrel[20].

Members of OPEC, of course, did not like the fluctuation of income or the deterioration of their revenues. At the second session of the OPEC fourth conference in June 1962, OPEC issued three of the most important resolutions in its history[21]. These three resolutions dealt with the basis of payment of income tax, royalties and marketing allowances.

1. Basis of Payment of Income Tax

Resolution No. IV-32, recommended that member countries enter into negotiations with oil companies '...with the view to insuring that oil produced in member countries shall be paid for on the basis of posted prices not lower than those which applied prior to August 1960'[22]. In case of failure of the negotiations, member countries '...shall consult with each other with a view to taking such steps as they seem appropriate in order to restore crude oil prices to the level which prevailed prior to August 9, 1960...'[23].

2. Royalties

Resolution No. IV-33 recommended that '...each member country affected should approach the company or companies concerned with a view to working out a formula wherein royalty payments shall be fixed at a uniform rate which members consider equitable, and shall not be treated as a credit against income tax liability'[24].

Royalty payments were different from country to country in accordance with its petroleum legislation and in many cases it differed in the same country between different operating companies. In Libya it was 12.5 per cent of the 'value of total field production'[25]. In Algeria it was 12.5 per cent of the oil sold from the field[26]. In Kuwait, as a result of an agreement with the Kuwait Oil Company in 1955, royalty was fixed at the rate of eleven shillings per ton. Iran's agreement with the Consortium referred to the royalty as 'stated payment' and it was fixed at the rate of 12.5 per cent of the value of the crude[27]. In Qatar, Shell signed an agreement in 1952, stipulating that the company would pay 4 shillings and 6 pence for each ton of crude oil exported from Qatar. Saudi Arabia was getting different rates of royalty from each company. For Aramco, it was 4 shillings per ton of produced crude, but for a Japanese oil company working under the name of 'Arabian Oil Company' it was 20 per cent of the value of produced crude. For a third company, Getty Oil, royalty payments was fixed at the rate of 55 cents per barrel produced. The second, most important, point of resolution No. IV-33 was a recommendation that members approach oil companies with a view that royalties 'shall not be treated as a credit against income tax liability'. This resolution meant that royalty should be treated as a cost and not as a part of the government's 50 per cent profit sharing. The justification OPEC gave for such a demand '...was simple: royalty should be expressed as a cost because it is a cost. The oil companies themselves treat it as such in their books and there is no reason why it should be treated otherwise when dealing with the government of host countries[28]. OPEC believed that royalty should be a compensation by oil companies to producing countries for the intrinsic value of a wasting asset [29]. Expensing of royalty, as was proposed by OPEC, would have benefited all member countries, with the exception of Venezuela, where royalty was already treated as cost. It '...would have given Middle East countries 11 to 12 cents per barrel increase in income' [30]. Furthermore, it would have changed - as it finally did - the tax structure of the oil concession, by making governments receive 12.5 per cent of the value of crude as royalty, then another 50 per cent of the profit.

To Libya, royalty was paid according to the petroleum law, as amended in 1961, calculated on the basis of posted price, but such royalty was deductible from the income tax companies had to pay. '...The concession hold shall pay to the commission such sum by way of surtax as will make the total of his payments equal to 50 per cent of the profits aforesaid [31].

3. Marketing Allowances

The third important resolution of OPEC's fourth conference dealt with marketing allowances, or the discounts. Resolution No. IV-34 said '...member countries should take measures to eliminate any contribution to marketing expenses...' [32]. In other words, to abolish marketing allowances given by oil companies from posted prices and consequently levy income taxes on the basis of posted prices. This resolution, too, would benefit all members, but in various degrees. Most countries in the Middle East dealt with major oil companies and considered posted prices as the basis for income tax. Iraq and Qatar based the calculation of profits subject to income tax on 'border values' which is just another term for posted price.

Venezuela was always in a different situation. Its royalties amounted roughly to 20 per cent; and its income tax was progressively based on the profits that arose from realised prices. Venezuela always wanted to maintain this kinkd of relationship with oil companies, and it changed its income tax law 'as a sovereign act of government without consulting the oil companies' [33].

Libya was levying income tax based on the realised price and a sizeable part of its oil was exported by independent oil companies who were giving heavy discounts on their oil sales. This meant that while such allowances were cost of sales in the Middle East countries, (they were about 1 per cent of the posted price) and '...to end them would fractionally increase the government revenues' [34].

It was clear from the beginning that Libya was going to receive the best deal per barrel, and Venezuela was not going to get much. Venezuela did not object, but on the contrary, it encouraged any action which would lead to a higher realised price for Middle Eastern oil. This gave her more demand for her oil, or at least it would not make her lose her customers or cut prices or income tax rates.

Certainly the effect of the three resolutions '...would be to bring the effective price of Middle East crude - which is bought mainly by European consumers - nearer to that of Venezuelan crude moved across the Atlantic[35]. Other Middle Eastern countries also wanted Libya to receive more for its oil, for they were watching Libyan crude oil undermine the crude oil price structure. The Libyans themselves '...despite pressure from their allies in OPEC, ...allowed the independents to continue selling crude oil at $1.60 per barrel as against Jersey's $2.16 late in 1964...'[36]. This was mainly because Libya wanted and needed more money, and the Oasis Oil Company convinced it '...that its tax revenues were rising more steeply than if they sold less at a higher price'[37].

By early 1964, major oil companies made offers to Libya, Saudi Arabia and Iran. Their offer to Iraq was on the condition that it '...would not be implemented until a settlement was reached on all matters outstanding between the government of Iraq and the IPC'[38], and restoring 'normal relations with concessionary companies'[39]. In Libya, the offers by the majors were conditional on being made applicable to the independent oil companies; '...unless everybody was put on the same footing, they would withhold the higher payment[40].

Member countries of OPEC were not able to maintain any kind of unity; those who received offers wanted to accept them, and did not want to wait for a united front. At OPEC's seventh conference held in Djkarta, in November 1964, 'OPEC resolved to leave the issue to the discretion of its individual Middle East member countries[41]. A resolution was adopted stating that oil companies' offers 'met the minimum requirement'[42]for Libya, Iran, Qatar and Saudi Arabia according to statements to this effect by their representative at the OPEC conference. Iraq rejected the offer because it was conditional and Iraq considered it as constituting ...a clear infringement on its sovereignty'[43].

What happened in 1964 was an example proving that OPEC was a group of countries with conflicting interests. For the moment offers came to few members, those members rushed to accept the offers and forgot about their fellow member countries.

'EXPENSING ROYALTY' AGREEMENT

The agreement known as 'Expensing Royalty' of 1964 was based on offers received by Iran, Kuwait, Qatar and Saudi Arabia from oil companies operating there. To Libya this offer was made by major oil companies operating in Libya as well as in the Arabian Gulf area.

The main terms of the agreement were:

1. 'Expensing Royalties', oil companies agreed to treat

royalties as cost at the level of 12.5 per cent of the posted prices at export ports. Meanwhile, governments agreed to moderate the cost of the new formula on oil companies by discounting the posted price used for tax purposes by 8.5 per cent for 1964. In 1965, the discount was reduced to 7.5 per cent for heavy crudes, with the gravity of 27 API degrees or below. For lighter crudes the discount went up by 0.13235 cents for each extra degree API. There were no specific provisions for reductions in the agreement beyond 1966. However, oil companies agreed that discounts should be charged after 1966 in the light of the competitive market situation and other economic factors.

2. Marketing allowances. The agreement also dealt with the question of marketing allowances. Oil companies agreed to reduce marketing allowances to a half-cent per barrel. As a quid-pro-quo, producing countries, except Iraq, accepted a 'quit-claim' provision, according to which they abandoned the OPEC resolution calling for the restoration of crude prices to their levels before August 9, 1960, for the period up to the agreement date.

3. 'The most favoured company clause'. This clause meant that countries in the Arabian Gulf could not give concessions to any new company unless such a company would accept the same arrangement which became applicable to companies which made the offer.

For Libya, the offer was more conditional than for others. The 'most favoured company' clause meant that unless independent oil companies operating in Libya agreed or were compelled to agree on the 'expensing royalty' formula, the majors would withhold the higher payments.

After a prolonged discussion and faced with the Libyan Government's determination to enforce the OPEC formula, independent oil companies reluctantly accepted the formula in January 1966 but the agreement was retroactive from January 1st, 1965.

Libya gained more from the agreement than any other country in OPEC mainly because by using the posted price instead of the realised price, '...made independents pay about 35 cents per barrel...' [44]. Libya also accepted a higher quid-pro-quo. First, the agreement was applied to Libya on January 1st, 1965, one year after it was applied to the Middle East countries. Libya's losses as a result of the late implementation of the agreement were estimated at more than 100 million dollars [45].

Second, Libya also agreed to relinquish its retroactive claims for higher posted prices until the end of 1964.

During the first decade of OPEC's life, Libya was a follower of OPEC, gaining some advantages like the expensing royalties and using the posted price as a base for calculating income tax. But Libya's major problem when it joined OPEC was a posted price which it considered unjust and under-valued compared to the prevailing prices in the Middle Eastern countries. Yet OPEC was not in a position to do much to help Libya in this matter. Libya's interests did not coincide all the time with those of OPEC mainly because Libya was a 'volume oriented producer' rather than a 'price-orientated one'. To Libya, more production was more important than higher prices at that time. It was the Libyan oil policy to attract oil companies to produce more, then the issue of the price dispute could be solved.

While Libya was a follower in OPEC, Saudi Arabia, Venezuela and Iran were sometimes collectively and sometimes individually assuming leadership of it.

LIBYA LEADING OPEC

When the regime of King Idris was overthrown, the country's role in OPEC changed. From the beginning, the revolutionary government was closely concerned with the handling of its political and economic targets. In oil, it started by establishing continuous contacts with Algeria with the purpose of co-ordinating their views regarding oil policies in the two countries. On December 22, 1969, a committee on pricing was established with the aim of making proposals and recommendations about the 'just price' of Libyan crude oil and negotiating with oil companies to adjust the Libyan posted price.

Libya's demand was to 'correct' the Libyan crude oil posted price which was under-valued. Oil companies first rejected Libya's demands and the government answer was to cut down production. In four months, Libyan oil production was cut by about 800,000 barrels a day. Esso was ordered not to export any liquefied natural gas, and to increase the prevailing atmosphere of uncertainty, the Libyan government nationalised the local marketing of petroleum products. Rumours were spread around that a complete nationalisation of the oil industry in Libya was imminent.

Occidental Oil Company was the first to come to an agreement with the Libyan Government. The agreement raised the posted price by 30 US cents per barrel and increased the income tax rate. The greatest achievement of the agreement was to end the myth that oil companies alone could decide the posted price of crudes. The deal brought to Libya, in financial terms, more than it received as a result of its membership of OPEC. It also made Libya emerge as the new leader of the oil producing countries capable of negotiating with the oil companies and persuading them to raise the posted price and the income tax rate.

CARACAS RESOLUTION

OPEC's twenty-first conference held in Caracas on December 9-12, 1970, was the first meeting of the member countries' oil ministers since Libya had concluded its settlement with the oil companies. At this conference, OPEC led by Libya adopted resolution XX-120 [46] setting out as objectives of the member countries:

1. To establish 55 per cent as the minimum rate of taxation on the net income of the oil companies operating in member countries.

2. To eliminate existing disparities in posted or tax reference prices of the crude oils in member countries on the basis of highest posted prices applicable in the member countries, taking into consideration differences in gravity and geographic location and any appropriate escalation in future years.

3. To establish a uniform general increase in the posted price or tax-reference prices in all member countries to reflect the general improvement in the conditions of the international petroleum market.

4. To adopt a new system for the adjustment of the gravity differential of posted or tax-reference prices on the basis of 0.15 cents per barrel for each 0.1 of API degree below 40 degrees and 0.2 cents per barrel for each 0.1 of API degree above 40.

5. To eliminate completely the marketing allowances granted to oil companies as from the 1st of January 1971.

The resolution called for member countries to establish negotiations with oil companies with a view to achieving the objectives of the resolution but because of the '...similarity of geographical location and other conditions in Abu Dhabi, Iran, Iraq, Kuwait, Qatar and Saudi Arabia...' [47], a committee was formed consisting of the representatives of Iran, Iraq and Saudi Arabia to negotiate on behalf of the six countries in the Gulf.

From the wording of the Caracas resolution, the leadership of Libya was clear. In its preamble the resolution stated that the conference '...having heard the statement of the head of the Libyan delegation with regard to the outcome of the negotiation carried out by that member country with its concessionaire companies to correct the unjustifiable basis on which Libyan posted prices had been calculated since their inception...' The operative points of the resolution followed the main terms of the September 1st, 1970 agreement between Libya and the oil companies, that is: to raise the income tax rate, to increase the price, to adopt a new system for the adjustment of the gravity and to eliminate the marketing allowances.

Libya's leadership of OPEC was due to two main factors: (a) The new realities prevailing in Libya and in the oil

industry;
(b) The tactics followed by the new Libyan regime.

(a) The New Realities: By 1970 several changes had taken place in Libya and in the world affecting the oil industry and improving the Libyan Government's bargaining power vis-à-vis the oil companies:

1. By 1970, Libya had become one of the most important oil exporting countries in the world. The size of Libya's production and the quality of its crude oil strengthened its bargaining power.

2. The Libyan negotiating power was also strengthened by the fact that Libya's oil potentialities were proven and consequently the government did not have to worry about inducing foreign investment by avoiding confrontation with oil companies.

3. The fact that Libya's oil prices were under-valued, and the old regime was protesting about them, made the government's legal position against the oil companies stronger.

4. The new government proved itself a tough and determined negotiator by compelling the American and British governments shortly after sezing power, to evacuate the military bases which they were using in Libya. This action served notice to the oil companies that the new government was serious in achieving its declared goals in the oil sector.

5. The continuing closure of the Suez Canal and the cut-off of oil flow through the Tapline Pipe-lines as well as the proximity of Libyan oil to the European market emphasised the importance of Libyan crude oil and further strengthened the Libyan bargaining position.

6. All these reasons, plus the fact that the world oil prices were frozen at their 1960 level, forced the oil companies to accept the principle of revising and increasing upward these prices.

(b) The Tactics of the New Libyan Government: The new government in Libya adopted in its negotiation with the oil companies new tactics based on:

1. The exploitation of the atmosphere of uncertainty and suspense which prevailed in that time where rumours were spread about an imminent nationalisation of the oil companies in Libya. This uncertainty was solidified by the nationalisation of local marketing of oil products in the country and the abrogation of a joint venture between the Chappaqua oil company and the Libyan Petroleum Corporation.

2. The new Libyan Government insisted on conducting separate negotiations with each oil company operating in Libya. It began with the most vulnerable one, Occidental Oil Company.

3. Libya, in its new tactics of negotiation, exerted different types of pressure on the oil companies, including reducing the amount of output of the company in negotiations

through the application of the conservation regulation.

4. It was also included in the government's new tactics to reward the companies accepting the agreement by allowing them to increase their rate of production.

THE END OF LIBYA'S LEADERSHIP OF OPEC

Libya once again wanted to adopt measures similar to those it had followed when negotiating the September 1st, 1970 agreement. Yet this time the companies, mindful of what happened to them before, tried to change the rules of the game.

To begin with, the companies wanted to face this round of negotiations collectively in order to avoid exposing the most vulnerable ones to pressure from exporting countries. US and Western European countries were rushing to support the oil companies. In the US, Attorney General John N. Mitchell gave anti-trust clearance to the US oil companies involved, permitting them to negotiate as a group with the producing countries [48]. Consequently, fifteen companies got together and sent a message to OPEC members. This message was described as '...an ultimatum of their own, outlining terms under which they would negotiate price increase...'[49]. Oil companies in their message proposed that '...an all-embracing negotiation should be commenced between representatives of ourselves, on the one hand, and OPEC as representing all its member countries on the other hand'[50]. Libya refused the oil companies' message while the Gulf countries accepted it.

The result of the Caracas resolution was the 'Tehran Agreement' signed on February 15th, 1971 between oil producing countries from the Gulf area and the oil companies. According to the agreement, the companies agreed to:

1. Increase the posted price by 35 cents per barrel at the Gulf terminals.
2. An increase of 2.5 per cent in the posted price plus 5 cents from June 1st, 1971, then another 2.5 per cent plus 5 cents increase for the years 1973, 1974 and 1975.
3. The treatment of gravity, 2 cents per barrel for each degree over 40 API and 1.5 for those under. It was to be applied on the basis of each one tenth of API degree.
4. The elimination of marketing allowances. The governments of the Gulf countries agreed to:

i) No 'leapfrogging', meaning the member countries agreed not to ask individually for better financial terms.

ii) No production restriction, aimed at better financial terms.

When the 'Tehran Agreement' was announced, it was not welcomed by Libya; on the contrary, it was considered unsatisfactory. The 'Tehran Agreement' stipulated a general increase in the posted prices of 35 cents per barrel; such an increase was not appropriate for Libya. Even before the agreement was signed with the Gulf states, Libya was able to sell the crude oil it was receiving from oil companies - in lieu of royalty payments - for prices higher than the posted prices (which were 2.55 dollars per barrel) by more than 35 cents per barrel[51].

The 'Tehran Agreement' was not only unsatisfactory, but it was also an infringement on Libyan sovereignty. Paragraph 'D' in the 'Tehran Agreement' limited the 'short haul' premium Libya could receive by 21.5 cents per barrel. This was, in fact, a ceiling established on the Libyan demand for short-haul premium. The idea of incorporating this provision came from the oil companies, who knew the tough negotiators they were going to meet in Tripoli, and who wanted to hedge behind the Gulf States. If Libya fought against such a provision and criticised the agreement, a split in the OPEC front would have taken place, thus endangering the future of the organisation - something oil companies, of course, wished to see. If Libya had accepted what was determined for her by 'her allies' in her absence, which was indeed not satisfactory from Libya's point of view (as we will see later), then it meant the negotiations in Tehran were as the oil companies wanted them 'all-embracing negotiations', a proposal Libya had rejected. Moreover, the establishment of a ceiling in Tehran for Libya's 'short-haul premium' would of course limit the support the Gulf states would render to Libya.

It was painful for Libya to see the oil companies united, and also to see her 'allies' in OPEC agreeing on what Libya should get in her absence. Mindful of the need for the existence of OPEC and determined to sustain at least the facade of unity, Libya criticised, protested and blamed behind closed doors those countries which signed the 'Tehran Agreement', but refrained from any harsh comments in public.

Libya was not happy with OPEC, even before this episode. Libya, since the revolution, has been considered an extremist and a hardliner by all the Gulf states, with the exception of Iraq [52]. When OPEC met in an extraordinary conference February 3rd, 1971, it limited its support of Libya to the objectives embodied in the Caracas resolution and '...the same minimum requirements agreed upon by the member countries bordering the Gulf, plus an additional premium reflecting a reasonably-justified, short-haul freight advantage for their crude oil exports...'[53].

OPEC members who were parties to the 'Tehran Agreement', and who were exporting part of their oil from Eastern Mediterranean ports (namely Saudi Arabia and Iran), after settling their problems with the oil companies regarding their Gulf oil exports, were able to afford to give full support to Libya to negotiate separately with the oil companies operating in Libya. This support came in the form of a joint communication issued after a meeting of the oil ministers of the countries exporting crude oil from the Mediterranean - Algeria, Libya, Saudi Arabia and Iraq - which took place in Tripoli, February 23rd, 1971. The next day, the Algerian Government took over 51 per cent of the oil companies in Algeria and nationalised all the petroleum pipe-lines. Because of Libya's close relations with Algeria, that action created further uncertainty as to what Libya's next step was going to be.

TRIPOLI AGREEMENT

On March 20, 1971, an agreement was worked out between Libya and oil companies which, although it was negotiated and signed by each company separately, was in the form of a uniform proposal submitted individually by the oil companies to the Ministry of Oil[54]. According to this proposal, which became known as the 'Tripoli Agreement':

1. Posted prices would be increased to 3.32 dollars per barrel of 40 API gravity.
2. Income tax was established at a rate of 55 per cent instead of 50 per cent.
3. The additional surtax payment, which was agreed upon in the first 'Tripoli Agreement', retro-active payment for the period 1965-1970 was to be replaced by a supplementary payment in respect of each barrel of the company's future exports.
4. The company's payments to the government - royalty, income tax, and surtax were converted from a quarterly basis to a monthly basis.
5. Allowances were totally eliminated.
6. Companies agreed to sell to the Libyan National Oil Corporation, pro-rata, sufficient quantities of crude oil for domestic consumption at a price of average cost plus a fee.
7. The government agreed to declare its satisfaction with the level of posted prices, taxation rates, retro-activity claims, methods of payment, reinvestment and supply to governments of oil and to quit all claims regarding the subjet for five years.

In fact, the 'Tripoli Agreement' was not different from the 'Tehran Agreement' in its basics and by signing it Libya's role as a leader of OPEC began to diminish. The Libyan Producers' Agreement not only enabled the oil companies to resist Libya's strategies and tactics, it also enabled them to make oil producing countries in the Gulf area limit their support for Libya to the terms of the 'Tehran Agreement' which fixed the freight premium Libya should get.

Libya's leadership of OPEC, short as it was, was nonetheless fruitful for Libya and the oil producing countries. Libya should take the credit for enhancing the role and the performance of OPEC as well as for creating a new reality in the company/country relationship. It was Libya which brought about the September 1st, 1970 agreement that led the OPEC countries to adopt the Caracas resolution. The latter became the catalyst for the adoption and implementation of the Tehran and Tripoli Agreements.

In concluding this paper, it can be stated that by the beginning of 1971 Libya's leadership in OPEC faded. Political factors, oil companies' collusion and market realities together played an important role in moving the leadership of OPEC from Libya to the Gulf States in general and Saudi Arabia in particular.

The oil companies' collusion as exemplified in Libya's producers' agreement rendered Libya's tactics and strategies virtually ineffective. At the same time, the market realities showed that while Libya's crude production was going down as a matter of government policy, other producers were increasing their crude oil output. Consequently, Libya was fading as an important producer, while Saudi Arabia was becoming the centre of gravity in the international petroleum market.

In the political realm, the Libyan leadership after 1970, devoted more of its time and energy to political issues relating to the Arab-Israeli conflict, Arab unity, African solidarity and Qaddafi's 'Third Theory', and 'People's Revolution'. Consequently, less time and energy were devoted to oil. At the same time, the Saudi Arabian oil Minister Ahmed Zaki Yamani was able to provide Saudi Arabia with the philosophical articulation and sophistication needed to lead OPEC.

REFERENCES

1. Lenczowski, G., 1960, *Oil and State in the Middle East*, Cornell University Press.
2. The Economist, Sept. 10, 1960, p.1,017
3. *OPEC Official Resolutions and Press Releases*, 1960-1980, OPEC Vienna 1980, pp.1-2
4. *OPEC Official Resolutions and Press Releases*, 1960-1980, OPEC Vienna 1980, pp.1-2
5. *OPEC Official Resolutions and Press Releases*, 1960-1980, OPEC Vienna 1980, pp.1-2
6. *The Economist*, Sept. 17, 1960, p.1,108
7. OPEC Resolution No.II 12 Caracas, January 1961
8. Memorandum from Esso Company to the Petroleum Adviser to the Libyan Government, February 26, 1926
9. The protest was announced on July 12, 1961
   Adelman, M., *The World Petroleum Market*, 1972, p.185
   The Economist, Oct.28, 1961, p.369
10. *Official Gazette*, Article 12, Paragraph C, Royal decree amending certain provisions of the petroleum law No.25 of 1955, July 15, 1961
11. *The Economist*, 'Libya rejoins the Middle East, Oct. 19, 1963, p.277

12. *Petroleum Intelligence Weekly*, Oct.22, 1962
13. *Middle East Economic Survey*, Jan.15, 1965
14. *Platts Oilgram News Service*, Dec. 2, 1964
15. *Petroleum Intelligence Weekly*, Dec.1, 1965
16. *The Economist*, Libya threatens the Independents', Oct.3, 1965, p.540
17. Adelman, M., *The World Petroleum Market*, 1972, p.185
18. *Petroleum Intelligence Weekly*, March 25, 1963
19. *Petroleum Intelligence Weekly*, April 1, 1963
20. Hartshorn, 1967, *Politics and World Oil Economics*, pp.21-22
21. It was mere coincidence that at this same session, Libya was admitted into OPEC as a full member.
22. Resolutions adopted at the conferences of OPEC, *op.cit.*, Resolution No.IV-32, p.46
23. Resolutions adopted at the conferences of OPEC, Resolution No. IV-32
24. Resolutions adopted at the conferences of OPEC, Resolution No. IV-33, p.47
25. *Official Gazette*, Article 12, Paragraph C, Royal decree amending certain provisions of the petroleum law No.25 of 1955, July 15, 1961
26. Sahara Petroleum Code of 1958, Article 63, Algiers, 1958
27. Article 22 of the Consortium Agreement with Iran of 1954
28. 'OPEC and the Principle of Negotiation', a paper presented by OPEC Secretariat to the 4th Arab Petroleum Congress, Cairo, March 16, 1965, p.9
29. See the Preamble of Resolution No.IV-33
30. *The Economist*, 'No Further', March 21, 1964, p.1,139
31. *Official Gazette*, Article 12, Paragraph C, Royal decree amending certain provisions of the petroleum law No.25 of 1955, July 15, 1961
32. Resolutions adopted by OPEC conferences, Resolution No.IV-34, p.48
33. *The Economist*, 'How much can they get?', Nov.16, 1963, p.695
34. *The Economist*, Libya threatens the Independents', Oct.3, 1965, p.540
35. *The Economist*, 'Oil's terms of trade' July 7, 1962, p.60
36. Tugendhat, C., 1968, *Oil the Biggest Business*, p.216
37. Tugendhat, C., 1968, *Oil the Biggest Business*, p.216
38. OPEC and the Principle of Negotiation, p.16
39. *The Economist*, 'Yes, But', Aug.22, 1964, p.740
40. Tugendhat, C., 1968, *Oil the Biggest Business*, p.216

41. *The Economist*, Middle East Payoff, Jan 23, 1965, pp.351-352
42. Resolutions adopted by OPEC conferences, Resolution No. VII-49, p.66
43. *The Economist*, Middle East Payoff, Jan 23, 1965, pp.351-352
44. *The Economist*, 'Milch Cows', Jan.15, 1966, p.232
45. Mosely, L., 1973, *Power Play*, p.328
46. See OPEC Annual Review and Record, 1970, p.21-23
47. Resolution XXI-120, *op.cit.*
48. *Wall Street Journal*, Jan.28, 1971, p.4
Oil and Gas Journal, Jan. 25, 1971, p.84
49. *Business Week*, Jan.23, 1971, p.71
50. *Petroleum Intelligence Weekly*, Jan.25, 1971
51. For an example, *Middle East Economic Survey*, Jan.29, 1971 - when the Shah of Iran in his press conference was describing Libya, though not directly, as an extremist and hardliner.
52. Resolution No. XXII-131. For the text of this Resolution, see OPEC Annual Review and Record, Vienna, 1971, p.32-33, Empahsis is added.
53. *Middle East Economic Survey*, April 2, 1971
Middle East Economic Survey Supplement, April 9, 1971
Petroleum Intelligence Weekly, Special Supplement, April 12, 1971
54. *Petroleum Intelligence Weekly Special Supplement*, May 6, 1974, pp.13-16

Chapter 12

A PRELIMINARY ASSESSMENT OF THE DISTRIBUTION OF NON-HYDROCARBON MINERALS IN LIBYA

Charles G. Gurdon

INTRODUCTION

Hydrocarbon minerals have dominated the Libyan economy for the past twenty years. In 1980, oil and natural gas contributed 65.3 per cent to the real Gross Domestic Product and about 95 per cent to Libya's export revenue [1]. By contrast, non-hydrocarbon minerals only represented 0.6 per cent GDP or 32.3 million Libyan dinars out of a total of 5,274.6 million [2]. Consequently the role of non-hydrocarbon minerals in the Libyan economy should not be exaggerated, but neither should its potential be overlooked. As oil-production, and therefore export revenues, begin to tail off in the 1990's, the country will have to utilise all its natural resources. Given the paucity of agriculture and the problems of developing a competitive industrial base,the role of non-hydrocarbon minerals is likely to increase in importance. It is therefore an apposite time to examine the distribution of non-hydrocarbon minerals in Libya and analyse their exploitation.

The objective of this paper is to assess the distribution of non-hydrocarbon minerals in Libya and their role in regional and national economic development. Having identified the mineral deposits, the paper will then analyse their current and future exploitation, with particular attention being paid to the iron and steel industry. The role of non-hydrocarbon minerals in economic development will then be examined, together with the problems of their exploitation. In conclusion, the paper will attempt to draw these themes together and high-light the considerable potential for non-hydrocarbon minerals in Libya's economic future.

THE DISTRIBUTION OF NON-HYDROCARBON MINERALS

Following the discovery of oil and natural gas, parts of Libya have been extensively geologically mapped and evaluated. From 1954-62 the US Geological Survey, under the auspices

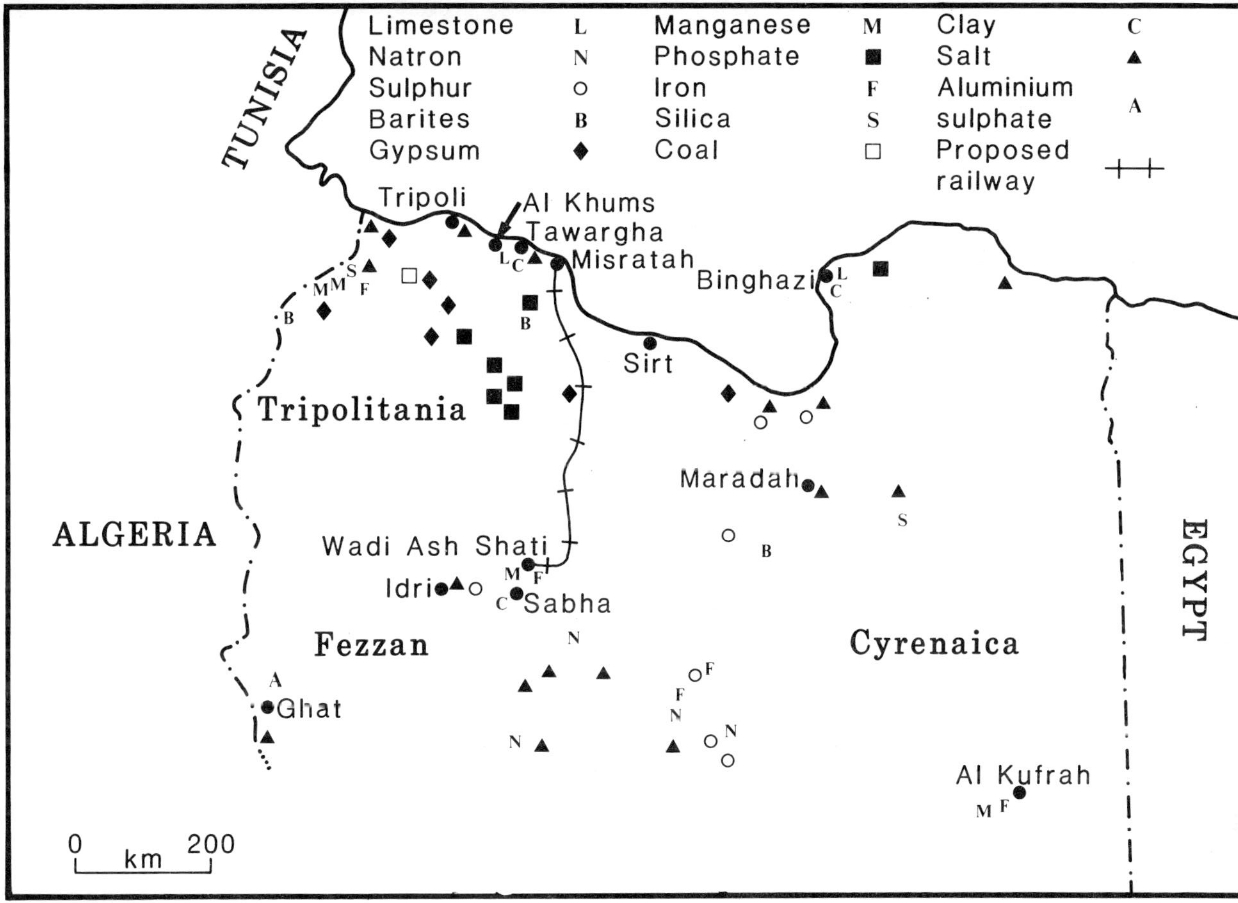

Fig. 12.1 Mineral deposits of Libya

Table 12.1: Non-hydrocarbon mineral resources in Libya

MINERAL	LOCATION	RESERVES & PRODUCTION	COMMENTS
Iron Ore	Wadi Ash Shati	722 million tonnes reserves 365 million tonnes reserves 290 million tonnes reserves	45 - 50% Iron Content 40 - 45% Iron Content 30 - 40% Iron Content 25 - 30% Iron Content
		Total=1,827-3,252 million tonnes reserves	
	Dor al Goussa, Jabal al Haruj al Aswad, Al Kufrah	-	Deposits of little economic value found south-west of Tripoli.
Magnesium	Nalut, Awbari, Wadi Ash Shati, Al Kufrah	-	Found in iron and limestone bearing zones in narrow bands. Economically insignif-icant.
Trona salts	Awbari Sand Sea	Production = 100t/a	Sodium carbonate found in dry lakes. Approx. 30% Sodium, 25% Chlorides, 20% Sulphates, 15% Carbonates & 10% Potassium.

Continuation of Table 12.1 (b)

MINERAL	LOCATION	RESERVES & PRODUCTION	COMMENTS
Sebkha salts	Maradah (Cyrenaica)	Reserves = 1.6mn tons of potassium salts	15sq. kms produce commercial quantities.
	Idri (Sabha)	Reserves = 2mn tonnes of common salt and 160,000 t. of potash	Salts accumulate on surface of about 35sq. kms.
	Mallahat (Tripoli)	30,000 t/a produced from limitless sea-water	Man-made evaporating pans use sea-water to produce salt.
	Ghat, Bu Kammash, Tawargha	-	Minor deposits - economically insignificant.
Gypsum	Bir al Ghanam, Nalut & Yifran in Tripolitania	Reserves = 98mn tonnes Production = 4,000 t/a	Reserves contain 90% gypsum.
Limestone	Al Khums and Al Aziziyah near Tripoli	Production = Approx 73,000 t/a (5)	Large deposits which can be used in the cement industry and at the Misratah complex.

Continuation of Table 12.1 (c)

MINERAL	LOCATION	RESERVES & PRODUCTION	COMMENTS
Clay	Al Khums, Sabha and Al Aziziyah	Approx 130,000 t/a of red bricks (5)	Used in cement and building industries.
Building stone	Qarqarish stone quarry, Tripoli	Reserves = 5mn tonnes	Used in building and cement industries.

Primary Source : Goudarzi G.H., 1970, Geology and Mineral Resources of Libya: A Reconnaissance.

of the Agency for International Development,[3] conducted investigations into promising mineral deposits with the co-operation of the Libyan Government. Detailed sampling and geological studies were only made on deposits of potential value, while general information was obtained about other mineral resources. A topographic map of Libya was published in 1962[4], and this was used as the base for a geological map which was compiled between 1960-62 with the co-operation of fourteen private oil companies. Since the 1969 revolution, the geological mapping programme has been extended and the gaps are gradually being filled in. However the work is incomplete,[5] therefore this assessment can only be considered to be a preliminary one.

IRON ORE

The only major non-hydrocarbon mineral deposit which has been discovered so far in Libya is the iron ore at Wadi Ash Shati. Located in the area to the west of Brak in the Sabha region, it was discovered in 1943. It lies in a depression which runs east-west for a distance of about 180 kilometres and is approximately 15 kilometres wide[6]. Iron ore bearing layers were found in the lower horizons of early Carboniferous sediments below clayey sandstones which range in thickness from 5 to 35 metres. There are three distinct layers of iron ore; the upper and lower ones comprising of siderite, chlorite and limonite and the middle one of magnetite and siderite. The iron content of the ore ranges between 25 and 50 per cent.

An area of 18 square kilometres was fully explored by drilling on a 400 by 200 metre grid, close to the town of Tarut. Due to the presence of sand-dunes futher south, it has not been possible to extend the drilling to the rest of the deposit. As Table 12.1 shows, initial estimates indicated that the iron ore reserves totalled 1,827 million tons[7]. However, in 1973 more optimistic estimates of 3,252 million tons, of which 52 per cent were described as promising, were made[8]. While it is impossible to produce an exact figure for the Wadi Ash Shati reserves, there is no question that they represent a major natural resource; not only for Libya but for the Middle East as a whole.

There are other deposits of iron ore in a number of locations. These include Dor Al Goussa and Jabal Al Haruj Al Aswad to the south-west of Tripoli and at Al Kufrah. They are, however, of little economic significance and the exploration and development of the iron industry is being concentrated on Wadi Ash Shati.

SALT

The mineral which is most wide-spread in the country is salt. Although its production is relatively small-scale, the 30,000 tons per annum currently represent the largest non-hydrocarbon extraction industry[9]. There are two types of salt deposit which are known as trona and sebkha. The less important of the two is trona or sodium carbonate which is formed as a crust on the bottom of several lakes in the Awbari sand sea. It is currently exploited at a rate of about 100 tons per annum during the dry season when the lakes completely dry up[10]. There are other trona deposits of little economic significance in other regions of the country. This type of deposit comprises of carbonates, sulphates and chlorides of sodium and potassium in varying ratios.

The sebkha deposits consist of a mixture of sand and clay which contain variable amounts of sodium, potassium and magnesium chlorides. The most important saline deposit is at Maradah which is about 125 kilometres south of Al Aqaylah on the Gulf of Sirt. Although the area covers 260 square kilometres, only about a tenth contains commercial quantities of salt. It has been estimated that the reserves of 1.6 million tons contain 40 per cent potash and a further 7.5 million tonnes of magnesium chloride[11].

Another important salt deposit is at Idri in the Sabha region in a closed depression about 135 kilometres west of Brak and Wadi Ash Shati. Formed as a crust which accumulates on the surface, it is estimated that Idri contains 2 million tons of common salt and 160,000 tons of potash[12]. There are also minor inland deposits at Ghat in the Fezzan and Bu Kammash in Tripolitania which are used for local consumption.

Traditional salt pans are worked throughout the coastal region; the brines being allowed to evaporate and the crystallised salts harvested. The largest and most important salt works are around Binghazi and at Mallahat to the east of Tripoli. The latter is in a depression below sea-level which is fed directly from the sea by a canal. It covers an area of 12 hectares and produces about 30,000 tons per annum[13].

GYPSUM

The only other mineral which is found on any large scale is gypsum. It is located in Tripolitania at Bir Al Ghanam, Yifran, Nalut and at Mizdah. Only the first deposit has been investigated in detail. This area comprises of a large deposit of gypsum and anhydrite of Jurassic age, which is inter-bedded with dolomite limestone. The reserves, which are estimated at about 98 million tons, are exposed in 400 metre layers along about 60 kilometres of steep hills. The output from the various gypsum workings in the country is approximately 4,000 tons per annum but is likely to be increased as demand from the building industry grows[14].

MANGANESE

There are deposits of manganese in a number of areas although none are under exploitation. They include those at Nalut, Awbari, Wadi Ash Shati and Al Kufrah. It is found in limestone or iron ore bearing zones in narrow veins and bands which range in depth from 5 centimetres to a metre. The association of the manganiferous veinlets and the Wadi Ash Shati iron deposits might permit their exploration along with the iron deposits.

NATURAL SULPHUR

Although there are substantial reserves of sulphur by-product, which is produced from the refining of crude oil and gas, there are also deposits of natural sulphur. They are primarily found in the Sirt and Sabha regions and they have a sulphur content of about 10 per cent. They do not appear to be economically significant however, when compared with the 47,000 tons per annum which is produced by the Al Brayqah gas liquefaction plant[15].

BUILDING MATERIALS

Except for very minor deposits of coal, barites and phosphatic limestone the only other non-hydrocarbon minerals found in Libya are building materials. The deposits which are worked are mainly those close to the urban markets of Tripoli and Binghazi. The main deposit of limestone and clay is located close to Al Khums where a limestone deposit, underlain by a clay bed, is exposed for a distance of 2 kilometres. The Tripoli building industry is also supplied with stone from the nearby Qarqarish quarry. The largest exposure of bentonite clay is in south Sabha where it covers an area of 2 square kilometres. While the reserves have not been accurately assessed, it is believed that these clays are suitable for ceramics. Although it has not yet been exploited, marble is also found in certain areas of the country. Silica sand, which could be used as a good source of raw-material for the glass industry, is found in sandstone hills of Jurassic age in Tripolitania.

SUMMARY

The distribution of non-hydrocarbon minerals in Libya is largely confined to the iron ore deposits at Wadi Ash Shati and various non-metallic deposits which are of little economic significance. The country could be largely self-sufficient in raw-materials for the building industry if coastal deposits of gypsum, limestone, clay and marble were developed. Besides the iron ore deposits, the most important minerals are those such as sulphur and ammonia which are by-products of the oil refining process. It is important to remember, however, that the search is far from complete. The geological exploration work is a continuing programme and it is possible that deposits of important minerals could still be found. Although it is very unlikely that any major deposits will be located, small quantities of strategic minerals could prove to be a very valuable asset for the country. It is for this reason that the search for minerals such as uranium is being continued. Given the location of important deposits in neighbouring countries such as Niger and Chad,it is possible that similar deposits could be found on the Libyan side of the border[16]. The search should therefore be continued in the future, particularly as oil revenues begin to decline.

THE DEVELOPMENT OF NON-HYDROCARBON MINERAL RESOURCES

The iron and steel industry

By far the most ambitious project which involves non-hydrocarbon minerals is the Misratah iron and steel complex. As oil exports and revenues begin to decline in the 1990's the Libyan government hopes to have created an industrial sector which is not entirely dependent on hydrocarbons. Therefore the 1981-85 development plan placed considerable emphasis on heavy industry and on the iron and steel industry in particular.

The original plan was to use the Wadi Ash Shati reserves to produce over 5 million tons of steel per annum. However, because of the small domestic demand and intense world competition, the plans were scaled down to 1.2 million tons per annum. This remains, however, the single most important project in the industry sector and, at over 2 million US dollars for the plant alone, by far the most expensive. When the 922 kilometre railway from Wadi Ash Shati to Misratah, the harbour and the industrial town are included, it is a very substantial investment. It is also convincing evidence of the government's commitment to the non-hydrocarbon industrial sector.

There are five elements in the Misratah complex; two steel mills, a hot and cold rolling mill, and a direct reduction iron works. The two steel plants alone will cost 1,267.5 million US dollars and have capacities of 670,000 and 650,000 tons per annum [17]. All the plants are being built by West German consortiums which have risked major investments in the complex. Four of the plants are, however, led by Voerst Alpine because the Austrian Government provided export credits which helped make the consortiums' bids more attractive to the Libyan clients.

In the first phase of the plan, iron ore will be imported through the Misratah harbour which is being built by a Turkish firm. Later when the railway, which was designed by Projekt Inzenjering of Yugoslavia, is completed, iron ore from Wadi Ash Shati will supply the Misratah complex. The first phase envisages an annual production of about 1.2 million tons of steel by 1986[18]. The expansion during the second phase will be largely dependent on market conditions and the relative cost of the Lybian product.

Despite the fall in Libya's oil revenue, following the OPEC price cuts of the past few years, the Misratah project does not appear to be too affected by the cut-backs. While the main complex's construction continues, however, the proposed railway from Wadi Ash Shati has been postponed because of the country's financial problems. While it has not been cancelled, it does mean that the complex will have to rely on imported iron ore for a longer period than was originally anticipated.

The market for iron ore is currently very weak and Libya is now able to by the raw-materials for its nascent iron and steel industry at very low world market prices. Furthermore, although demand should reach 7 million tons per annum by 2000 AD, until Misratah is finished demand will remain very low[19]. At present it is therefore uneconomic to develop the deposits at Wadi Ash Shati, or elsewhere. The very weak steel and finished product world market prices also undermine the rationale for developing the Misratah complex. As steel capacity is being cut throughout the western world and the new industrial countries of the Far East develop highly competitive metallurgic industries, the viability of a Libyan steel industry must be questioned. Is it economically sensible to develop an indigenous steel industry which may not be competitive and which has enormous obstacles to surmount?

The iron ore deposits at Wadi Ash Shati are 922 kilometres from the Misratah complex and a railway will have to be purpose-built to transport the ore. The cost of the railway will be very high because of the difficult terrain and inhospitable climate through which it has to pass. Rather than building an expensive and comprehensive double-track system, a single track with passing loops is now envisaged. Besides the iron ore, other goods which would be carried include construction materials fuel and postal packages[20]. Under current market conditions, it is probably uneconomic to develop the railway when iron ore can be imported cheaply from Australia, Brazil and other countries. As the recession in the western world ends it may well become far more logical. Since this is likely to coincide with increasing demand for, and therefore revenues from, oil Libya should be in a better position to afford to develop the railway and the deposit in a few years' time.

Besides the distance and the cost involved in developing the steel industry, there are other factors which should be considered. The ore is of a comparable quality to that in the rest of North Africa and the world's principal exporting countries.

It would therefore not be a problem to use indigenous ore once the economics of its recovery made the use of imports unnecessary. The Wadi Ash Shati deposit can also be exploited by strip-mining which is the cheapest method of extraction. The US geological survey indicated that the iron ore reserves extend outside the test zone so that the reserves could be far larger than originally estimated. Besides the iron ore, limestone and groundwater, which are necessary in the steel making process, are both available in the coastal region near Misratah [21]. Being a major oil and natural gas producer, Libya has no shortage of cheap fuel for the metallurgic industries. Therefore, while there may be temporary problems with the development and exploitation of the Wadi Ash Shati iron ore deposits, in the long-run it appears to be generally both a practical and economically viable plan. Not only will it reduce Libya's dependence on imported iron and steel products, but also it could act as a catalyst for further non-oil development; both at Wadi Ash Shati and Misratah and ultimately throughout the country.

BUILDING MATERIALS

Besides the Wadi Ash Shati iron ore deposit the only non-hydrocarbon mineral deposits which are worth exploiting on a large scale are various building materials. These include gypsum, limestone, clay and marble. The construction industry, which includes the production of cement, is one of the most important non-oil sectors of the Libyan economy. The scale of the government's commitment to housing, health and education, as well as other economic sectors, has led to a substantial increase in the demand for cement and other building materials. As the table below shows, the 1981-85 development plan called for a substantial increase in the production of industrial supplies including building materials. The indigenous sources of raw-materials will help to meet these targets, although the importation of some products will continue as demand increases.

Development planners have given serious consideration to non-ferrous minerals in Libya. Steps are being taken to encourage the use of indigenous building and facing materials. In this way, it is hoped to preserve the character of Libyan towns and villages which are being spoilt by the over-use of cheap, mass produced, imported materials. The long-term regional plans intend to increase the production of non-hydrocarbon minerals. The Ras Lanuf petro-chemical complex will eventually also produce 8,000 tons per annum of gypsum, 19,835 tons of potassium, 30,000 tons of magnesium and 37,905 tons of sodium chloride [22]. In order to ensure that each plant is commercially viable, however, it was recommended that a thorough study should be undertaken before decisions were made on the construction or capacity of each plant.

Table 12.2: Production of selected industrial commodities 1981-85 [23]

Building Material	Unit of Prod.	1980	1985	Index 1980=100	Annual Compound Growth Rates
Cement	000's tons	1,9000	4,6000	242.1	19.3 %
Lime	tons	73,000	270,000	370.0	29.9 %
Red Bricks	tons	113,000	300,000	265.5	21.5 %
Gypsum	tons	3,000	5,000	166.7	10.8 %

Source: Secretariat of planning, Summary of the Socio-Economic Transformation Plan 1981-85, S.P.L.A.J., p.23, Table 6.

THE ROLE OF NON-HYDROCARBON MINERALS IN REGIONAL ECONOMIC DEVELOPMENT

It has been seen that there are very ambitious plans for the exploitation of non-hydrocarbon minerals. They currently play a small role in the Libyan economy, contributing only 0.6 per cent of the Gross Domestic Product in 1980 [24]. Their potential should not, however, be overlooked. Although the capital cost of developing the mineral deposits is very high, they serve two essential functions. Besides acting as a catalyst for regional economic development, the minerals can also supply the nascent industrial sector. Given the decline in oil revenues in the 1990's it is essential that they are developed both effectively and successfully.

The 1981-85 development plan placed great emphasis on industry and it was allocated 23.1 per cent of the total budget. By attempting to achieve an annual growth rate of 22.4 per cent throughout the plan period, it is hoped to raise industry's share of the G.D.P. from 2.5 per cent in 1980 to 6.3 per cent in 1985 [25]. The Misratah iron and steel complex is the most important project in the industrial sector and the use of indigenous sources of iron ore is a crucial element in its development. For this reason the development plan for the Sabha region, where the iron ore reserves are located, is crucial to the long-term national goals. In the non-hydrocarbon mining and quarrying sector of the five-year plan, the national policy is divided into three elements. They are:-

'to intensify exploration for exploitable minerals by means of a wider spread of geological survey'

'to increase the contribution of the nation's natural resources in the raw-material demand of the industrial programme

'to achieve self-sufficiency and wide geographical availability in building materials'[26]

The Sabha region preliminary regional plan 1981-2000, which was drawn up in 1982, recognised the need for a long-term strategy for the extraction of the iron ore at Wadi Ash Shati. It was seen as a national issue which depended on cost and benefit analysis of its contribution to the development of the Misratah-based steel industry. Besides the extraction of approximately 100 million tons of ore in the period from 1985-2000, which represent 6 per cent of the usable reserves, the regional plan saw other implications of the project[27]. These include the construction of the Misratah-Tarut railway, together with a branch line from Ashkidah to Sabha, a new town for 5,000 people in the Tarut Al Qardah area and greater consumption of groundwater and electricity. It also calculated that the multiplier effect of the 500 jobs created in mining could result in a total increase of up to 3,000 jobs.

Some of the costs and problems of exploiting the Wadi Ash Shati reserves were also recognised in the preliminary regional plan. In its most pessimistic and low-growth strategy it concluded that the iron ore and railway projects should be shelved until their economic viability was assured. Given that the costs and value of Misratah-produced steel manufactured from Libyan ore compared with imported ore had not been adequately analysed, it was felt that the economic realism of the project in the post-oil period was doubtful. This dissenting strategy also called for feasibility studies and stringent cost benefit analysis to be applied before any mineral extraction projects were implemented[28].

When considering all aspects of a major project, the impact on the rest of the region has to be considered. It appears that the Wadi Ash Shati project could createserious problems unless considerable care was taken to prevent them. Because of the lack of a skilled pool of labour in the mining area, the demand for labour could become over-stretched. Wage levels would probably rise as the mine competed with other sectors of the local economy for workers. This and the demand for local goods and services would cause inflation in the area. In addition, the mine's demand for water and electricity could have an adverse effect on other sectors, most notably agriculture. Since there is no slack in the labour market the mine could not therefore act as a growth pole. Its expansion is likely to be at the expense of the local economy unless the mine is serviced from outside the region which will probably happen anyway.

The extraction of iron ore from the Wadi Ash Shati mine could bring many benefits to the national economy. It will supply the vital Misratah complex with raw-materials which will, in turn, act as one of the lynch-pins of the country's national industrial programme. Provided that it is economically viable to use indigenous, rather than imported, iron ore then the project seems to be rational and advantageous for the national economy as a whole. It is, however, likely to bring few benefits to the regional economy, for the reasons outlined above. Its effect will probably be like that of so many other mining projects in developing countries. It will be a purely extractive industry which will compete with, rather than assist, other sectors of the regional economy. Given its scale and national economic significance, the other sectors are likely to decline in importance as they are unable to compete for labour and other inputs. The area is therefore likely to become almost a single-commodity economy. It is ironic that, in trying to reduce the overwhelming role of oil and gas in the country, the extraction of iron ore from Wadi Ash Shati is likely to lead to the same conditions which are found in the oil-bearing regions of the rest of Libya.

The importance of the production of building materials was emphasised by the Sabha region preliminary regional plan [29]. The high cost of transporting cement and other products has acted as a constraining factor on the regional economy for many years. The ambitious goals of the five-year plan cannot be achieved if the building programme cannot be fulfilled through the lack, or high cost, of building materials. For these reasons, the preliminary plan considered that the exploitation of such products was more important that the extraction of any other minerals, including iron. Certainly on a regional, if not national, level the benefits would be greater than those of the Wadi Ash Shati project and quarrying. Although it would not provide a base for a metallurgic industry, the mining itself would act as a stimulus for employment and the development of ancillary services which could benefit the region. For these reasons, the construction of a cement works at Sabha and Al Jufrah and a brick and tile works in the region were seen as priority projects [30].

Besides the production of cement and bricks, through the use of indigenous raw-materials, the exploitation of the small-scale salt deposits was also recommended. By developing the trona deposits in the Awbari sand, sea, and the Idri and Traghan sebkhas, incomes could be supplemented and the local economy stimulated.

By examining a single region, albeit the most important mineral - producing area, it is possible to see the role which non-hydrocarbon minerals can play in the economy. As outlined in the preliminary regional plan, there are major problems which have to be overcome if any large-scale development is to be undertaken. Unless certain safeguards are implemented it is likely that the project will be developed to the detriment of the local economy albeit to the benefit of the national economy as a whole. The region will, however, benefit from the production of building materials and particularly of cement. When the exploitation of non-hydrycarbon minerals is evaluated all these factors should be taken into consideration. The national and regional costs and benefits are not necessarily the same and it is essential that this is recognised.

CONCLUSIONS

It has been seen that Libya is endowed with a number of important non-hydrocarbon minerals, of which the most important are the iron ore deposits at Wadi Ash Shati. The government plans a very ambitious programme for their development and exploitation. The current economic problems which the country is encountering have, however, delayed the use of indigenous iron ore for the Misratah iron and steel complex. Given the significance of these reserves for the national economy, there is little doubt that they will be developed when the economic climate is more favourable. It appears that the government believes that the advantages for the national economy outweigh any and all of the local problems which the development is likely to cause. In the meantime, the exploitation of building material products is to be expanded and the search for other non-hydrocarbon minerals accelerated.

REFERENCES

1. Secretariat of Planning, 1981, *Summary of the Socio-Economic Transformation Plan 1981-85 A.D.*, Tripoli, pp.7 & 9.
2. *Ibid.*, pp.7 & 9
3. Goudarzi G.H., 1970 , *Geology and Mineral Resources of Libya - A Reconnaissance*, United States Government Printing Office, Geological Survey Professional Paper 660, Washington, p.4.
4. *Ibid.*, Plate No.1.
5. Secretariat of Planning, *op.cit.*, Table No.6, p.23
6. Goudarzi G.H., *op.cit.*, p.54
7. Secretariat of Utilities, 1982, *Sabha Region - Existing Conditions October 1981*, Finnmpa OY, Helsinki, p.60
8. *Ibid.*, p.60
9. Goudarzi G.H., *op.cit.*, p.90
10. Goudarzi G.H., *op.cit.*, p.93
11. Habashi F. and Bassyouni F.A. 1982. *Mineral Resources of the Arab Countries*, Chemecon Publishing Limited.
12. Secretariat of Utilities, *op.cit.*, p.62.
13. Goudarzi G.H., *op.cit.*, p.90

14. Habashi F. & Bassyouni F.A., *op.cit.*, p.13
15. Habashi F. & Bassyouni F.A., *Op.cit.*, p.32
16. The significance which Libya has given to the settlement of border disputes with its neighbours is partially a result of the location of mineral reserves in the border areas. It is already known that the disputed Aozou Strip in northern Chad and the Libya-Niger border area are both mineral rich.
17. 1982, Middle East Economic Digest, *West Germany and the Middle East*, February, p.78
18. Middle East Economic Digest, *op.cit.*, p.78
19. Secretariat of Utilities, May 1982, *Sabha Region - Preliminary Regional Plan 1981-2000*, Finnmap OY, Helsinki, Vol.4, p.105
20. *Ibid.*, p.77
21. Goudarzi G.H., *op.cit.*, pp.68 and 69
22. Secretariat of Municipalities, 1980, *El Khalij Regional Development Plan 1980-2000*, Draft Report, Tripoli, SPLAJ, pp.11-20
23. Secretarial of Planning, *op.cit.*, p.23, Table 6
24. Secretarial of Planning, *op.cit.*, p.9, Table 4
25. Secretarial of Utilities, *op.cit.*, p.45
26. *ibid.*, p.61
27. *ibid.*, p.105
28. *Ibid.*, p.106
29. *Ibid.*, p.61
30. *Ibid.*, p.105

PART FIVE: DEVELOPMENT OF AIR TRANSPORT

Chapter 13

AIR TRANSPORT IN LIBYA 1951 TO THE PRESENT DAY

Amin Marghani

Probably the first visual contact with the aeroplane for most of the Libyan public was when the Italians came to end the resistance of the Libyan people, using military aircraft in their operations. However, they were also among the first people in the world to see the first commercial jet ever to be put into operation carrying passengers, mail and cargo. This was the Comet A-1 which landed at Tripoli airport, on an inaugural flight from Paris to pick up fuel on its way to West Africa. It took four decades after the first experience and two decades after the second for Libya to become directly involved in owning and operating aircraft in its own airforce and national airline.

Upon independence, Libya was among the poorest countries in the world. Its population was just over one million, living mostly on the Mediterranean coast in two areas: in and around Tripoli and in and around Binghazi. Foreign aid and rent from military bases had made the existence of a government possible but it could not contribute much to the development of the country.

Poor in resources and sparsely populated - .65 persons per square kilometre - Libya had no prospects for development. Only its location and strategic importance led to the maintenance of suitable airports that could handle military operations, civil aircraft in transit or landing to pick up fuel, British or American military personnel, and, to a much smaller extent, the residue of the Italian community still in the country.

The activity of oil exploration started in 1954, thus some traffic started to develop on the existing air services with Libya as its destination. By the beginning of the 1960's there was enough traffic to tempt most European carriers to send their aircraft to Tripoli and to a lesser extent, Binghazi to pick up passengers originating from, and terminating their journey in Libya.

BOAC, BEA, Lufthansa, Alitalia, Sabena, Misrair, UTA and TWA all began to serve the Libyan airports of Tripoli and Binghazi. Their passengers were those participating in the

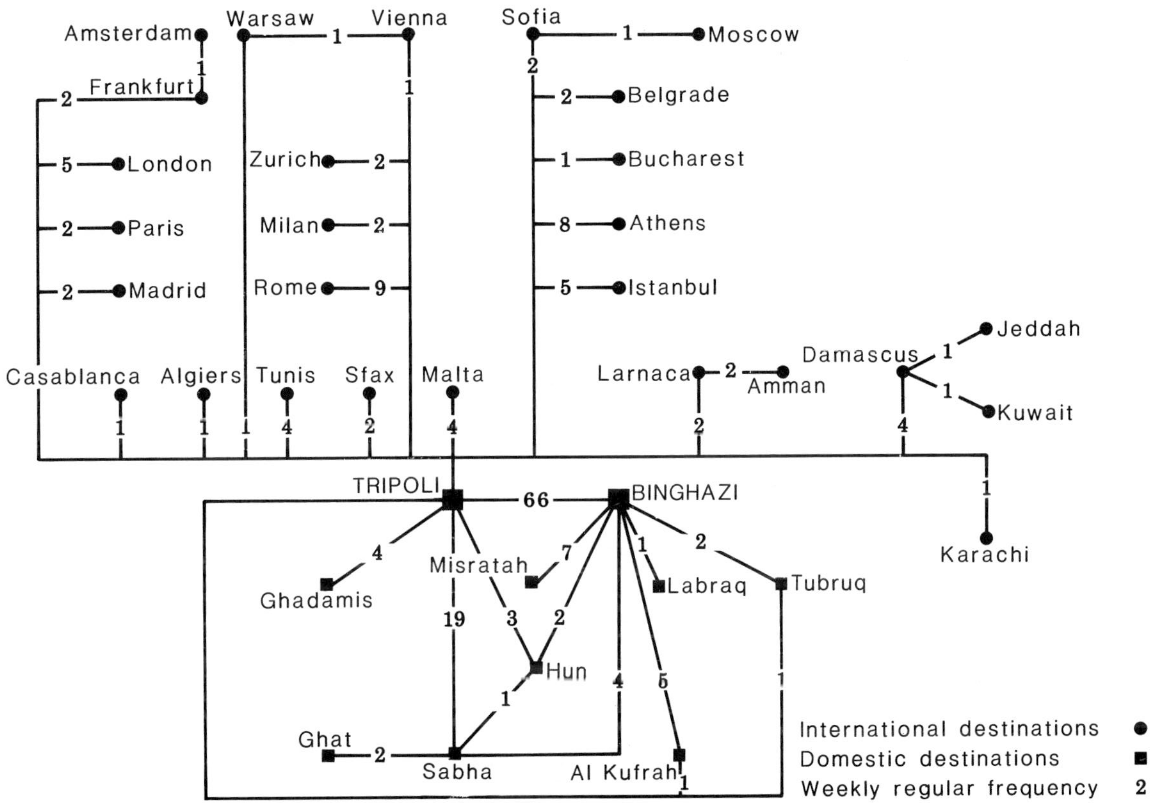

Fig. 13.1 Libyan Arab Airlines: International and domestic services, winter 1983 - 84

oil boom and Libyans travelling both within their country and abroad for business or pleasure. The idea to establish privately-owned airlines, became evident that the government alone could afford such an expensive business.

It is possible to identify two areas of air transport development in Libya since its independence in 1951. The first is that of Libya's airports becoming important middle points between European colonies in Africa and the metropolitan states. The second is the era of air transport growth within Libya as a consequence, and in support, of the economic and social development that accompanied the discovery and export of oil.

The movements through, and from, Libyan airports have shown continued growth from the time of independence until today. However, in the early sixties, there was a fundamental change in the source and character of traffic. Since independence, traffic through Tripoli and Binghazi airports had been mainly that of aircraft using them for the purpose of refuelling. This is because flights between the UK and East and West Africa had to stop en route, due to their limited fuel-capacity, and in order to pick up passengers - mainly British or American troops travelling home on duty, or leave. BOAC and its associated carriers WAAC and EAA were the main operators through Libyan airports in this era, with flights between Europe and points in West Africa like: Kano, Lagos, Abidjan and Accra; or in East Africa like: Nairobi, Dar es Salaam and Khartoum.

In their report on the economic development of Libya, published in 1963, described the internal transport system as being adequate; with air transport playing a supplementary role to road transport between the, then provincial, capitals of Tripoli, Binghazi and Sabha[1]. At that time, the flights between Tripoli and Binghazi amounted to six a week, operated by foreign airlines. Tripoli-Sabha was operated by a single, weekly service (DC-3). The study team preparing the World Bank Report noted the existence of landing-strips in the desert at Ghadamis, Hun, Brak and Ghat, in addition to certain other temporary landing-strips built by the oil companies near their camp sites. Military airfields like Wheelus, near Tripoli, and Gemal Abdel Nasser (Al Adam), near Tubruq, were exclusively used for military training and operational purposes by the NATO forces.

The aircraft movements at Tripoli airport in the fifties were predominantly of a military nature. However 14,000 movements in 1960 and 6,000 in 1955 were of civil aircraft - the difference has been attributed to the aircraft movements associated with oil exploration activities. Binghazi (Baninah) airport was significantly less important. While passengers to and from Tripoli airport were 23,000 in 1955 and 80,000 in 1960, Baninah airport totalled only 7,000 in 1955 and 10,300 in 1960.

Far from accurately predicting the future of air transport in Libya, and the association of such a future with the discovery of oil and the fundamental necessity for a substantial air transport network - particularly in view of the evident inevitability of the growth of a dominant oil sector, given prosperity activities in the previous decade - which would facilitate both the oil sector and the economic development of the country as a whole, the IBRD Report did not see the potential for the establishment of a national airline. The predictions of the World Bank were based on the fact that a national airline would only have operated three or four services between Tripoli and Binghazi that is to say that international airlines would continue to operate the scheduled services between these cities: the recommendation of the World Bank to discourage the formation of a national carrier was based on the poor prospects for operating commercially on an already substantial route like that between Tripoli and Binghazi. However, the assumption that such a local service would be operated jointly with other international airlines and that there was no potential for it as a consequence of the discovery of oil, or even in its possible share of existing international traffic, must be questioned.

Oddly, the Report did recommend light aircraft services between the desert oases in Fezzan, focussing on Sabha with a connecting, single, weekly service to Tripoli. The purpose of this recommendation was to connect these oases by air rather than build roads; the argument being that air services could be more quickly established, and that they would cost less to subsidise. Such a proposal would certainly, on the face of it, have facilitated movement between the desert oases on the one hand and Tripoli and Binghazi on the other. The link between the provincial capital Sabha and Tripoli was very limited - one DC-3 a week. Thus the connection between any two oases in the south would have been of the same frequency, but with a yet smaller aircraft. It is difficult to believe that such a link would have been of any significance, other than in transporting government officials every now and then. While upgrading the desert tracks into secondary roads might prove expensive, and possibly unnecessary, the introduction of air services in such a fashion would have proved a total loss and served no economic purpose. Contrary to its practical recommendations, the final opinion of the Mission which prepared the World Bank Report was optimistic of the potential for developing an air transport system: '...the existence of air facilities will rapidly make people air-minded'.

However, it remains a mystery why the development of a national airline was not suggested, with such a growth-rate [2] the fact that regular services between Tripoli and Binghazi already existed [3], the expectations of improvements in education, health and agriculture, which would involve a substantial number of foreigners and Libyans needing transport, and above all, the increasing activity in oil exploration. It is equally remarkable that the Mission's recommendations to link the three provincial capitals by air in preference to road with those of the numerous oases nearest to them [4]; establish an air ambulance service [5]; and to exploit the country's potential for tourism [6], did not lead it to recommend that a national air transport system should be set up.

Ironically, the World Bank Mission's Report based such a recommendation on 'economical justification', but in the same Report it blamed the lack of advanced skills for holding back Libya's development or, to put it in the Mission's own words: '...the whole country's development efforts may be held back by shortages of the more advanced skills, which can only be acquired through a long process of education and training'[7]. It might be suggested that transport and, above all, air transport, taking into consideration the sparsity of Libya's population and its vast area, could be an important tool for development. In this case, ought air transport to be excluded from being part of the education and training process? Or was the team convinced that flying was too much for the Libyans to master!

Fortunately, soon after this, the importance of air transport to the development of Libya, in the form of a national carrier, was emphasised. In 1964, Doxiadis, a consultant employed by the Libyan Government, rightly explained the weakness of the domestic air transport system to have been a consequence of the absence of a national carrier. This consultant noted the adequacy and full development of the international services to Libya, but notes that the '...lack of domestic services, despite the large comparative advantage which air transport has in Libya, seems to be due to the non-existence of a national carrier...' noting further that '...extensive domestic air services can only be run by a national airline.'

The significance and importance of air transport to development had clearly been recognised by the Libyan Government and in October 1965 a national Libyan airline commenced operations on both domestic and international services with two jet Caravelle aircraft. Firstly, the route between Tripoli and Binghazi was assigned to be exclusively operated by this national carrier. The international services of the airline were daily to Rome, and twice-weekly to London via Geneva. The domestic service was extended to cover Sabha with two flights, in addition to flights from Tripoli to Ghadamis and from Binghazi to Al Bayda and Tubruq. Right from the start, the airline began to expand its international and domestic networks, and has continued to do so until the present day.

The airline was obliged to seek the assistance of expatriate, professional executives and technicians on secondment from other airlines. Such assistance was necessary since the operations of foreign airlines through Libya did not create a basis for technical and administrative training, nor did these airlines extend a helping hand in training Libyans. Libyan Airlines, when formed, could only have filled the lowest category of its staff with Libyan nationals, with the exception of a handful in supervisory positions. Training programmes for Libyans were implemented in the form of on-the-job training. A number of young men were sent as pilots or mechanics to the UK to study at the Air Training Services School in Scotland. In the meantime, pilots, mechanics and even stewards were on secondment from Air France. The administration and commercial sector management were supplied through KLM and BOAC.

A landmark in the history of the carrier was March 1975, when an Air France crew went on an illegal strike in protest against the arrest of a French steward, accused of responsibility for the theft of a gold shipment. In response, some qualified Libyan captains took control of the operation of the airline and mounted successful certification programmes for other Libyan crews who had already received training and were about to be qualified as pilots and flight-engineers. Royal Air Maroc came to their help with Moroccan crews and flight instructors. By the end of that year the technical crews were growing in number and standard of qualification, in pace with the growth of the fleet.

The continuing remarkable growth-rate of almost 20 per cent every year since the formation of Libyan Arab Airlines has several times placed it amongst the top ten fastest-growing airlines, in tables published annually by the International Air Transport Association (IATA). The airline's fleet is currently thirty-one aircraft. The distribution amongst the various types is shown below:

BOEING B -707	3
BOEING B -727	10
FOKKER F -28	3
FOKKER F -27	15

Besides these aircraft the airline operates a number of executive jets including one Boeing 707, two Grumman Gulfstreams and a number of Lockheed Jetstars.

Libyan Arab Airlines today run scheduled services to the capitals of most Arab countries and many destinations in Europe, it would have extended its operations to the Far East had it been able to obtain the aircraft it needed. In 1979, three Boeing 747's were ready for delivery in Seattle when the United States administration denied the export licence of these aircrafts to Libya. This decision has caused considerable disruption to the operations and continued development of the airline, and continues to do so. The United States administration have used the 'Export Administration Act' to stop delivery of the aircraft to Libya from domestic, political motives, in order to demonstrate its disapproval of Libyan policies in Africa. The American restrictions continued to escalate, particularly after the airline had looked to Europe and signed a contract to buy ten aircraft from Airbus. The restrictions had been specifically aimed at preventing the Europeans from meeting their contractual obligations towards Libya, by means of the controversial extra-territorial powers the US seem to enjoy. The main problem for the Europeans was that the ordered aircraft were powered by American General Electric, engines. The extra-territorial powers being exercised by the US administration with regard to Libya have had a significant impact on the thinking of the Europeans and future aircraft now being developed in Europe. The Airbus A -320 will have all - European equipment with the exception of a partial American participation in the two types of engines which are expected to power it, the CFM 56 -4 or the V -2500 [8].

OPTIONS FOR DEVELOPMENT OPEN TO LIBYAN ARAB AIRLINES

My opinion of the options open to Libyan Arab Airlines, if it wishes to recover from the current stagnation of its development, is made in the hope that by the time this paper is published a decision on which path to follow will have been made. My line of thought will not necessarily lead to the correct solution since the opinion formulated in this case is based on published material, experience and common-sense rather than inside information and solid facts - normally the basis for any good decision.

The availability of commercial aircraft suitable for international operations is confined to the United States (which produce the majority of such aircraft), Western Europe (who have continually attempted to remain in the industry and challenge the American domination) and, lastly, the Soviet Union which only provides such aircraft for its own carrier, in addition to selling some to a number of carriers belonging to countries within the sphere of Moscow's influence.

In considering the various options open it is necessary first of all to understand the requirements. For example, the economics of operating an airline should be considered: while the airline must use the type of aircraft that suit the structure and composition of its network best, up-to-date equipment should not be neglected in the name of economy. Nor should the investments made to train technical and managerial staff and the effective utilisation of the skills they have acquired at high cost and over a long period of time, be excluded from consideration. Equally, the question of communalism with other airlines in the region, or standardisation of equipment and procedures should not be ignored. The waiting time on aircraft delivery and the necessity for long-term planning are also fundamental issues and requirements for good airline management. In a nut-shell, the commercial viability and profitability of the airline have to be closely examined.

The fleet of Libyan Arab Airlines is composed mainly of aircraft which are no longer being produced. The Boeing 707 will shortly be banned from flying to most parts of the world in order to stop the contribution of its the engines it carries to noise-and air-pollution. Production of the Boeing 727 has ceased and the older aircraft within the fleet have been restricted to smaller pay-loads and operational capability thus they are becoming increasingly more costly to operate. The Fokker F -27, possibly the least affected, may still serve for some time to come with proper management and maintenance. The Fokker F -28 has only recently been received and is welcomed as a substantial improvement on the F -27, by which the oil industry was previously served.

This assessment of the current fleet of the Libyan national airline clearly indicates the acuteness of the problem, since 90 per cent of the seat per mile capacity lies in the jet fleet which is ageing and becoming uneconomical to operate. The decision to purchase three Boeing 747's in 1978 - whose delivery was denied in 1979 - can only be attributed to the opening of new markets, particularly in areas where the bulk of labour is imported in order to participate in the construction of various economic and industrial projects. Destinations like Seoul, Manilla, New Delhi and Karachi in addition to the fat routes of the existing network would have been served by such aircraft. However the purchase of the Boeing 747's would not have taken care of the replacement requirement of the existing fleet, since they are only suitable for long distances which are busy enough to fill its seats and cargo capacity.

After attempts to persuade the Americans to sell aircraft to Libya had become decisively unsuccessful, the Libyans turned to Europe and in September 1981, ordered some Airbus A-300's and A-310's. It is uncertain whether, when it placed this order, the airline perceived how unrealistic Airbus' undertaking to deliver aircraft with American engines was, but it is certain that Airbus and the French Government wanted to challenge both the American Government and the American aircraft manufacturers.

Having discovered that such a contract could not be fulfilled by Airbus, the second option currently open to the Libyans is to take advantage of the possibility of building the latest version of the Airbus A -300 - that is the A -300 -600, powered by Rolls Royce RQ -211 -524 engines. In taking this option, the airline would sacrifice three years of obligatory waiting-time before receiving the first aircraft, to allow for necessary development procedures. But once available many countries, especially those choosing to follow policies of independence from the United States, (this does not necessarily indicate policies consistent with those of the Soviet Union) would certainly find this new balance attractive not only as a means of escaping American ruthlessness, but also because it would deter the US from depriving other countries of this important tool for development.

If the Libyans select the European Airbus option, they will certainly have lost ten whole years during which they could have developed their national airline, by the time they receive the first aircraft. That is between 1978 when they received their last B -727's and 1987 when they would expect to receive their first European Airbus, if they decide to buy them. However, they will certainly have won the battle by proving that they could break the Americans' monopoly and by encouraging Europe to develop the Airbus A -320 away from the control, and thirst for imperialism, of America.

The third option is to turn to the Soviet Union who can offer inferior technology, aircraft which are unsuitable in range and capacity, and uneconomical in operation due to the high rate of fuel consumption. Furthermore, it would lead to a sacrifice of the investment made in training hundreds of technicians and, above all, to residual traffic from competitors offering more up-to-date aircraft and services than the Libyan airline.

There is a fourth option, that of waiting for the American administration to possibly change its mind and ease its control in defiance, once more, of the Europeans. I find this option too insulting even to discuss in view of the torture the airline has been made to suffer.

The Libyan national airline will have to survive for three or four more years with uncertainties about how best to serve the public and contribute to the development of the country. But I can confidently predict that it will not have to endure this frustrating experience again provided the priorities are set right and a far-sighted, mature and courageous decision that supplies the long-term needs of the airline is made at a reasonable speed. That decision would be the selection of the second option - that of buying from the Europeans. The Airbus A -300, the A -320 and the F -100 have no American strings attached to them and cover fully the requirements of a carrier like Libyan Arab Airlines. Many airlines in the region would follow this step as has previously occurred.

I have concentrated in this paper on the national airline which forms only a part of Libyan air transport. There is enough material to write many books about air transport in Libya - the achievements of the Department of Civil Aviation and its role in the legislation of this industry and the development of the various airports is worthy of much research and comment; the aero-club and the role it plays not only as a conventional aero-club but also as a substantial participant in the category of general aviation activities is in itself very interesting; and so on. But because the problem of a national carrier is the most urgent, that is the one I have selected to discuss at greatest length in this brief paper.

REFERENCES

1. International Bank of Reconstruction and Development, 1960, Johns-Hopkins, Baltimore.
2. *Ibid.*, p.245
3. *Ibid.*, p.246
4. *Ibid.*, p.247
5. *Ibid.*, p.246
6. *Ibid.*, p.216
7. *Ibid.*, p.252
8. Marsh D., March 19th 1984, 'Airbus plan angers U.S. parts makers' *Financial Times*.

PART SIX: PLANNING RESOURCE USE

Chapter 14

A CASE STUDY OF REGIONAL PLANNING IN LIBYA

W.S. Watkins and R.V. Price

ABSTRACT

In this paper practical aspects of regional planning in Libya are discussed, with specific reference to the Sabha regional planning study. The aims of the study are summarised and the practical applications necessary to fulfil the aims are outlined.

Organisation of the study and the methodology adopted were formulated to suit local conditions. It is postulated that the art is in the marriage of sound theoretical concepts with the constraints imposed by the actual physical, social, economic and political environment. The science is in the formulation of physical directive plans with sufficient in-built flexibility to allow for changing circumstances without betrayal of basic concepts.

The authors wish to express their gratitude to Finnmap Oy of Helsinki, Finland with whom they are working on the El Khalij and Sabha regional planning studies. Gratitude is also sincerely expressed to the various levels of administration in Libya and to all those without whose assistance the planning work would not have been possible.

Finally it should be stated that any views expressed are the personal views of the authors and do not necessarily reflect the official views of the authorities concerned.

PREAMBLE

As a preface to the discussion of regional planning, the following fundamental questions and answers need to be considered:

(1) Is it reasonable to strive for development?
Yes, however ambition should be based on realism; beware of over-ambitious, ill-conceived schemes.

(2) What form should development initially take?

Fig. 14.1 Jamahiriya - planning

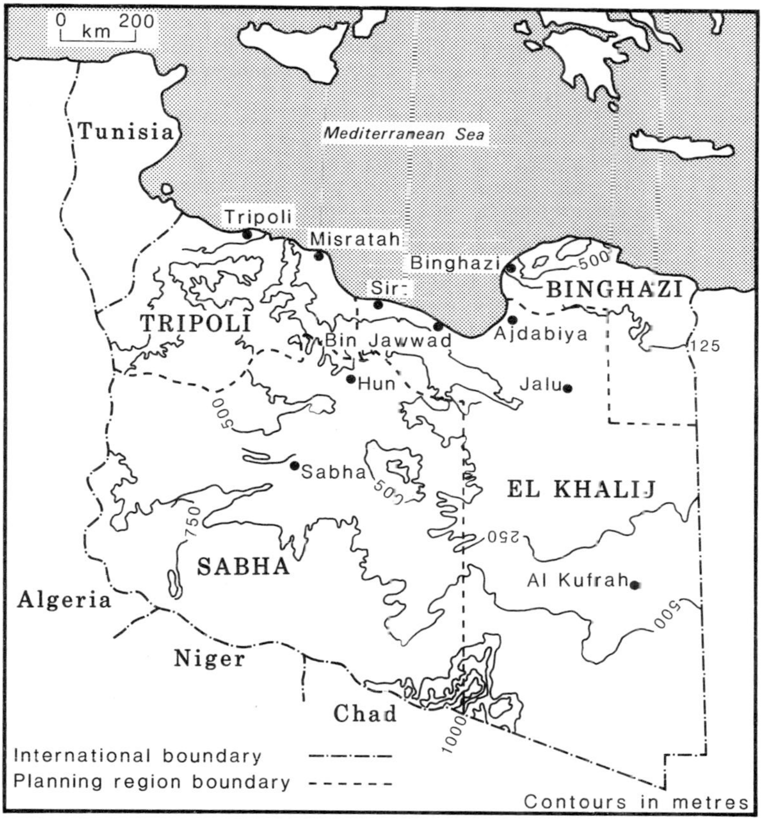

Improvement of the economic climate to enable increased social and spiritual welfare. The distinction between economic growth and comprehensive socio-economic development should be drawn.

(3) Is there an optimum rate of development?
The rate of development is very difficult to control since it depends on such factors as national income, national resources and stage of development.

(4) Is there a fool-proof method of preventing mistakes during development?
No, only by no development which itself is a mistake. The aim must be to minimise them by avoiding previously-made mistakes and by learning from those of other people.

(5) What should be the fundamental principles upon which any plan is based?
Realism and flexibility.

(6) Is it wrong to allow foreigners to prepare your plans?
No, initially an outside view may be more objective. However, in the long-term, local involvement is essential if plans are to be successfully implemented.

It must be stressed that dogma is a major enemy of planning. Sometimes planners are handicapped by pre-conceived, fixed ideas. Sometimes those for whom plans are prepared are unwilling to consider all solutions. Objective study of the existing situation together with sound analysis of potential enables imaginative development concepts to be formulated. The link between these theoretical concepts and practical implementation will always be compromise. Since realisation is the ultimate aim of any plan, it is necessary to strike the optimum balance between what is ideal and what is most likely to be implemented.

In the quest for excellence the planner's tools are sound theory, flexibility and compromise. The planner's judge will be time - long after the planner has lost his influence over, and responsibility for, events. With the benefit of hindsight it may be tempting to lay more blame than is due at the planner's feet, the planning profession may argue. Or is it that by the time the mis-judgements become apparent the planner is no longer accountable?

THE SABHA REGIONAL PLANNING STUDY

The Sabha regional planning study formed part of a physical planning programme for the whole Jamahiriya [1]. As such it required to take into consideration national economic and social policies. The national physical perspective plan 1981-2000 provided guide-lines which suggested the implications of national policies in relation to long-term planning in Sabha region[2]. These guide-lines were taken into account during the formulation of social and economic goals for the region. It was also necessary to study all existing physical, social and economic factors in order to develop a physical planning programme aimed at achieving the established goals[3].

In other words, the social and economic planning required its physical planning counterpart, they could not be divorced into two separate processes. The starting-point was social and economic planning, the end result was physical planning and, organisationally, there had to be a common framework into which both were integrated. Moreover, social and economic policies should, in their formulation, take into account their spatial effect on the environment and people's lives, just as physical planning should have regard for sound social and economic policies.

The Sabha planning study, then, was considered a multi-purpose exercise aimed basically at:

- introducing a spatial pattern of social and economic activities in accord with environmental conditions and future life-style;
- optimising capital project location according to the region's resources;
- reducing inequality in income levels and standards of living between sub-regions;
- intensifying and optimising inter-sectoral linkages
- decentralising development planning and management and mobilising more fully local human and physical resources.

The consultant's brief was to make a thorough study of all aspects of the region's physical, social and economic structures; prepare topographical maps at various scales; draft several alternative strategies for regional development up to 2000; prepare a detailed regional plan for the chosen strategy; and design twenty-year urban plans for fifty-nine towns and villages. This was the first such comprehensive planning study carried out in the region. The broad scope required that an integrated approach to the region's development for all the planning agencies concerned would result at both regional and local planning levels. Hitherto much physical planning and project allocation in the region has derived from unco-ordinated sectoral decisions. How far the Consultant's efforts will be able to establish a regional framework for development is discussed below.

In order to identify intra-regional disparities (key local problems) and incorporate solutions for these into the alternative strategies, it was necessary to carry out the regional analysis, development potential analysis and predictive aspects of the plan at a sub-regional level.

The settled portions of each baladiya were considered as sub-regions not only at the administrative level but also satisfying many functional and formal classification criteria. This is inevitable since in the political sub-division of the country account was taken of population distribution, ethnic groupings and economic resources. Decentralisation of administrative powers and a policy of rationalisation of investment by locating most higher-order services in one centre has led to the emergence of each baladiya town as a local 'central place' serving its own hinterland.

The settled portions of the baladiyas of Al Jufrah, Ash Shati and Sabha qualify as distinctive physical and functional sub-regions. However, Awbari and Murzuq baladiyas are too large and their settlement pattern too dispersed to be considered individual and homogeneous sub-regions. Wadi Al Hayah and its continuation westwards as Wadi Irawan constitute both a homogeneous economic activity zone and a distinctive physical zone. This can be considered as the Awbari sub-region. The south west corner of the region with settlement located between Al Awaynat and Al Barkat in a linear pattern along Wadi Tanezzuft is again of a separate and distinctive character, both physically and ethnically.

Similarly, in Murzuq baladiya, the central linear zone of settlement stretching from Tsawah in the west to Tmassah in the east is relatively homogeneous, although owing to the greater distance involved and the need for accessibility to services, several minor service centres such as Traghan, Umm Al Aranib and Zuwaylah have developed as well as the major 'central place' of Murzuq.

The Qatrun oasis also constitutes a distinctive sub-region in view of its physical isolation from the main activity axis in Murzuq. Equally, the Uzu area - the settled wadis on the northern slopes of the Tibisti Mountains - is a particularly distinct physical, economic and social entity.

Thus eight spatial sub-regions could be identified within the existing settlement pattern. The vast tracts of unpopulated desert separating these also required statistical analysis of their development potential. These could be broken down into five broad physical sub-regions. The region was therefore subdivided into the thirteen zones or sub-regions listed below.

Table 14.1 Sub-regions

Zonal No.	Zone Name
1.	Al Jufrah
2.	North (Al Hamadah Al Hamrah)
3.	North-West (Awbari sand sea)
4.	North-East (Jabal Al Haruj Al Aswad)
5.	Wadi Ash Shati
6.	Sabha
7.	Awbari
8.	Murzuq
9.	South-East (Sarir Tibisti)
10.	Al Qatrun
11.	South (Murzuq sand sea)
12.	South West (Ghat)
13.	Uzu

The establishment of a data bank and its subsequent monitoring was a major aspect of the assignment. Available sources of data required for planning were frequently out-dated, incomplete or inaccurate. There was a lack of consistency in official records held by the five baladiyas concerned. The consultant was therefore obliged to set up his own information system which was acquired by a painstaking initial field survey coupled with aerial photographic reconnaissance.

The analysis of gathered information was geared to identifying the region's most critical problems and establishing which zones possessed greatest physical development potential. Particular emphasis was laid on groundwater availability studies[4]. A brief outline of the physical development potential of each sub-region is summarised below:

AL JUFRAH

Water resources within the Hun graben are limited and quality is poor.

East of the graben, potential is very limited. Only small localised agricultural projects can be recommended for Zallah and Al Fuqaha.

West of the Hun graben, studies are currently being

undertaken to establish groundwater resources. Prospects appear favourable - in which case transportation of water to the Al Jufrah oasis will ensure prosperous agriculture in a zone of relatively good economic potential in view of its location and road and possible rail links.

WADI ASH SHATI

Water resources in the Brak area are over-exploited.

In the Wadi as a whole it is estimated that up to 90 per cent of water is being wasted by leakage from artesian wells.

The future effect of iron ore mining on water consumption/pollution/recycling requires study.

The possibility of production projects east of Brak, west of Barqan and north-west of Idri must be considered.

A water management policy is critical to the future of agriculture in this sub-region.

SABHA

Existing projects enjoy relatively high technology.

The market for local production is large and expanding. Productivity is low, however, due to the competition for labour presented by more highly paid secondary and tertiary sector employment in Sabha.

Cost of water extraction is high.

Projects in this area, including Ghudwah, should specialise in horticulture.

AWBARI

Water reserves in Wadi Al Hayah are being grossly over-exploited. There is rapid decline in the level of the upper reservoir caused by existing wells and projects being too closely spaced. The lifespan of some existing projects has been put as low as twenty years.

Solutions to this problem, which do not involve large scale movement of settled population, should be put forward.

The recommendation will be to transport water from newly-drilled, spaced wells up to 10 kilometres from existing cultivated areas.

Further production projects along the lines of the Maknusah Project are possible in the Nubian Sandstone area located between Wadi Al Hayah and Wadi Atabah.

WADI IRAWAN

Favourable groundwater conditions exist.

The new Ghat road will provide direct access.

Development along this route will strengthen the west-east economic axis and help integrate the Ghat area with the region.

Large-scale resettlement in this area should not be proposed and projects should be orientated towards production.

MURZUQ

Development will be restrained by labour shortage, although the large number of migrants from Chad represent a useful supply of manpower.

Salty water lenses are commonly found in the upper reservoir.

There is much sabkha on the northern edge of the sand sea.

The scattered character of settlement has resulted in a poor over-all service level where rationalisation is inevitable on cost grounds.

The present official policy is for small-scale settlement projects to consolidate services in rural areas. This policy is correct.

The potential for some larger production projects also exists e.g. Wadi Barjuj.

SOUTHERN SUB-REGIONS (GHAT, AL QATRUN, UZU)

These zones suffer, and will continue to suffer, from high marketing costs and the poor supply of labour.

Each zone should have a goal of self-sufficiency (regional autonomy).

The area of cultivated land required by 2000 to achieve this goal can be forecast.

The potential for larger-scale development should not be excluded.

EASTERN EDGE OF MURZUQ SAND SEA

South of Al Qatrun a high potential for water extraction exists.

The axis along the proposed road link to Chad could be strengthened by the establishment of production projects.

SOUTHERN BORDER ZONE

Not a great deal is known of the area along the Niger border but the indications are that groundwater is plentiful.

The area is of strategic importance and its economic development should be considered.

ALGERIAN BORDER ZONE

A road link from Ghadamis to Al Awaynat has been proposed.

The area is known to have mineral potential.

Water is available although soil conditions are variable.

Studies should be recommended regarding agricultural potential.

In response to the local problems identified, the following long-term regional goals were proposed:-

Key Problems	Goals
GEOGRAPHICAL ISOLATION	
High marketing costs High cost of imported goods	- Completion of present programmes to improve inter-regional communications.
High cost of construction Administrative difficultes	- 50 per cent reduction in the Tarabulus-Sabha road journey time (1981) upon completion of the Mizdah-Brak link.
	- Investigation of the feasibility of other inter- and intra-regional roads and international routes.
	- Consideration of the long-term re-orientation of trade links with West and Central Africa.
	- Maximise utilisation of the projected Misratah - Ash Shati railroad for the importation of fuel etc.
	- early completion of projects for establishing a cement and building material industry in the region to lower construction costs .

Key problems	Goals
GEOGRAPHICAL ISOLATION (cont):	
	- Decentralisation of administration, particularly in agriculture.
CLIMATE:	
Desertification	- Effective water-management policy.
Water wastage	- Control of unrestricted grazing.
SOIL EROSION:	- Policy of afforestation where feasible. - Design of urban areas to take into account climatic factors.
ECONOMIC:	
Labour shortage Low skill levels Low average incomes Under-exploitation of minerals Dependence on imported fuel Settlement pattern daters economic provision of services	- Emphasis on mechanised, agricultural projects with low labour demand in remote zones of high physical potential. - Reduction of manpower levels in non-productive service and trade sectors. - Vocational training programmes. - Diversification of economic base - Rapid Libyanisation of secondary sector work-force. - Mineral investigation

Key Problems	Goals
ECONOMIC (cont):	
	- Exploration for oil in the region to be intensified, with the primary aim of achieving fuel self-sufficiency.
	- Consolidation of services and employment growth in selected, medium-sized towns.
	- Rationalisation of investment in infrastructure by resettlement project policies.

SOCIAL:	
Sub-regional imbalance	- Provision of an even distribution of services to all sub-regional centres.
Illiteracy	
Access to services	
Housing shortage	- Distribution of new projects in accordance with social need as well as physical development potential.
	- Per capita allocation of annual budgets for development of social services to be directed to geographical areas of greatest need.
	- Programme of adult education in rural areas.
	- Construction of low-cost agricultural roads in rural areas.

Key Problems	Goals
SOCIAL (cont):	
	- Priority to be given to providing planning solutions for the villages with lowest service levels.
	- Priority to be given to the rehousing of families currently living in 'marginal' dwellings (tents, shacks, huts). - Urban utility design studies to be carried out for every planned settlement. - Evaluation of a policy of refurbishing older housing rather than replacement. - Annual housing construction targets to be realistic and guided by the practical capacity of the construction sector.

Three strategies were proposed as models for social and economic development of the Sabha region up to the year 2000. It was recognised that the basis for all development strategies would be the approach adopted in the future agricultural policy for the region. Once a decision had been made on this, the development of all other socio-economic sectors of activity in the region could be integrated to form a comprehensive, regional plan framework.

The three options proposed were:

(1) Extrapolated Trends - the maintenance of the policy direction of the current five-year transformation plan

throughout the planning period.

(2) Modified Trend - whilst the national objectives of Strategy 1 would be taken as a guide-line, it was proposed to achieve this by an evolutionary approach with a lower over-all level of investment.

(3) Economic Viability - a stringent option in which only those projects within the long-range plan which could be firmly justified on economic grounds would be recommended for implementation.

In order to assist the decision-makers, the basic physical, social and economic implications of each strategy were simulated. Furthermore, the resultant physical outline plans were evaluated to show their relative advantages and disadvantages.

Subsequently Strategy 2 was preferred. This development policy satisfied current aspirations for economic diversification and realistic growth potential. However, strategic planning is a flexible means of coping with changing circumstances. Events may, in fact, bring pressure for the more stringent development policy, Strategy 3, in the future.

The regional plan is not limited to physical resource distribution proposals. Its more far-reaching role is the statement of sectoral policy modifications required to achieve balanced and fully-integrated regional development[5]. The national planning system currently in force in Libya, whereby five-year transformation plans set sectoral targets for growth and investment, does not adequately take into account the specific needs of each region.

Will the Sabha Regional Plan have the desired impact of ensuring co-ordinated socio-economic development? Is the administrative machinery available for inter-sectoral liaison? Here the Committee comprises senior representatives of a wide range of development-interested bodies. At best, the regional plan could be a blue-print for the region's economic survival in a post-oil national economy. At worst, the plan is a framework into which viable local plans fit.

Ultimately the level of practical usefulness of the plan is outside the consultant's control. Currently there is no statutory support for regional plans in Libya and no multi-sectoral administration at a regional level. Implementation of recommendations relies entirely on inter-sectoral co-operation, which, hitherto, has lacked co-ordination.

At the local planning level, the new urban plans will greatly assist baladiyas in their continuous development control functions. Again a cautionary note should be sounded. Urban plans only hold good on a long-term basis if their implementation is efficiently carried out. Baladiya technical departments have this responsibility.

In summary, it should be stressed that the four current

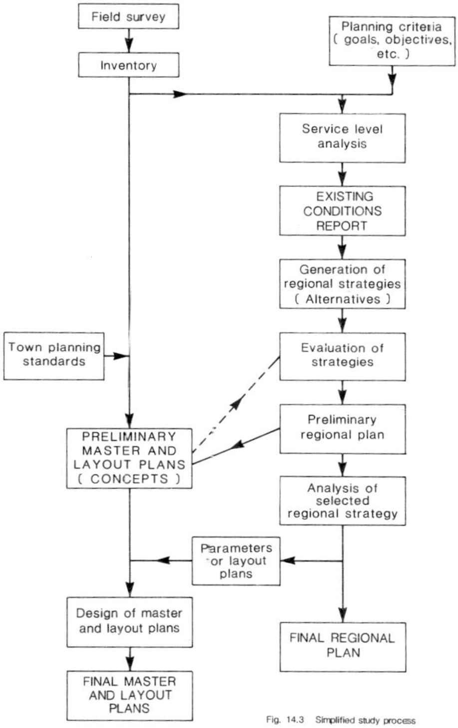

Fig. 14.3 Simplified study process

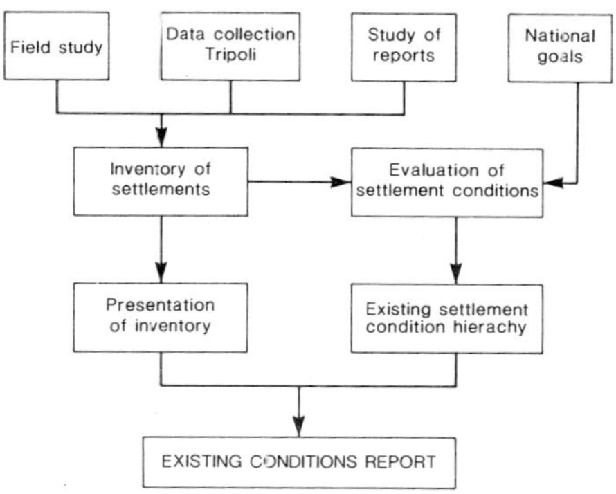

Fig. 14.2 Existing conditions report

Fig. 14.4 Master and layout plan process

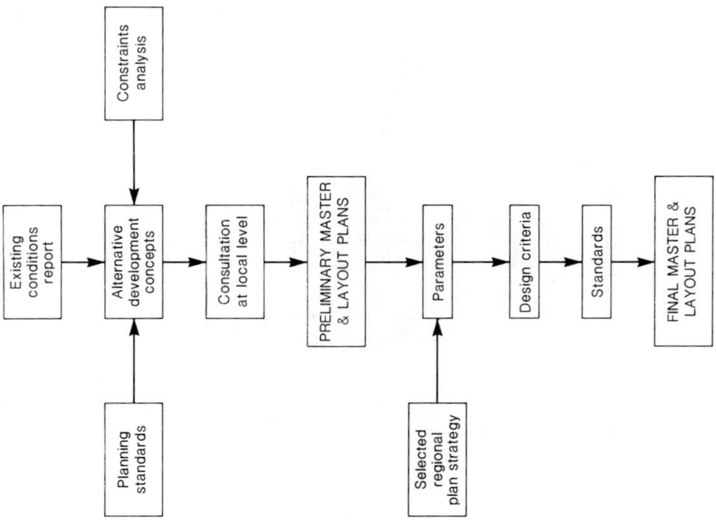

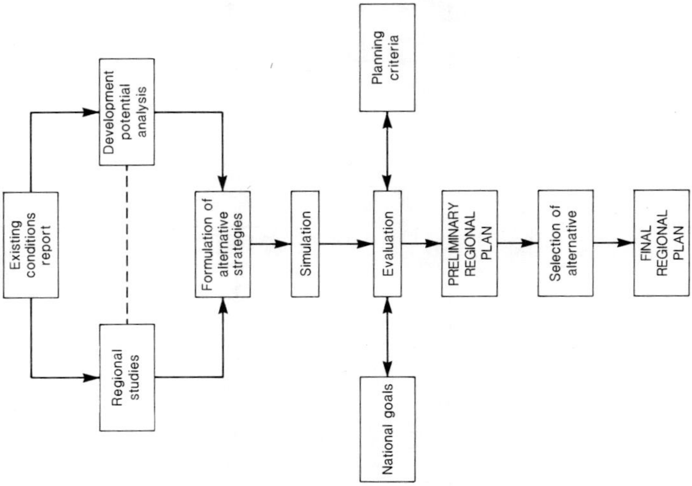

Fig. 14.5 Regional planning process

regional planning studies do not combine to provide an end-state, national plan for Libya for the year 2000. Rather they represent the application of tried and tested planning theories and techniques to meet today's particular development needs. Data inputs, goals and objectives and over-all strategies will require continual monitoring and review as part of the continuing process of change. In the Sabha region, the onus now falls on the decision-makers and technical officials to ensure that the consultant's proposals are implemented on a realistic and rational basis.

REFERENCES

1. Secretariat of Municipalities, 1977, *Terms of Reference for Regional and Master Plans for the Libyan Arab People's Socialist Jamahiriya*, Tripoli.

2. United Nations Technical Co-operation, Physical Planning Project, August 1979, *National Physical Perspective Plan, Guide-lines for the Sabha Regional Plan (Draft for Consultation)*, Tripoli.

3. Finnmap Oy, October 1981, *Sabha Region, Existing Conditions*, Reports 1 and 2, Helsinki.

4. Finnmap Oy, May 1982, *Sabha Region, Preliminary Regional Plan 1981-2000*, Report 4, Helsinki.

5. Finnmap Oy, 1984, *Sabha Region, Final Regional Plan, Summary Report, Report SF1, Helsinki.*

Chapter 15

CHANGING PLANNING POLICIES IN LIBYA

Shukri Ghanem

PLANNING BEFORE THE REVOLUTION

Agriculture was always the backbone of the Libyan economy. Before oil, it provided food and work for the majority of the population; it also constituted the bulk of the country's exports. The exploration and subsequent discovery of oil, together with the presence of foreign military bases in the country, stimulated the local demand for agricultural and industrial products. Demand for services has also grown continuously since the second half of the fifties.

When the country became an oil exporter, it was thought that Libya's permanent financial troubles had been put to an end. The country, which was among the poorest nations of the world, had finally found a natural resource capable of balancing the everlasting deficit in its economy.

Since the income from oil goes directly to the government, the government became responsible for finding the best way to spend the revenue from oil. Consequently, it turned to planning, hoping to use oil as the leading sector in the economy and oil cash receipts as an engine for economic growth. The first organised planning scheme in Libya, after oil, came in 1963 when the government announced the first five-year economic and social development plan. The total funds allocated were 169 million Libyan dinars to be spent on the different sectors of the economy.

Although the plan was thought to be over-ambitious and the estimated income from oil was considered over-optimistic, the real income from oil during those five years exceeded all expectations. The plan was revised a few times, to match increases in the real income from oil, that year, then extended to cover 1969. By the end of that year, the allocation of funds for the plan reached 625 million dinars, while the total actually spent amounted to 542 million dinars, as the following table shows.

The first economic and social plan was centred around a basic philosophy limiting the role of the government to

Table 15.1 Development expenditure 1963-69, (LD millions)

	1963	1964	1965	1966	1967	1968	1969	Total
Agriculture and livestock	1.3	1.9	7.2	10.1	17.3	4.4	13.2	55.4
Industry and minerals	0.1	0.6	2.0	4.7	7.4	7.4	6.3	28.5
Electricity	1.7	2.9	3.7	5.8	14.1	16.8	11.8	56.8
Transport and communications	4.4	6.4	13.1	10.2	18.7	24.3	14.5	91.6
Housing and utilities	4.1	7.5	12.1	23.0	42.1	34.1	39.3	162.2
Local administration	–	–	2.9	9.9	6.8	14.6	12.1	46.3
Education	.6	1.0	5.6	10.7	8.1	13.6	8.0	47.6
Public health	.7	.2	.8	2.1	5.5	4.9	2.9	17.1
Labour and social offices	.7	1.6	3.5	3.4	5.3	5.3	1.0	20.8
Information and culture	–	.1	.4	.4	.7	3.0	2.0	6.6
Economy and tourism	.1	.6	.5	.6	1.0	1.1	.4	4.3
Planning	.1	.2	.6	1.4	1.1	1.0	.6	5.0
Total	13.8	23.0	52.4	82.3	128.1	130.5	112.1	542.2
Total allocation of funds in the plan	21.7	32.5	87.0	90.8	105.0	143.3	145.0	625.3
Total income from oil	38.5	75.2	125.4	186.7	223.3	357.8	419.7	

encouraging the private sector to develop both itself and the economy. Consequently, the plan's priorities were infrastructural projects: roads, ports, electricity, housing and public utilities. These were aimed at making the private sector benefit from the external effects of such an infrastructure.

During the implementation of the first plan the government made a deliberate effort not to become directly involved in economic projects and whenever such involvement was necessary it was kept to a minimum. The sum allocated in the first plan for agriculture and industry was very cautiously defined, as a result, and thus was mainly for the preparation of research and feasibility studies on certain priority projects. The role of the Ministries of Agriculture and Industry was that of a research centre providing the private sector with information on the different projects and guidance about how best to implement them.

The government also embarked on a scheme of credit facilities with low - and in some cases free - interest loans. It also followed certain protective measures such as tax exemption, subsidies and customs duties. Sometimes it assigned import quotas in order to encourage local agricultural, or industrial, products and help them compete with imported commodities.

As a result of the first economic plan, oil-production developed rapidly to become the dominant sector of the economy. Furthermore, there were increases in agricultural and industrial output; government revenue from oil; the Gross Domestic Product; per capita income; and standard of living, all of which grew at an impressive double-digit rate. The increase in income generated a continuous growth in demand which could not be met, in spite of recent improvements, in local agricultural and industrial production. The situation necessitated the growth of imports which was further accelerated by an increase in the marginal propensity to import. This increase in imports was also a result of development projects and expansion in the oil industry, which required heavy machinery and transport equipment from abroad.

Table 15.2 Increase in food and total imports (LD millions)

Year	Food Imports	Total Imports
1963	10.2	85.3
1964	13.4	104.5
1965	16.2	114.4
1966	19.7	144.7
1967	26.3	170.0
1968	27.6	231.3
1969	30.7	241.4

Although dependence on the foreign market to bridge the gap in local demand increased, the government kept its interference to a minimum, hoping that the market would correct itself naturally leading, in the long run, to the creation of a healthy economic environment conducive to development and prosperity through the framework of a free-enterprise system. However, towards the end of the sixties the economy started showing clear disparities in the distribution of income, not only among people but also among different economic sectors and geographical regions. The economic plan favoured people working in the agricultural and oil sectors. The cities in the north, mainly Tripoli and Binghazi, were benefiting more from the economic boom than the rest of the country. The result was migration from rural areas to the northern cities, increasing the pressure on the different sectors of the economy.

PLANNING DURING THE FAT YEARS

The Libyan revolution of 1969 changed the planning policies of the country. Although the first few years were a continuation of the previous economic policies and the private sector flourished even more than it had done before the revolution, it was clear from the first that significant changes were to come sooner or later. The new regime advocated socialism, more self-reliance and self-sufficiency in food. Although socialism in the Third World meant different things to different countries, in Libya it was felt that it meant expanding the public sector and cutting-back the private sector.

The new government directed its efforts to the oil sector, insisting on a correction of the Libyan oil posted price which was undervalued in comparison to similar crudes exported from other countries. The revolution ushered a period of continuous price increases. During the seventies, the Libyan oil posted price jumped from 2.23 US dollars per barrel in 1969 to 56.34 US dollars per barrel in January 1981. The price increase during that period was due not only to the Libyan revolution, but also to devaluation of the US dollar, the October war and its aftermath and the Iranian revolution. The Libyan Government's income from oil increased and planning continued, but with a different strategy. The first plan after the revolution was a three-year economic and social plan (1970-72), followed by another three-year plan (1973-75). Then, in 1976, came the five-year 'transformation' plan. Through these three plans, covering a period of eleven years, 11.225 billion Libyan dinars were spent on development projects distributed among different sectors of the economy, as the following table shows.

The role of the government in economic activities was enhanced following the first three-year plan (1970-72). Direct government intervention in the agricultural sector took place

Table 15.3 Total expenditure on development plans during the years 1970-80 (LD million)

Sector	1970	1971	1972	1973	1974	1975	1976	1977	1978	1979	1980	Total
Agricultural including land-reclamation dams and water-resources	23.4	47.8	63.8	88.9	223.9	242.2	288.1	263.7	281.8	379.7	446.0	2349.3
Industry	15.0	29.0	65.1	62.5	107.0	100.0	165.5	160.7	157.1	210.2	557.0	1629.1
Oil and gas	1.5	15.3	27.8	28.5	56.8	52.9	67.3	67.6	80.0	93.4	59.1	550.2
Electricity	14.9	27.1	38.3	42.3	86.5	83.4	129.2	146.8	159.9	288.8	276.2	1293.4
Education	6.6	16.1	31.6	36.8	56.5	81.5	80.9	79.9	72.0	112.0	120.0	693.9
Information and culture	1.5	1.0	2.0	4.2	5.4	4.5	13.0	16.0	24.2	28.5	38.3	138.6
Labour force	1.0	1.8	3.5	3.4	7.5	4.8	5.7	7.5	9.8	9.6	10.6	65.2
Public health	4.9	3.7	15.4	9.8	15.9	20.9	28.3	36.3	53.5	69.8	70.9	329.4
Social security	-	-	-	3.7	8.8	3.8	2.5	1.9	3.9	1.9	6.6	33.1
Sports	-	-	-	-	-	-	1.6	8.5	6.0	18.7	16.9	51.7
Housing	37.5	39.4	72.2	60.9	146.9	128.3	143.9	181.4	159.3	172.4	206.5	1348.7
Public utilities	26.5	31.4	34.0	34.3	55.7	87.2	109.9	126.3	149.7	231.6	273.4	1160.0
Transport and communications	12.3	25.2	40.3	33.8	89.8	102.6	135.4	165.3	198.2	236.6	350.9	1390.4
Economy	.4	8.9	2.2	2.3	2.6	2.6	1.9	2.5	5.8	6.4	87.6	123.2
Planning	.3	.7	.7	1.3	1.7	4.8	5.4	2.0	2.8	3.0	4.0	26.7
Total expenditure	145.8	247.4	396.9	412.7	865.0	919.5	1178.6	1266.4	1364.0	1862.6	2524.0	11182.9
Total allocation of funds	224.5	301.6	442.9	545.0	916.2	1124.7	1407.7	1520.0	1785.0	1573.0	2527.4	12368.0
Total income from oil	482.6	593.6	514.0	663.6	1176.0	1510.3	2220.4	2620.0	2486.8	3848.7	6785.2	23501.2

with the hope of increasing output and achieving self-sufficiency in food through government-run agricultural projects. Industrial projects were established and run directly by the public sector. Throughout the ten years 1970-80, priority was given to agriculture and 2349.9 million Libyan dinars were spent on the establishment of five main agricultural projects: Jifarah Plain, Jabal Al Akhdar, Fezzan, Al Kufrah and Sarir Salul Elkhudor. The projects were run directly by the government, which simultaneously continued its policy of assisting the farmers by means of subsidies and protection.

Government involvement in industry also grew fast during this decade. 1629.1 million Libyan dinars were spent on industry with more than a hundred factories being established and run entirely by the public sector.

During the first years of the revolution the public sector co-existed with the private sector, the latter continuing to flourish and benefit significantly from the credit facilities offered by the banks but in the second half of the seventies, the government tightened its grip. First foreign trade then local, both wholesale and retail, was nationalised.

Although the government did not nationalise private sector factories the workers, encouraged by the 'Green Book' view of industrial ownership, took over the plants they were working at, proclaimed themselves 'partners and owners' and assumed their management. By 1979, the private sector in the country was almost totally abolished. Ownership ceased to exist except in agriculture. Furthermore, people were not allowed to own more than the house in which they lived. This situation put tremendous pressure on the state, for it became responsible for providing all the needs of society. It had to decide on what industry to establish; what commodities to import; from where to import; where to sell and for what price. It also had to build schools, hospitals, roads, hotels and, with very little exception, all the houses needed by society. Consequently planning expanded to cover all sectors of the economy and all aspects of social life; and this was not easy in a country lacking skills and having serious management problems.

The increasing income from oil eased the strain on the state. There was so much money that it was not difficult to follow a policy of 'all things to all people'. The planning was indiscriminate with industrial projects being undertaken with little regard paid to their economic feasibility. Roads, ports, airports, hospitals, schools and hotels were built simultaneously, and the major cities began to look like large construction sites! In the trade sector commodities were imported from all over, with no attention to whether or not they were necessary. Imports jumped to unprecedented, and unthought of, levels as the following table shows.

The government also directed its efforts to heavy industry. A steel-mill in Misratah, an aluminium-smelter in Zuwarah and a number of petro-chemical projects came under construction.

Table 15.4 Imports of food, compared to total imports

	Total imports in US Dollars	Total imports in Libyan Dinars	Food imports in Libyan Dinars
1970	555	198.0	39.3
1971	707	250.4	47.6
1972	1043	343.2	53.0
1973	1723	539.9	58.1
1974	2762	817.8	129.8
1975	3542	1048.7	87.8
1976	3212	950.8	66.6
1977	3773	117.1	190.2
1978	4603	1362.6	205.3
1979	5311	1572.4	238.1
1980	9923	2958.0	

Some of the industrial projects bore very little relation to the country - the machines were imported as were the technical knowledge, raw-materials and labour. Negative value added in such projects is, of course, normal. Although money was continuously being funnelled into agricultural projects, little attention was paid to the economics and productivity of the agricultural sector. Self-sufficiency in food continued to be an unattainable goal. Only in barley and eggs did the country become self-sufficient, but at a cost which was almost prohibitive and with the existence of bottle-necks in the supply from time to time. By the end of the seventies, mainly due to its relatively small population and the increasing income from oil, it was not difficult for Libya to satisfy the different needs of the plan as well as importing all kinds of consumer-goods and meeting security demands. It was possible to follow a policy of financing 'gun and butter'. Oil export value increased, as did the Gross National Product and per capita income.

Although the agricultural and industrial sectors grew because of the high priorities they received in the different plans and the huge amounts of money allocated to and actually spent on them, the achievement of these sectors did not meet the target of self-sufficiency in food. But some goals were partly achieved, such as a reduction in income disparities between people and regions. Agriculture problems were a result of low-productivity and the shortage of water resources; skilled manpower; and capable management to run the public sector agricultural projects. Industry faced other problems besides the lack of skilled labour and capable management. It faced many difficulties and sustained high costs as a result of the administrative procedure and delays in obtaining work-permits and visas for the foreign skilled workers. Other problems for industry such as the poor rate of attendance among factory-workers, due primarily to the lack of adequate transport and housing and military service, in addition to electricity cuts, caused significant losses in that sector.

The statistics for agricultural and industrial output have to be studied carefully for, although they show a continuous increase, one cannot see this increase reflected in the foreign trade statistics; which are more accurate and show a continuous increase in imports and a continuous decrease in non-oil exports, as the following table shows.

Table 15.5 Libya's imports and non-oil exports, (US $ millions)

	Libya's imports	Libya's Non-Oil Exports
1977	3773	11
1978	4603	8
1979	5311	8
1980	9923	8

PLANNING DURING THE LEAN YEARS

By 1980 the different measures taken by industrialised countries within and outside the International Energy Agency, aimed at reducing their dependence on OPEC oil, started gaining a real momentum. The demand for OPEC oil began its continuous downward trend aggravated by the international economic recession. While OPEC oil production reached 30.928 million barrels a day in 1979, it went down to 26.878 million barrels in 1980, 22.49 million per day in 1981 and 18.398 million in 1982.

Libya's oil production followed the same path, from more than 2 million barrels a day in 1979, down to 1.827 million barrels a day in 1980, 1.1 in 1981 and 1.017 in 1982. Not only did the volume being produced go down, but the market-price of crude-oil could not resist the drop in demand and had to be reduced. In 1983 OPEC itself had to accept a general reduction of 5 US dollars in the government sale price of crude on the prices of February 1983. While the price of Saudi crude, Arabia light, which is the market crude for OPEC, became 29 US dollars per barrel from 34 US dollars per barrel, the Libyan crude-oil 'Brega' government sale price went down to 30.5 US dollars per barrel, 5 US dollars less than the price of February 1983 and 10.5 US dollars per barrel less than the price prevailing in January 1981.

The income from oil went down drastically as a result of this drop in prices and a decrease in production. From 22.527 billion US dollars in 1980, it dropped to 15.7 billion in 1981 and 14.35 billion in 1982. In 1983 it is estimated to have been less than 10 billion US dollars. Oil income reduction came in Libya at a time when the government was assuming all economic activities. It was the government which spent some of the oil money on development projects, imported commodities needed in the local market and military hardware. Furthermore it directly employed the majority of the work-force. For, with the exception of private farmers, the entire work-force is attached, directly or indirectly, to the government.

This loss of income affected the country's ability to continue its 'gun and butter' policy. Priorities had to be re-arranged in order to balance income and expenditure. As a result of Libya's dependence on foreign markets and the fact that it had developed a 'big-spender' attitude in response to its increasing income from oil, the country's imports jumped from 5.311 billion US dollars in 1979 to 9.923 billion in 1980 and 15.466 billion in 1981. The government felt it could no longer finance this high level of imports and declared its priorities in general terms under the slogan of 'maximum arms and minimum food' - policies unlikely, incidently, to encourage widespread popular support. The new 'more guns, less butter' policy meant that military expenditure would not be subject to any reductions and that any economies would be directed towards consumption. The government's first measure was to stop the importation of a number of commodities which it considered 'unnecessary'. It also started preparing what it called the 'commodities budget' which was a sort of quota system for imported goods, including only those it considered 'necessary'. Cars, televisions and videos were 'temporarily' excluded from the list of imports for two years. Despite these efforts, austerity measures on imports did not help to save much money and the government had to resort to applying an austere policy to development. While the value of projects signed in Libya as part of the five-year plan which was drawn up before the sudden fall in oil ressources,was 11.827 billion US dollars in 1981, the value of the projects signed in 1982 went down to 1.374 billion US dollars or about 12 per cent of the value of the projects signed in 1981, as the following table shows.

Table 15.6 The value of project contracts signed by the Libyan authorities from 1981-82 (US $ millions)

	1981	1982
Industry (non-oil)	1467.3	45.7
Oil industry	381.1	85.4
Agriculture and irrigation	553.3	132.7
Water and electricity	684.6	593.3
Housing and construction	6160.8	244.2
Transport and communications	1870.4	120.4
Health, education and welfare	335.5	144.6
Miscellaneous	373.7	7.3
Total	11826.7	1373.6

It is clear from the above table that no sector was exempt from drastic cuts. Although it looked as if the priorities of the plan changed - industry and agriculture lost their priority to water, electricity, housing, construction, transport and communications - it should be noted that most of the projects in these sectors were meant to serve and support industry and agriculture.

Although the government thought at first that it could concentrate on industry and agriculture in general, the income reduction was more than had been anticipated and the government had to choose between heavy and light industry. In 1983, a decision was made in favour of heavy industry, with no reasons for such a decision being given. The current trend is for the government to stop all new projects except the steel-mill in Misratah, an aluminium complex in Zuwarah and the petro-chemical projects in Brega. In agriculture, the policy is to concentrate on what is officially called the 'great man-made river' a pipe-line to carry 2 million cubic metres of water a day from a huge underground reservoir in Sarir and Tazerho in the south-east of the country to the north where it will be used in agriculture.

It seems that this is not going to be the end of changes in Libya's planning policies, since oil income is not going to increase, crude-oil prices are not expected to rise and neither is the demand for OPEC oil. Furthermore, because of the increase in the prices of other commodities, the real income is going to erode. Meanwhile the economics of the big projects are very shaky since they depend on foreign expertise, technology, markets and, in some cases, raw-materials; hence there are fears that these projects might become a drain on the economy. For a country like Libya, with a very small market and a low level of skills, has very little chance of building heavy industries which are economically viable. It is for this reason that it should concentrate on the smaller industries and aim to satisfy local consumption.

REFERENCES

Figures appearing in this chapter are taken from:
Export statistics published by different authorities in Libya.
The OPEC Annual Statistical Bulletin 1981
Reports by OAPEC 1981 and 1982
IMF International Financial Statistics August 1982
IMF International Financial Statistics 'Supplement on Trade and Statistics' 1982

INDEX

Index